RUGBY
IN OUR BLOOD

EDITED BY ANGUS POWERS

Tafelberg

Tafelberg
An imprint of NB Publishers,
40 Heerengracht, Cape Town
www.tafelberg.com

Commissioning editor: Annie Olivier
Cover design: Mike Cruywagen
Cover photo: Gallo Images/AFP
Book design: Nazli Jacobs
Copy-editor: Alfred LeMaitre
Proofreading: Carola Meyer

Printed and bound by Interpak Books, Pietermaritzburg
First edition, first impression 2011

ISBN: 978-0-624-04876-3

ALASTAIR MACDONALD AND OWEN BEVAN

You have always been in others and you will remain in others.
And what does it matter to you if later on it is called your memory?

Doctor Zhivago, Boris Pasternak

Contents

Introduction

Everyone from South Africa has a story about rugby. Try it. Chat long enough to any South African you might meet, anywhere in the world, and a rugby story will invariably emerge. Most will be about people's favourite teams and the extraordinary events that have occurred while supporting them. Players themselves never need much prompting to recall the many hilarious incidents that seem to punctuate life at the top of the game. But the most powerful stories will probably relate to rugby's role in forming, or changing, people's attitudes and perceptions. In South Africa, rugby is like the rain or the wind. Over the years, the force it exerts ends up altering the landscape. Rugby helped form us. It is a powerful sport.

I've only ever scored one try in my life. It was for the U13B team, and my fellow flanker and I barged over from a maul close to the try line. We were unstoppable. We were also both holding onto the ball so tightly that when we thumped over, it was impossible to tell who had dotted down. In truth, we both had. I guess that means I've only scored half a try in my life. An hour later, in the match that followed, our U13A flyhalf staggered off the field with concussion. I remember both incidents with unusual clarity, just as the events in the rest of this book – some of which occurred almost 40 years ago – are narrated as if they happened just yesterday. When you play rugby, it demands everything of you. It's not an experience that is easily forgotten.

Before watching rugby became part of my job, I watched rugby. As a kid, Currie Cup rugby on TV on stifling Saturday afternoons, the volume turned down while the house slumbered. At King's Park,

Natal persevering in the B-section. At university, matching the Springboks' epic journey to the Rugby World Cup final with an equally epic consumption of beer. In Twickenham, where I lived while the Springboks tied the world record for consecutive Test wins. At Lansdowne Road, seeing the All Blacks *bliksem* Ireland. In New Zealand (where rugby really is a religion), with my hosts in their basement bar, complete with big screen, surround sound, and pre-rolled marijuana joints. In the streets of Cape Town, where the national anthem spontaneously erupted when John Smit held aloft the William Webb Ellis trophy in 2007.

Then I became a sports writer, and I began to think more carefully about the game. What is it about rugby? Why does it have such a hold on us? That it was virtually a compulsory sport at most South African schools is no doubt part of the explanation, but what about all those women crowding into stadiums to watch the Springboks or their favourite Super Rugby team? They don't look like they ever played.

So, where do all our rugby stories come from?

Rugby owes much of its magnetism to being, in many ways, the original war game. It is an arena in which a team's physical, mental and strategic ability to counter the onslaught of the opposition is tested to breaking point. To those who play, it offers a rollercoaster ride of euphoria and pain. To those who already know the limits of their bravery, it is the most visceral, thrilling spectator sport available.

If players hurt so that spectators may know how wonderful it is not to hurt, the exhibition of brute force also throws the subtleties of the game into even starker relief. Poetry in the context of violence can be extremely seductive. Mazy runs, slick handling, swerves, sidesteps, off-loads, goose-steps, hand-offs, grubbers and perfect clearance kicks . . . players operating on instinct while under constant threat are an intoxicating sight.

More than its participants care to admit, rugby is an emotional game. Players must routinely weigh their courage, whether in the face of a huge opponent, getting up from a punishing tackle or kicking for poles with the match in the balance and the crowd hushed. Fans are also bound by rugby's code of respect. Just as every player needs an opposite number to test himself against, so supporters need the antagonism of the opposing fans to define their own identity. What would be the point of wearing team colours to a match if there were no rival fans to respond and to resist?

The eternal logic of sport dictates that without a loser, there cannot be a winner; without an enemy, there cannot be a friend. But the unique sportsmanship of rugby allows both players and fans to furiously vent their energy while the game is on, yet when the final whistle blows, to call it quits and have a beer together. No hooliganism, and no hard feelings.

Rugby's appeal extends beyond the spectacle. The game itself is endlessly flexible. Like all great sports, its first principle is simplicity itself: carry the ball over that white line 50m downfield. Rugby, however, rapidly gets more complex, with basic running, dodging, passing and tackling skills being expanded to include scrumming, mauling, rucking, line-out and kicking craft, depending on a player's position. The game can be played in any conditions (including waterlogged fields in Rugby World Cup semifinals) and in a variety of ways: keeping the ball among the forwards, spreading it among the backs, kicking for territory, kicking to give away possession or refusing to kick at all. The standard 15-man format can also be altered to ten-man or seven-a-side rugby (the version that will feature at the 2012 Olympic Games), and can even be shorn of tackling altogether to produce the most free-flowing game of all, touch rugby.

The reaction of school kids on encountering rugby for the first time is worth noting. Not only does rugby accommodate players of all shapes and sizes, it actually depends on them. A rugby team cannot be successful without the correct balance of skinny tall guys, strong fat guys, small brave guys, and skilful fast guys. No one gets banished to lonely goalkeeping duties or is left to twiddle his thumbs on the touchline. Every position is different yet crucial . . . and, better still, generates infinite opportunities for humiliation or heroism if you're caught out of position and have to deal with a situation you're ill-equipped for.

On reflection, is it possible to conceive of a team sport better suited to South Africa's renowned ethnic diversity?

Rugby has always been a game that adapted well to South Africa, chiefly because it was so often used to divide people, exclude them and set them against each other. Afrikaner against Englishman, white against black and, more recently perhaps, black against white. But now, freed from its history, the sport is uniquely placed to take advantage of the contrasting physical attributes and traits found in our extravagantly multicultural population.

In fact, the process is already well under way. Although many of the stories in this book recollect the tensions which traumatised our society, many more find themselves revelling in rugby's achievements, big or small, that could only have been possible in a liberated South Africa.

Can you imagine a black Springbok being named the world's best player in the bad old days of apartheid? Could a female South African doctor have collected two Rugby World Cup winner's medals (in a row)?

Hardly likely.

Not in our wildest dreams back then could we have contemplated winning not one but two Rugby World Cups. Now we expect it. Even demand it. If that's a measure of how far rugby has come in the twenty-odd years since the Springboks played the All Blacks in 1992 in their first Test since readmission, imagine what rugby can accomplish in the next 20 years. That's another reason why rugby fascinates us. South African rugby represents hope.

This book is a collection of stories exploring what rugby means to South Africans from all walks of life. They may be revealing, nostalgic or entertaining stories, but above all they are personal. We all have a story, because we've all been touched by rugby. Not only is it part of our political, economic and sporting landscape, it is part of our national identity and psyche, too. It's part of our lives, part of who we are. It is deeply ingrained. Rugby is in our blood.

ANGUS POWERS

PS.

Without the commitment and passion that each of the 43 contributors has for the game of rugby, this book could not have happened.

Of course, there were some interesting episodes along the way:
Meeting singer and model Inge Beckmann in a smoky bar was a good start.
Rob van Vuuren took our relationship to a whole new level in one of his shows.
Tony Leon corresponded from Argentina.
John Smit and Joost van der Westhuizen were open and generous.
Sherylle Calder found a gap between international clients.
Jacques Kallis and Mark Boucher put aside time on the eve of a Test match.
Schalk Burger invited me down to his local bar.
John van de Ruit took a break from launching *Spud*, the movie.
Oscar Pistorius is quite simply a remarkable individual.
Jake White didn't have a holiday over Christmas.
Bantu Holomisa dodged the mayhem of the opening of Parliament.
Simnikiwe Xabanisa filed his story while on tour with the Springboks.
Obie Oberholzer mulled over his text in the desert.
Leon Schuster had to tone his down to avoid a lawsuit.
Claire Mathonsi wrote in from Zimbabwe, Fraser Thomson from an oil rig somewhere in the North Sea, Riaan Manser from at least five different countries, and Twig Baker from wherever the biggest waves were.
And that's not even the half of it.

BRING IT ON!

JOHN SMIT

The Journey

Compared to most Afrikaans guys, whose love for rugby probably begins in the womb, I was a late starter at ten years old. I was a *laat-lammetjie* (late-born child), and although my much older brothers played rugby, my games were soccer and tennis. Especially tennis. That was all I played.

I was born in Pietersburg (now Polokwane), but when my family moved to Rustenburg there wasn't a lot of tennis going on and rugby was much more important. By the time I got to Pretoria Boys High, it was the same old story: we were all English-speaking soccer players from Pretoria, Boksburg and Johannesburg; they lined us up, shortest to tallest, fattest to thinnest, and then picked the forwards and the backs.

When I was in Standard 8, I was selected for the first team. It seemed a big decision to make: between playing first team and going to *veldskool* (high school bush camp). But it turned out to be not so difficult after all, and that's when I realised how much I enjoyed rugby. That was in 1994, and in my first match for the first XV we were thumped by Jeppe High, who were coached by Jake White.

From my first game as a Standard 6 pupil for the U14A team to my last game in matric, my parents would come all the way from Rustenburg – an hour and a half away – to watch. We played on the main field, Brookes Field, and while I was warming up I would only feel at ease when I'd seen that my parents had arrived safely and were sitting in their folding chairs in their customary spot on the right-hand side of the field. For five years, I wouldn't be able to concentrate until I'd seen them. Then I could play.

Once, they still hadn't arrived by half-time. Our coach came up to me and ranted, 'What on earth's wrong with you? You're nonexistent on the field!'

I said, 'No, it's just that I can't find my folks. I think they've had an accident.' And he said, 'No, man, they're sitting on the other side!'

My parents hadn't been able to sit in their usual spot because someone else had got there first, so, completely unaware of what it meant to me, they'd gone to sit on the other side of the field. It was such a relief, and the next 30 minutes of rugby were probably the best of my school career. When the game was over, I had words with my parents and told them never to sit in a different place ever again!

In Standard 9, I was in the Pretoria Boys first team who toured Zimbabwe: three or four matches against all the good Zim schools. It was an awesome tour – we were billeted out and got to know plenty of local people. The last game was against one of the prestigious schools in Harare, Prince Edward, and because we hadn't lost up until then it turned into the biggest game of the tour. The problem was that I had been too lazy to do my washing, and I had run out of clothes, specifically jocks. I had no underpants for the match. There was massive hype around the game, and the touchlines were packed with spectators, to the point of encroaching on the corner of the in-goal area. I had no choice but to run on in my first-team shorts and hope that everything remained intact.

Just before half-time, we had a scrum, right in front of the try line, down in the corner, directly in front of all these people. I was playing tighthead prop, so I bound with my hooker, crouched and my lock put his hand through my legs – as locks do – to grab the front of my shorts. But as he did so, the drawstring of my shorts snapped and I was revealed in all my glory to an entire corner of spectators. The prop in front of me started laughing, and then everyone burst out laughing. It was a really humbling experience. I was laughed at for about a month afterwards at school. Rugby has ways of humbling you – normally you get dumped or tackled hard – but it was hard to live that one down!

The Sharks contracted me in Craven Week in 1996, straight out of matric. I finished my finals and drove to Durban. In November I had been writing exams; in December I was playing for Natal U21 in Wales; and in January I was on a field warming up with James Small, Gary Teichmann, André Joubert, Mark Andrews, Adrian Garvey, Robbie Kempson and Ollie le Roux. These were the guys whose pictures I'd had stuck up in my cubicle just a few months before. Heroes. The legendary team of the 1990s.

In 1996, Natal had just won the Currie Cup, and I felt slightly out of place. I needed to pinch myself all the time. This was my education in life: being fortunate enough to be a youngster in the presence of these guys, even though they were near the end of their reign. I got all my advice from them. I was one of the few youngsters around. Now you can be 19 or 20 and make the Springboks and no-one bats an eye, but back then it was quite a thing.

Eight years later, in mid-2004, Jake White got the Springboks together in Bloemfontein for the first time since the 2003 Rugby World Cup failure and Kamp Staaldraad. Jake had just brought Os du Randt back, which was quite a big call, and he had told us three days before, on the Sunday, that we were going to win the Rugby World Cup in 2007. We all thought he was crazy.

At our 6pm meeting on the Wednesday, sports psychologist Henning Gericke, our *kopdokter* (psychologist) had us sitting in 22 chairs in a circle. Holding a Springbok jersey, he started walking around the outside of the circle. He stopped behind Os and put the jersey in Os's hands, and said, 'Os, I want you to start and to tell this team what this jersey means to you.'

Everyone else was relieved that the older oke had to go first, but it took Os a while because he held the jersey for quite some time before speaking. It wasn't an awkward silence; we thought he was pondering what to say, but actually he was composing himself. Os started talking about his career: winning the World Cup in 1995; the things he had done wrong while playing in the Springbok jersey; his injuries; how he'd wasted certain opportunities; going to the Bulls; his comeback for Free State. As he began telling us how much the jersey meant to him, tears were running down his face and he became unable to talk. I looked at him and I was on the verge of crying myself because Os was my hero – he is still my hero, to this day. Os was the big dog of Springbok rugby: he'd won a World Cup, he'd won a Tri-Nations, he'd done everything, and still this had brought him to tears.

Suddenly I had to reassess what the Springbok jersey meant to me, as did the guy next to me, and so on round the circle. It was the start of something special, because that team became a family and a brotherhood in half an hour, all because one man with massive stature showed his emotions about the jersey. We spoke about that circle many times in the years that led up to the 2007 World Cup. What it did was to allow guys to feel comfortable about expressing themselves, especially in the times of trial and tribulation that would follow. It was a really special moment.

When we eventually got to the 2007 World Cup, the pieces finally just started to fall into place as we went along. Before we left, my last speech on South African soil was to tell the team that we were going to get on that aeroplane as though we had already won the World Cup. We were going to behave like world champions, and we were going to train and play like world champions. We had to believe.

So we arrived in Paris and the Eiffel Tower was lit up in green and gold. It was probably yellow and some other colour, but we saw green and gold. We got to our first hotel, and the road was named 'Jacques' something or other, but we saw 'Jake'. Small things, but you make your pathway by seeing what you want to see. When Schalk Burger was cited for a high tackle in our first match, we saw it as a conspiracy to get rid of our best player because he was a real threat. Instead of worrying about what we'd do without our best player, we became intent on showing what we could do even without Schalk, and when he came back we knew he'd be even fresher and more of a threat. Our confidence grew as we turned everything to our advantage by sheer determination.

To a degree, we were trying to convince ourselves that we were champions, because there was no getting away from the fact that D-Day was still 20 October, the day of the final. I stopped sleeping well from the semifinal onwards. As captain (or coach) you worry more about the members of your team than you do about yourself. I had my wife with me, but I was still struggling to sleep. The reason my mind was so active was that every night for that whole week I was thinking about how this had been a journey four years in the making.

It had begun on that Sunday four years earlier in Bloem, when Jake told us we were going to win this. We thought he was mad. Then we got to know each other three days later with Os du Randt, who was still a key player in our team. We missed out on back-to-back Tri-Nations triumphs in the last three minutes at Dunedin in 2005, and we had survived all the heartache and the criticism of 2006. Then in 2007 I'd injured my hamstrings in the Tri-Nations; the more I thought about my injuries and whether I'd make it to the World Cup, the longer I stayed injured.

It had been a four-year journey, and when it came to the culmination of it all, the World Cup final was a blur. It was a thrilling game, but not for one moment did I think we were losing it. I felt in control for the whole 80 minutes, and at that final whistle I could do nothing but drop to my knees. The emotions that went through me – it wasn't just about hearing the whistle go and the fact that we'd won the grand prize. It was that we had achieved something amazing that had taken years to build. The satisfaction was all about what we as a team had done. Lifting that cup was the ultimate memory for me. I thought that night would have been the night of my life – and it was one of *the* nights – but little did I realise . . .

When we returned to South Africa – it was a long flight, and we emptied that British Airways aeroplane of alcohol of any kind – we didn't have any idea of what would be waiting for us. We were so excited to be home, to show off what we had won and to see the fans, but when we got to the airport and realised what was happening . . . all those people. And then that bus tour around the country!

That was when I realised that our victory meant much more than any individual or team achievement. The whole country was like a different place. Every report that had said I was a rubbish hooker or a bad captain just evaporated. To see the elation, and to realise what an impact those four years had had, made everything worthwhile. It was like reliving the satisfaction of 20 October times ten.

I would never have dreamed in 2007 that I might have another crack at it. I went into that World Cup thinking I would be playing for a French club the following year. In those days, when you made that kind of decision, it was like saying, 'This is my last Test match.' That final was it; there was no tomorrow. And then to be recalled by a new coach and to still be in the mix, playing for the Springboks and hoping to have another go at it if I'm fit and strong . . . that's a fairy tale.

A lot of people close to me say it's a risk to try again. What if I don't succeed? But that's certainly not reason enough not to try. You can't duck the challenge because you're scared of ruining what you've already achieved. That 2007 Rugby World Cup is ours forever. Not to take another crack at it for fear of ruining your reputation is a cop-out.

I haven't become the John Smit of today because of all the things I've achieved. I've also become the person I am because of all the things I've had to learn along the way.

That's life.

———— *As told to Angus Powers*

JOHN SMIT has won more Tests as Springbok captain than any other Bok has played as captain. He is South Africa's most capped hooker, has made the most consecutive Test appearances for the Boks, and holds the world record as the most capped skipper in international rugby. John has won the Currie Cup, two Tri-Nations titles, beaten the British and Irish Lions, and lifted the Rugby World Cup. He has also scored six Test tries.

ROB VAN VUUREN

My Game

I love rugby. Seriously, I flippen love it. I think it's the best sport there is. No contest. I love watching it, and I loved playing it. I constantly replay moments from the rugby games I have played throughout my life in the 'best of' catalogue of my memory. They shuffle through my mind like a playlist I never tire of.

My first sidestep. Actually it was a succession of sidesteps strung together in a stretched-out moment of pure instinct as I flummoxed each vainly lunging opponent. I felt like Michael du Plessis. It took place on the broken-beer-bottle-strewn field of the Gonubie Farmers' Hall, the home ground for my tough-as-nails school, Lilyfontein Primary. Yes, that is actually the name of the school, and no, I'm not saying we were tough as nails because of the name. We were tough farm-school types with snotty noses and calloused bare feet.

I remember one instance on that same field, when our entire barefoot ragamuffin squad had to hit the dirt during practice to avoid the attentions of a passing swarm of bees. It was just like the 2010 Currie Cup semifinal between the Sharks and the Bulls, except we didn't have Darren Scott trying to buy time while talking kak on the side of the field.

I became aware from a very young age that rugby provides you with valuable life lessons. Important lessons, like if you shave your knees, your roasties won't get infected. It was during my first away game for Lilyfontein that I learned the most important lesson of all – that my dad didn't know everything.

He was watching forlornly from the sidelines as the imposing man-sized star player of the opposing team ran through us like the proverbial hot knife through butter. My dad, the makeshift linesman with a Peter Stuyvesant hanging limply from his mouth, shouted out to his beleaguered and quite terrified son, 'Tackle him low, my boy! Tackle him low and it won't hurt! Take him round the ankles and you won't get sore. I promise!'

Like a fool, I believed him, and so the next time the kid came careening through our defences I flew at him like a midget avenger, scything at his ankles. Moments later, as I limped to join the rest of my battered team behind our posts, I screamed through a sheet of tears at my dad who was there with us to bear witness with his sad little flag as more points were piled upon us. 'You lied, Dad!' I wailed. 'You said it wouldn't hurt. It hurts a lot!'

Before my first rugby game: small, but dangerous.

Then there was high-school rugby. I can still hear the spine-chilling percussion of studs on concrete, accompanied by the portentous smell of Deep Heat, in the change rooms at Maritzburg College before every game.

I can feel my heart beating as I recall ranging in on cover defence on a runaway winger and the triumphant collision as we cascaded across the sideline in a mess of limbs.

I am transported by the rush I felt one day in training when, as an arty outsider in an extremely cliquey bunch of jocks during my brief foray into the College first-team squad, I managed to break through the defence and leave the 'stars' sprawling. That only happened once. But hey, it felt good.

One of the best variations of rugby in high school was called *domp*. What a jol. We'd wait for a heavy rain and then head out onto the most waterlogged field and pummel the living polony out of each other until we couldn't any more. There were no rules, only big hits, lank mud and the world's longest and messiest rolling maul. The guy who got nailed in the most violent fashion was normally the winner. Awesome.

I can still taste the bitter pill of defeat in my last game for College against Durban High School – a taste made even more unpalatable by the fact that it was the only time I had ever been on the losing side in my entire high school rugby career.

I am humbled by the memories of that somewhat brutal transition from schoolboy rugby to varsity level when I played for Rhodes U21A and lost to pretty much everyone. I remember playing against Police in Port Elizabeth and Despatch in Despatch and getting *dik gemoer* both times.

I look back on the carnival atmosphere of inter-res rugby as some of my happiest memories of the sport, and I remember that sad day when I hung up my togs for good. I had to turn down both the captain and coach, who had wanted to groom me for a position in the Rhodes first team, so that I could pursue my studies in the theatre in earnest. Let's be honest, though – it was Rhodes. I was pretty much over losing to everyone in the Eastern Cape.

As you can probably tell, my rugby memories are dear to me, but none more so than my very first rugby game. That's where it all started.

I've always been small, but as a little kid I was practically a pygmy. There we stood, these barefoot *laaities* from Altona (just outside PE), nervously fidgeting in anticipation before the big game, and me the lightest *laaitie* of them all. The imposing trees stood sentry alongside the field like the giants of Eastern Cape rugby (Danie Gerber, Garth Wright, and um, that other guy . . .) as we, the future, were about to take to the battlefield.

The actual game is a blur, except for one glorious moment that forever defined the spirit of rugby for me. There was a kid on the opposing team who could best be described as gargantuan, and he was having a field day. This locomotive of lard, this beast-like expanse of a child, was running over my teammates like they were nothing. He was swatting them away like they were flies; he was squashing them like bugs. And then there was me . . . the last line of defence and the smallest oke on the field, playing in his first-ever rugby game.

The massive child-beast saw me coming and smirked like a rampant troll at a badly barricaded village gate. I felt like a Lilliputian about to take on the Stay Puft monster from *Ghostbusters*. I was clearly out of my league. But then he did something he never should have done to a child in the early stages of developing his very own brand of short-man syndrome. He put his tongue out at me. The cocky fat bastard actually put his tongue out at me. Big mistake.

I wouldn't call it a tackle exactly. It was more like me having successfully got in his way. But I got in his way with every inch of my tiny little body and every mile of my unconquerable spirit, and I brought him down. I brought him down to tiny-guy town. He came crashing to the ground like a detonated building, like a chubby Goliath, like an over-confident fat kid who had just put his tongue out at the smallest kid on the field with the biggest heart.

I was hooked, and I would never look back. Rugby was *my* game.

ROB VAN VUUREN is a theatre director, producer, playwright, stand-up comic and actor. His accolades include taking a record-breaking 13 shows to the Grahamstown National Arts Festival in 2008, triumphing in the TV show *Strictly Come Dancing* and performing at Nelson Mandela's ninetieth birthday bash in Qunu. Rob's disturbingly real alter ego is Twakkie, from *The Most Amazing Show*, but in his youth Rob was better known for his sniping breaks around the base of the scrum and his ferocious tackling.

Lost Love

I've only recently quit rugby. In 2009, to be precise. As a full-time, professional Paralympic athlete, maybe I shouldn't have told you that.

I'd go to rugby practice psyched up after athletics training; it was good for fitness and a bit of a jol. I played two games as a substitute for the Pretoria Boys High Old Boys team in the intra-varsity league at the University of Pretoria. We had 35 guys on the team, so each guy probably got ten minutes on the field. I didn't play as aggressively as I could have and I made sure that I tackled correctly and had warmed up properly. My athletics coach didn't seem to mind. I love rugby, and I really miss it.

But let me start at the beginning.

My father is Afrikaans and my mother was born in Kenya. We grew up with my mother, so we grew up speaking English, but my Afrikaans is decent. I still consider myself half-Afrikaans. Growing up in an Afrikaans family meant growing up with rugby. We watched rugby on TV every weekend. Rugby was king. My grandfather on my mother's side grew up in Kenya, and captained his club rugby side there. Much later, when he moved out of his house in Bryanston, I inherited three pigskin rugby balls. Those things are so heavy that I can't imagine playing with them.

My other grandfather, on my father's side, was a champion boxer. I don't know how much work he does there, but he still goes into the office every day, even though he's now 93. Until the age of 86, he could do 120 skips in a minute. He has 26 grandchildren, and whenever he sees one of the boys – there are 14 of us – he gives us a friendly punch. That's his way of greeting. He's a tough man. A fighter.

I tried a lot of sports when I was young: boxing, wrestling, soccer, cricket. I never got out LBW so I enjoyed cricket. I blocked my stumps with my legs so well that the other kids wanted 'pads' like mine because I could blitz between the wickets, too. I'd take quick singles but I always forgot that my batting partner couldn't run as fast and I would end up running him out. That didn't make me very popular, and I was soon dropped to the B team.

Boxing was our family's sport, and I enjoyed it immediately. I also played a lot of water polo while I was at Pretoria Boys High. I always found it funny – the guys would see me climb into the pool without prosthetics and for the first two or three minutes, they'd take it easy on me. Only when I started dominating them would they step up to the plate. I always wanted that. I have never asked to be treated differently. I believe the only way you can get stronger is by competing with guys who are better than you in every respect.

That is what is unique about a team sport: when you win a game, you feel like you've accomplished something as a group or a team or a brotherhood, and when you lose, you all share the loss. Nobody blames an individual, even though it may be evident that somebody slipped up. You all take it together. That is the respect you learn from sport, which you can't learn in any other walk of life.

At Boys High, I was in the same hostel as John Smit had been. John was ten years ahead of me and had left before I arrived, but Chiliboy Ralepelle and I were in hostel together. Chili once picked me up and held me over his shoulder in a move straight out of Wrestlemania . . . and then dumped me onto one of the wooden hostel beds. The bed fell out of its frame and the legs stood there wobbling.

When I arrived at Boys High, which is a big rugby school, we were offered loads of new sports, but the first opportunity I got, I started to play rugby.

First I had to adapt my prosthetics. We had to find a softer casing, and I needed carbon feet that were better suited to high-intensity sport. I was a year older than my classmates, so in 2001, in Standard 6, I was already U15. Two years later, in Standard 8, I was playing fifth-team rugby. We had ten Open teams at Boys High, so in the greater scheme of things I was a mediocre rugby player.

When I was sixteen, I weighed the same as I do now – 80kg – and because of boxing, I had massive lats. (I've had to lose them since so that I can run a decent 400m on the track.) I started out at inside centre because I had some size on me and was quite quick, but by the time I was playing fifths, I had moved to the left wing. My hands weren't that safe, but I could run.

You know how it goes at school: if you're in fifths, you want to be in fourths; if you're in fourths, you want to play thirds, and so on. Because I was big and fast and tended to be able to read a game fairly well, I would have been very happy if I could have ended up in thirds by the time I was in matric. But I was never going to be a professional rugby player. In fact, after I got a hospital pass in a match against King Edward VII School (KES), I wasn't going to be any kind of rugby player at all. But I didn't know that at the time.

It was a typical hospital pass. The ball popped up really high from the outside centre. I was waiting, and as I took it I saw the opposition had me lined up. The ball seemed to take forever to reach me; I had already considered letting it go because the tackler's eyes were virtually popping out of his head in his eagerness to get to me. But I grabbed the ball, and as I took it I attempted to sidestep him. He took me round the legs; I tried to hand him off, with the ball tucked under my arm, and then another guy tackled me round the shoulders. I landed on my back, and made an effort to turn over and place the ball. But the damage had been done. Getting up was bloody sore.

By now the fathers who had spent all afternoon in the beer tent were getting pretty loud. I was on the KES supporters' side of the field, and one father yelled at me, 'Walk it off! Don't be a sissy! Get a life, come on!' As I stood up and tested my weight on the knee, I knew it was buggered. I took a limp or two, and my ego got the better of me as I tried to jog it off. But it was no good, and I had to take a slow walk off the field. Somehow I still cycled home that day.

The next morning my knee couldn't fit into my prosthetic leg. It was massively swollen. I was taken to an orthopaedic surgeon, and although my anterior cruciate ligament was torn and my meniscus was slightly cracked, it was decided that they didn't need to operate. My biokineticist suggested that I get involved in an athletics programme to start my rehabilitation and to regain my fitness in time for the 2004 rugby season. He took me down to the athletics track and introduced me to an athletics coach, Ampie Louw. I was adamant that I was not going to do athletics, but Ampie (who still coaches me today) had other ideas.

Ampie had trained athletes for the Paralympics before, but he neglected to tell me that. Athletics was the one sport I had never wanted to get involved in. Previously, when I had tried the sport, my legs had always been too heavy, with high resistance and low energy feedback. Basically they were just wooden feet coated with rubber. I would forge sick notes, complete with spelling mistakes and written in cursive in pencil: 'To whom it may concern. Oscar is feeling slightly ill today and won't be able to participate in athletics. Yours truly . . .'

Every year I'd get busted and my mom would give me a whack when I got home. 'It's not about winning,' she said. 'The loser isn't the one who gets involved and comes last. It's the one who doesn't get involved at all and sits on the sidelines.'

After I first met Ampie, I walked away convinced that I would get back to rugby. No ways was I going to do that soft sport on the track. While on holiday at Plettenberg Bay, I gave it some more thought. I was hungry for rugby and didn't want to have just a mediocre season when I got back. I like to do things properly, so I met Ampie again on 4 January, and we started training the next day.

But Ampie tricked me. At the end of January, he entered me into a North Gauteng trial . . . just to see how things went. I ran the 100m in 11.72sec and 11.78sec that day; the world record was 12.20sec. I'd only been running for three weeks.

'Ah! You broke the Paralympic world record,' said Ampie.

I didn't even know what the Paralympics was. I knew it was a bunch of disabled dudes who ran in a competition that coincided with the Olympics, but I had a mental block against identifying with them, as I'd never seen myself as disabled. I had always participated in able-bodied sports. That's cool, I thought, but I'm still set on rugby.

At the end of February, Ampie entered me into another meet and I won, in 11.51sec this time. Then I ran my first 200m in Durban. I ran a crap time, 23.8sec maybe, but for the first time I realised how tough it was to sprint flat out for 200m. April arrived and I was getting ready for rugby season. Then Ampie produced an invitation for me to run in America.

I grew up in a very modest home, so going overseas was something special. The Athens Olympics were two months away and here I was, beating the world champion over 200m – even though I'd only been running for six months. As soon as we got back to South Africa, I started gearing up for rugby season. Then Ampie phoned me with the news that I'd been selected for South Africa's Paralympic team for Athens. That was the moment when I had to say goodbye to rugby and embrace an individual sport instead. It was also the moment that I had to start taking my sport seriously.

My rugby career had not been without incident, but those were serious in a different way. One was even captured on film by the father of a friend of mine. I was in Standard 7, playing U16 rugby against St John's, and a long pass found me on the wing. It was a miracle that I caught it, but I spotted my would-be tackler and I thought to myself: Buddy, I am going to ram you down! I had been standing deep on the wing, so I had a good 25m to build up momentum before impact. I was ready to pick my knees up and mash this guy. Sure enough, he came in for the tackle, checking which side I might try to sidestep him, and as he tried to take me I literally mowed him down.

The try line was right there. I scored my try, and added a Breyton Paulse celebration to do it justice. I was still getting up from the ground when my opposite number, about half a foot taller than me, came up and, intent on revenge, shoved me in the chest. I overbalanced, and as I toppled over one of my prosthetics came off. In a rush of adrenaline, I pulled the other one off so I could balance properly, wound my arm back and hooked him with a massive flattie.

I nailed him so badly you could hear the echo on the 22m line, which is where my friend's dad was standing with his camera. We've watched the replay a hundred times and you can hear his dad exclaiming, 'Oooh! That's my boy!' My guy took a couple of steps left and a couple to the right, then fell onto his knees. That was the end of his game. He didn't know what was happening. He had to sit on the sideline and kept asking the ref if the match was over. Twenty seconds later, our deputy head of sport came storming over, screaming my name.

What did I do that for, I kept thinking. I was now in major trouble. Later they brought the other kid over from St John's for a disciplinary hearing and I ended up getting caned by the boarding house master. The weirdest thing was that I got caned, and then he congratulated me. That was the first and last time I took someone on in sport. When you play rugby, you learn to keep your emotions in check.

Boys High is across the road from Loftus Versfeld, so it was natural that I became a Bulls supporter. Francois Hougaard is one of my best mates. Even if his pantry is stocked with rugby boots instead of food, he is actually quite a down-to-earth guy. I enjoy mocking him about his mullet and how precious he is about straightening it. When I really want to piss him off, I'll give it a tug. I've also dragged Bryan Habana out for a couple of sessions on the track, and he'll tell you himself he hasn't made the end of them. Running 300m sets is completely out of his league, as his sprints are a maximum of 30–40m long.

Receiving a Bulls jersey from Ettienne Botha, the centre who passed away in a car accident in 2005, is what converted me into a real Bulls fan. Ettienne had heard that I was coming to a Bulls game, and he requested that I come down on to the field to receive a jersey he'd had the team sign for me. I met up with him a couple of days later for coffee. He was an individual who took a real interest in people's lives.

Sport teaches you to be hard on yourself, but also to be humble when you come out on top. In a way, I think rugby is one of the most gentlemanly of sports. Even if you were crunched in a tackle and the whole world saw it, you still shake hands with the opposition after the game. It really is a matter of respect for the guys you have shared the field with. Look at football. I love it, and it's got almost everything that rugby has, except for that crucial element of physicality. If you take a hard knock in rugby and your face hits the dirt, your mate will help you up because he knows that in a couple of minutes it could be his turn.

I've learned from Paralympic sport that it's not about winning. It's about being the best that you can be, and I think that's incredibly important. But when you put your body on the line for a common cause, you form a bond with your teammates that is difficult to replicate anywhere else. Ever since I quit the game, I've really missed rugby. Even thinking about it now gives me goosebumps.

——— *As told to Angus Powers*

OSCAR PISTORIUS was born without fibulae, and underwent a bilateral amputation of his legs below the knee at the age of eleven months. He received his first prosthetic legs at 17 months. Twenty years later, he won four Paralympic gold medals; smashed multiple Paralympic world records; received the freedom of the city in Rome and Milan; and was named by *Time* magazine in their Top 100 list of the most influential people in the world (one spot ahead of Oprah Winfrey).

RIAAN MANSER

What I Could Never Leave Behind

Rugby is an almost embarrassing addiction that I cannot shake.

When I was seven, the older boys in our street were always talking excitedly about this awesome game that they played. I wanted to see what it was all about, so I tagged along to an U9 practice. It was madness and chaos and screaming and aggro . . . at least, as much as eight-year-olds could muster. I was hooked. I missed ten tackles, had my head smashed into the ground, was kicked in the teeth and never touched the ball. But I was hooked.

The coach asked me at the end of practice if I was sure I wanted to play with the 'big' boys. He thought it might be more sensible to wait until I was slightly older and had grown a bit. I didn't agree, and the next week I was playing flank for the C team.

Growing up in Zululand, there wasn't much scope for misplaced loyalty. Yes, the Afrikaans community loved Uli Schmidt and Ray Mordt as much as the next guy, but we loved Natal first. B-section rugby, warts and all.

With my foster granddad and my friend's dad, we would make the long haul to King's Park on the weekends to watch the Banana Boys take on the likes of Northern Free State and Eastern Transvaal. A chunk of Eric Herbert's 1 402 Currie Cup points surely came against Hugh Reece-Edwards, Wynand Claassen, Ronnie Haarhoff and company. When Natal eventually broke back into the big league in the late 1980s, we didn't miss a game. And winning the Currie Cup for the first time – on Natal rugby's centenary in 1990 – was unforgettable.

One Saturday stood out more than most. I was competing in a

regional schools athletics meeting at King's Park athletics track, right next door to the rugby stadium. Our school had bussed the dozen or so of us down early that morning. Too early, in fact. We had some time to kill, so, characteristically, I broke a couple of school rules.

We were supposed to stay put at the athletics track until the other schools arrived, but I decided, along with two accomplices, to escape and hitchhike to the Pavilion shopping centre in Westville for breakfast. We had just ordered at the Wimpy when Wahl Bartmann sat down at the table next to us. All 95kg of the semi-hunchbacked Natal captain and superstar. We couldn't believe it. As usual, my friends forced me to approach him. In my croaky pubescent voice, I asked the only man in the world who looked like that if he was the only man in the world who looked like that.

Wahl turned out to be genuinely friendly. We didn't have cameras, but he gladly signed the backs of our ties. Unbelievable.

We soon headed back to the track and got stuck into our respective events. I had more field than track events early on and managed to win the discus and place in the shot put. Wahl had fired me up. The problem was that the Natal game was going to kick off at 3pm next door, which unluckily coincided with the final of my track event. I heard later that my teacher almost burst into flames when she couldn't find me. That was unfortunate, but I got to watch a Natal comeback win, sealed with a stumble-and-crawl try by Jeremy Thomson.

A couple of years later, the 1995 Rugby World Cup etched itself indelibly into our collective memory. I had the privilege of watching the torrential-rain saga play out at King's Park; apart from the nerve-wracking match itself, I must make mention of the impressive engineering of the Cadac *skottel*, which allows it to braai wors and chops even when the rain is bucketing down.

Fast forward one World Cup: in October 2003 I was having breakfast with Namibia's World Cup team on the morning of their departure for Australia. I had been on my bike since leaving Cape Town one month earlier on my trip around Africa, and sitting down at a buffet with Kees Lensing, Wolfie Duvenhage and the boys was a totally unexpected bonus. The president of Namibian Rugby managed to sour their send-off by using his five-minute speech to lecture the team and threaten them with immediate repatriation if they so much as stuck their heads out of the bus window while in Australia. The players thought he was a joke and concentrated on the fact that they were on their way to the greatest rugby spectacle on the planet. Good for them. I then joined them in their parade through Windhoek, in the captain's car.

While circumnavigating Africa on my bicycle, with many a war zone and other dangers to negotiate, I remained ultra-aware of the 2003 Currie Cup schedule. Without any idea of what kind of terrain I had to cover, I cycled like a man possessed in the last few days before the Currie Cup final, through jungles and minefields and across flooded rivers with my bike slung across my back. The rocky jungle roads became tarred roads, which represented hope. How I managed to reach Sumbe, a coastal town near Luanda in Angola, which had both electricity and the possibility of satellite television, on the day of the final remains a mystery.

I asked around for DStv like a crack addict. I harrassed every soul I bumped into. No one knew what I was talking about. Eventually the manager of a small hotel bar directed me to someone's house, advising me to look out for the dish on the roof. The only satellite dish in Sumbe, he said.

I sat myself down outside the house with the dish, kickoff drawing rapidly nearer. With five minutes to go, I began preparing myself for the fact that I would not see the final between the Sharks and the Bulls at Loftus. Jeez, this is not fair, I thought. I have not been lazy. I deserve this.

One minute before the match started, a man and his family arrived. Armed with a smattering of Portuguese ('*Obrigado!*'), and despite his fragments of English, I got him to switch on his TV and let me play around with the remote. It was amazing how this fellow allowed me to take over his living room. The game was on, and soon I was sitting right in front of the TV, his beer in one hand, a bowl of chips in the other, totally ignoring this group of bewildered people. The Sharks got thumped by the Bulls that day. But the fix I needed, I got.

Early in 2004, while passing through the Ivory Coast, I hoped to meet Max Brito, the Ivory Coast winger who broke his neck during the World Cup we hosted in South Africa. But he had been assisted by the French Rugby Federation and was receiving medical care in France. Neck injuries can happen anywhere, any time. A friend of mine broke his neck in a game in which I played while in parachute battalion in Bloemfontein.

A related, more famous case in Springbok rugby involves Bok legend André Venter, who was left paralysed from the waist down after developing a rare degenerative disease. Little did I know it then, but when I eventually met André, I would not once feel pity for him, nor would he seek it. In fact, I was inspired beyond words. It is the responsibility of those of us who have played and fallen in love with the wonderful game of rugby to offer something back.

It's strange how these things work out. Thousands of kilometres from the Ivory Coast, I was on a tram in Alexandria in Egypt, heading to an outlying suburb to explore, when I heard American-accented English being spoken at the back of the carriage. One guy had rugby togs slung over his shoulder, exactly as you'd imagine they carried their gear 50 years ago. The Americans turned out to be a group of Mormon missionaries who had joined the local rugby club. A club that was coached by a South African! I had no choice but to change my plans and immediately head to practice with them.

Barefoot and in trousers and a button-up shirt, I gave it a good bash with the enthusiastic Egyptians. These guys were running through tackling drills and practising ball steals with the hearts of lions, but their timing and execution was desperately lacking. What I saw at that practice reinforced for me what a critical role experience plays in sport. If I had hung around any longer in Alexandria, I probably would've run out for the team, one of the major sides in the national league, that weekend. But I had to get going.

When I reached Cairo, I managed to catch the infamous Springbok vs Ireland Test on TV, when the New Zealand ref Paul Honiss awarded a penalty to Ireland and then ordered John Smit to give his team a talking-to. Smit did so, and the Irish flyhalf took the gap with a quick tap, and darted over untouched to score a crucial try. Like Bok fans all over the world, I was gutted when we lost by five points.

I looked up the Cairo Rugby Club and was presented with an Egyptian rugby jersey by the club captain. I've often worn that jersey with pride. I wish more African teams would start to thrive. If only the big corporates would spend some serious money on rugby in Nigeria, we'd have more than one African nation in the running at the World Cup.

My next roadside rugby incident occurred in Mozambique, when I bumped into a bunch of kids passing an over-inflated rugby ball around in a circle. I stopped, of course. I chatted to them for a while and then we began backline drills on the small section of tar. I even had one of the guys film us as we went about our rugby practice in between the smoke-belching trucks and spluttering Peugeot station wagons.

Once I had rested up from cycling around Africa, I attempted another world first in 2008: this time paddling around Madagascar, the fourth largest island on earth. Very near Lavanono, a famous Malagasy surf spot, I bumped into four large Frenchmen. They had brought a team of French kids over on a junior rugby tour of Madagascar, but for their five days off the four of them had taken a road less travelled, hence our meeting.

We had beers, then they moved on to the famous rum, and eventually we were scrumming down against each other in a tiny beach restaurant. The owner cheered us on as we, all front-rowers, shared tips about the goings-on in the darkest place on a rugby field.

Watching the Currie Cup final that year was an incredible experience. Two cyclones, blowing in back to back, had me bunkered down in probably the only place I'd get to see it. Again, it was the Sharks vs Bulls, but this time it was all in French. But the Sharks were winning, so I understood everything!

To this day, I cannot explain how I convinced the entire bar to change channels from the soccer to a game they did not understand and cared even less about. But by the end of the comprehensive Sharks victory, the patrons were slapping me on the back as if I'd played in the game myself and contributed in some way. Maybe I had!

RIAAN MANSER put his name on the map when he rode his bicycle, solo and unaided, 37 000km through 34 African countries on a two-year quest to become the first man to cycle around the continent's perimeter. Four years later, after an eleven-month battle against the elements and extreme isolation, he cemented his place among the adventuring elite when he became the first man to circumnavigate Madagascar by kayak. When he's not enjoying the great outdoors, Riaan is South Africa's premier motivational speaker.

WAYNE FYVIE

Tell Them Your Brother is Coming

As a South African boy born in the small town of Harrismith in the Free State, what else could fill my head but the wonderful game of rugby? Rugby in my blood? From the very first day until now, nothing has changed. I vividly recall, many years ago, my dad, my brother and I waking up in the early hours of the morning to watch our beloved Boks competing against the All Blacks. With a cup of coffee and an Ouma rusk in hand, we turned on the telly, only to see images of the New Zealand public protesting and not allowing our team to take the field. With tears in my eyes, I looked to my dad for an explanation of why this was happening. It didn't make any sense to me. After all, for a five-year-old, this was sport, not politics.

As a six-year-old, I would go and watch my older brother Gary practise with the Harrismith junior primary school team. I loved the game. Then one day, I heard the coach call, 'Come here, my boy!' I ran over, and he asked if I'd like to play. 'Yes!' I exclaimed.

'We're short a centre for the game on the weekend,' he said. 'If you can make it, we'd like you to play.'

This was it. I was in the mix. Four more sleeps and I would be running out for the Harrismith U8 team . . . as a six-year-old. I was too excited!

We were playing the match in Bethlehem, which was about an hour away. Before my dad came to wake us up at 5am, I was already in my gear and ready to go. A bright orange jersey with green cuffs: I wore it with pride because I was part of a team. I had earned this jersey. I must say now that the colours don't rank up there with my favourites, but at the time it was the best outfit in the league.

Arriving at the ground, I looked around at the frosted pitch. As the sun rose, more of the glistening white frost would turn into wet brown grass. Nothing could stop me. I was going to do some damage out there. What fun mixing it with your *maatjies* on a frosted field against the enemy in another strip from another town. All we had to do was get the oval-shaped ball over the line, and the enemy was what we had to get through to do so. The more we did this, the better our chances of winning. What a game!

My dad once reminded me of how one of the mothers of our team picked up the corner flag and chased the ref because the opposition had dropped the ball over the try line and the ref had allowed the try. There was always lots of passion for winning rugby in the Free State.

I remember telling Gary, when he was off to boarding school at Clifton in Nottingham Road, 'Take a photo of me, and tell your friends that your brother Wayne is coming and he is a rugby player!'

A year later, I was at Clifton, and life was all about sport. School work was there so that we could play sport in the afternoons, in my opinion. Once we were writing mid-year exams and had a match that afternoon against Michaelhouse. My focus was certainly not on the exam and, as snow was expected, I had to ask our coach at break, 'If it snows, will we still play this afternoon?'

'My boy,' he said, 'this is not cricket. Rugby we play in any conditions!'

During the next exam, the snow came bucketing down. And we played the game, even though the field was covered in snow. What I remember most about that game was that we had to have a cold shower before we could have a hot one, because a hot shower would have burned as we were so iced up.

Because I was too small for any other position, I played scrum-half and was captain of the U11 team. Like all scrumhalves, I was full of shit. Once when we got a penalty on the opposition 22m line, I tapped the ball, looked at the ref and said, 'Mr Ref, there is no way these guys are 10m back,' and I started to walk, counting off the steps. One, two, three, four, five . . . The opposition started to retreat until one of their fathers shouted, 'Tackle the boy! He's already tapped the ball!' I came close to walking over and scoring a try untouched, which would have been one to talk about if it wasn't for that father.

The lack of school work and too much focus on sport eventually caught up with me, and I decided to do Standard 6 for the second time at Hilton College. At the time, this was a real embarrassment, as failure at school was something that was laughed at by your peers. School was still hard work, but I got through. I played scrumhalf for the U14 and U15B teams, because the 'A' team scrumhalf was none other than Hentie Maartens. (And only one of us became a Springbok at No. 9!)

As a late developer, a move from the backline to the forwards was inevitable and my lack of speed contributed to my shift to flank forward in my senior rugby years. I played for the third team in my first match, and after a spate of injuries after the first weekend's rugby my second game was on the flank for the first XV. That was a proud moment for me as I played with my older brother, who was on the other flank. But it was back to the thirds for the rest of the year after that one game.

Rugby is a very special game which taught me many things about life. All you need to do is take a look at the make-up of a rugby team to see why this game is unrivalled. The men wearing the No. 1 and 3 shirts are normally two plumpish fellas. The No. 2 jersey is occupied by the mad guy. Anyone who's happy to pack down in a scrum like that can only be mad.

Then, 4 and 5 . . . what can I say? Long, skinny and can jump, but not well enough to have made it on the basketball court. These unique individuals can also have an aggressive streak once tested. But it does often take a lot to test them.

At 6 and 7 you get the good-looking guys who have all the charisma and love getting stuck into whatever is on offer. The No. 8 position is normally taken by the person who wasn't tall enough to make it at lock, was too slow to play in the backline, and who wasn't good-looking enough to play at flank.

In the No. 9 position, you get a Troublemaker – with a capital T – and the cheekiest member of the team. Always causing kak and running behind the big boys and shouting loudest, but from a distance. I know. I was a scrumhalf once.

The glory boy, a favourite with the ladies and who normally leaves the field with clean pants, is the No. 10. Unless his name is Henry Honiball.

Numbers 12 and 13 also fancy themselves a bit and will often find themselves crossing the try line thinking it was all their hard work that got them there – and boy, do they lap up the glory.

The wings are 11 and 14. 'Wing' says it all. They want to fly around as fast as they can with as little contact as possible. 'Contact' is almost a swear word for them, and in fact they are often just plain scared.

In the No. 15 jersey you'd normally find another nutter, because anyone who throws himself into the air to collect an up-and-under with eight big forwards bearing down on him definitely needs to be a little nuts – and also a bit of a loner, floating around at the back of the field.

Then you get the reserves, waiting patiently for one of their mates to get injured so that they can get out onto the pitch. And the coach who moulds this bizarre collection of individuals into a team.

Who can say rugby is a simple game when you look at those guys? You've got all sorts: fat, long and thin, good-looking, short and cheeky, smooth and fast – and of course the nutters. That's complex, not simple. It's a lot like a successful business.

Rugby teaches you many life skills. For instance, it teaches you how important it is to plan ahead. Adrian Garvey, the tighthead prop who came down from Zimbabwe to Natal, was told by coach Ian McIntosh that if he didn't weigh 110kg by the start of the next year, he wouldn't make the squad. So he gym-ed hard and ate as much as he could, but with weigh-in day approaching Garvey was still 2kg short of the magic number. So he planned ahead and got two 1.5kg weights from the gym and put them in his pockets for the big weigh-in. Mac was ecstatic when he saw the 111kg at the weigh-in, saying, 'I knew you could do it, my boy! Well done!' Forward planning is crucial.

I also recall Ian McIntosh and his selection panel calling me in one day and telling me that I was too small to play flank, and that I wouldn't make it if I stayed in that position. Sean Gage, one of the best hookers I had seen play, had recently and tragically died, so Mac and his team asked me to switch to hooker. They would 'work with me and help me with the transition', but I said to them, 'I will play flank for Natal. Flank is my position.' They were happy with that but informed me that I was the eighth-best flank in the province. Nonetheless, I played my first game for Natal that year . . . at flank. I was glad I stood my ground and believed in my own ability.

Rugby also teaches you how to handle disappointment. When I was in the prime of my rugby career and had just returned from a tour with the Springboks in 1996, we were in the middle of another Currie Cup season. Natal were playing against Eastern Province. I told my roommate, Dieter Kriese, that it was only a matter of time before I was injured, having played 72 games in a row for the Sharks with only one break (when I attended my brother's wedding). Don't tempt fate. I got the injury: I ruptured all the ligaments in my knee and damaged my medial meniscus cartilage. It meant ten months out of the game, lots of rehab and a long, hard climb back to recovery. When you're out of the mix, it's a lonely place and it's up to you to get back in.

Getting dropped from the Sharks also made me realise that the jersey is only on loan to you and belongs to the person who wears it the next week. I was very disappointed by the axing, and I phoned my dad to hear him say to me, 'My boy, you can either cry about it or get your jersey back. It's your choice.' I went back to basics, trained really hard and got my jersey back. The team is always bigger than the individual.

The world was opened up to us with the end of the apartheid. We were fortunate enough to be able to travel the world and do what we loved – play rugby. But for me, it all ended after a year in Wales playing for Cardiff Rugby Club.

I called a mentor and friend of mine and asked him if he thought I should continue playing another season in Cardiff. He asked if I was enjoying it. 'Not really,' I said. 'My body's sore and I don't have the drive left in me.'

'Why waste a year?' he said. 'Get back and get involved in your business.'

I took his advice, and after my last game for Cardiff I took all my kit off, gum guard included, and walked out of the change room to start a new life in the business world.

Does rugby stop there? As one of the better armchair critics you'll find, I always say, 'The longer we're out the game, the better we were.'

Will the passion for the game ever die? No ways!

––––––––––––––––––––––––––

WAYNE FYVIE played over 100 games at flank forward for the Natal Sharks and three Tests for the Springboks, captaining both his province and the Springbok mid-week team. Wayne hung up his boots in 2001 and now runs his own business, greenOFFICE. He also serves as a trustee for the Chris Burger Petro Jackson fund, which assists injured rugby players in South Africa. He remains a passionate supporter of a sport which has done so much for so many.

SCHALK BURGER

Accidental Hero

If I had to find the essence of rugby in one moment, in one game, it would be the 2009 Currie Cup semifinal against the Blue Bulls at Newlands.

It was Western Province's first home semifinal for a while, and I was on the bench after breaking a rib in the Tri-Nations earlier in the season. I came on after half-time, and midway through the second half I put in what was probably the biggest tackle I've ever made in my life. Fourie du Preez, one of my best friends, was on the receiving end.

Obviously I didn't target him personally; I was targeting the man with the ball. When the tackle was completed, I was incredibly psyched up. Fourie managed to get up – bravely, because I thought there was no way anyone could get up from a tackle like that – and as he came over to the scrum resulting from his knock-on, I gave him a little wink. He's one of my best mates, but he's playing for the opposition. What can you do? On the way to the next line-out, I jogged past and said, 'Fourie, I'm sorry it was you. I wish it was someone I don't actually like!'

The match continued, and after Morné Steyn produced one of the greatest kicks ever seen at Newlands from the 10m line, we lost by two points. After a few beers with my teammates, I thought I'd check up on Fourie, so I walked across to the Bulls' change room with a beer in each hand. I gave one to him, and said cheers. Listen here, he said. When he felt that tackle come in he didn't think it was me, because he didn't think I could tackle that hard! He saw a blond shock of hair and thought it was Duane Vermeulen.

That is what's fantastic about rugby. As tough as it is on the field, you can still crack a beer and have a laugh about it. What happens on the field stays on the field. Very seldom has stuff been taken off the field.

The Springboks work like that, too. In the 2007 Super 14 final, the Sharks lost in the 81st minute to a Bryan Habana try. The next day John Smit had to skipper all those guys – including his gutted Sharks teammates and the victorious Bulls – in the lead-up to the Rugby World Cup. That's a great example of what unique man-management skills are required in rugby, especially South African rugby. You need super social skills to get a group of fat okes, skinny okes, short okes, coloureds, blacks and whites – all speaking different languages – to pull in the same direction.

As we know, a team with less talent but more commitment will regularly beat a team of superstars. How to achieve that special bond with your teammates is something more difficult to put your finger on. But when you get it together, the results are amazing.

It's also amazing that my rugby career ever came together in the first place. You could say I was a late developer in rugby. At school, my rugby wasn't great but my cricket was magnificent. In Standard 6 at Paarl Gym, I was playing first team cricket at school and first team at Wellington Cricket Club. By matric, I was cricket captain, opening the bowling and batting No. 3. (I was also surfing every weekend, down at Blouberg or Big Bay or Melkbosstrand.)

It wasn't that I was terrible at rugby. I played Craven Week as a reserve lock for Boland. But accolades came easier in cricket than in rugby. I finished school with a cricket contract at the Boland Academy, and when I started university in Stellenbosch I went straight into the varsity first cricket team.

However, I couldn't say no to a game of inter-res rugby. Unfortunately, I tore my biceps, which ruled me out of cricket for a while. When they found out, Boland Academy dropped me to their fourth team, and although I worked my way back up I eventually lost my cricket contract because I had carried on with another game or two of res rugby. But in the meantime I had received a call from Stellenbosch rugby.

Although Maties knew I was concentrating on cricket, they needed extra reserves because the U19 and U20 sides would be playing simultaneously at the intervarsity tournament in Bloemfontein. No problem, I said. I was actually quite keen on some contact. I had been bowling at small okes batting, which was great, but I wanted the chance to *donner* some *ou*.

It was very lekker travelling up on the train. I had four or five beers the night before – nothing serious, because my teammates were checking me out. The next day our U21 captain went down with a stomach bug. So they said, 'Schalla . . .'

I was amped up: 'Guys, I am *so* ready for this!'

I was thrown in at the deep end and it was a great little game. We lost on the hooter – 24-23 or something – and from then on, my rugby picked up. I still played cricket, but the next weekend Maties selected me to play again. Same position – open-side flank. This was in 2002. I'd just left school and here I was playing three games for Maties U21.

A few weeks later, I happened to play in the curtain-raiser for the Maties second team, who played in the first division along with the university first team. In that second team game, a friend of mine (who's now at Racing Metro in France) got injured in the first half. They put me straight on. I'd just played 80 minutes of rugby, and now it was another 40 minutes straight away. On the Monday, the new team sheets were pinned up and my name was down for the second team. And that's how I got into the senior ranks.

I played four or five games for the second side, and then they drafted me into the first team. Through the Maties first team, I was invited to Jake White's South African U21 training squad. I played all the trial matches, but I didn't make the final squad. I was still only eighteen. I remember Jake telling me not to go back to cricket, and that I must keep playing rugby. Sure, I said, but when December came, I was playing cricket again. Cricket was lekker.

But by now I had also played two U19 games for Western Province, turned out for the Province U21 team, and had been selected for the Stormers squad. In 2003, my second year out of school, I didn't play a single game for the Stormers, but played Vodacom Cup rugby instead and then captained Jake's South African U21 team.

When I got back to Province, I played five Currie Cup games, and then took a phone call from Springbok coach Rudolph Straeuli. 'You're going to the World Cup,' he said. Then rugby completely took over. The decision between rugby and cricket had been made for me.

I haven't driven to a rugby game at Newlands for seven or eight years now. I live right across the road from the stadium, so I walk. In shorts, slops, and if it's raining with an umbrella. Under the railway line, across the field and into the Province change room. If it's a five o'clock game, we've got to be there at twelve. I leave at five minutes to.

Once the team's assembled, we go to the Vineyard Hotel for lunch. Since I started playing for Province, the menu hasn't changed. Lasagne, drumsticks, bolognaise, boiled eggs, Greek salad, sweet chilli sauce, peanut butter, buns, Appletiser and Grapetiser. That's it.

Playing at home is magic. But home or away, it's a pretty special feeling when, after you've given everything in 80 minutes of rugby, you sit in that change room, open a beer and start exchanging stories about *this* tackle or *that* move or *that* turning point . . . it's a fantastic environment to be in. And this is what goes down every single weekend.

However, winning a big trophy is what bonds teammates together forever. I've won the world championship with the South African U21 side and I've won the Tri-Nations and the World Cup with the Springboks (I don't have good memories from the British and Irish Lions tour!), but at Western Province we haven't won anything yet. We've had some good teams and some great seasons, but if you look back there isn't anything that stands out. We need that one big achievement to cement our bond at Province.

I've been involved with the Boks for a long time now, and that team has come a long way. A player never forgets the first time he becomes a Springbok, but it's something else when the team really bonds. After we won the 2007 Rugby World Cup, our group was as tight as anything. We didn't go out after winning the final. We just sat in our little team room and exchanged stories. We had so much energy and emotion to let out, we just sat there – until 7am the next morning – drinking beer and telling stories. Well, not all of us made it to seven in the morning. But I did.

The one sad thing about rugby is that I find we don't mingle enough with the opposition, and by that I don't mean at after-match functions. No one socialises there. I mean actually having a few beers with the guy you've played against ten or twelve or 20 times in your rugby career, and just having a laugh with the guy. After all, we've got so much in common.

Let's be honest, we all have certain preconceptions about players from Italy, Argentina, New Zealand or Australia or wherever. Take a guy like Chris Latham. His socks were always down and his shirt was always hanging out, so we South Africans thought he was a bit of a *skollie*. But spend some time with the guy, and you realise that's he's actually a really relaxed, down-to-earth family man. There's always a surprise when you get to know the guys you play against. Hang out with them and it'll probably be one of your best experiences ever.

People always speak about how in the old days there were so many great characters in the game. I think one of the reasons was because players were allowed to be characters back then. Modern players don't really get the opportunity to express themselves. If you're a character nowadays you'll probably end up in trouble more often than not.

I've made a lot of friends in the game, from school right through varsity and provincial rugby. Usually I get to know the loose forwards first because we're in direct opposition. And obviously we make friends at international level in Australia and New Zealand because we play there so often. Nonetheless, playing for the Barbarians was one of the greatest rugby weeks I've ever experienced. I've been privileged enough to play for them on three occasions, but I'd play there every year if I could.

If you had asked me when I was a *laaitie* what I wanted to be when I grew up, I would have said either a South African cricketer or a Springbok rugby player. Not a policeman or a lawyer or a fireman. A sportsman.

And if I wasn't a rugby player, I would be a rugby supporter. I'd love it. It's fantastic how rugby as a sport and an industry has developed. There's rugby on 24/7. Even on Sundays – you can watch Heineken Cup. For a rugby fan, it's just amazing. My brother is the biggest rugby fan out there, and when the season starts winding down, he tells me to keep on playing. Just keep on playing!

But eventually you have to draw the line somewhere. As a player, the season does get long. Even I need to go on holiday!

——— *As told to Angus Powers*

SCHALK BURGER is one of the most recognised and remarkable players in world rugby. He played for the Springboks before he had represented the Stormers; scored a try on his Bok debut at the 2003 Rugby World Cup; and returned from a career-threatening neck injury to resume his influential role in the 2007 World Cup-winning side. Schalk's toughness – for instance, scoring a try and playing until the final whistle of the 2010 Currie Cup final despite a broken rib – has become the stuff of legend.

BEVAN CULLINAN

Rugby Taught Me Shit

I was a fat seven-year-old and was in Sub B when my father was transferred from Johannesburg to Port Elizabeth. I joined a new school at the beginning of the second term, right when rugby season started. I was a reserved kid, and scared of getting involved in anything that might open me up to more ridicule beyond the obvious: Porky McPorkenstein. I got through the first two weeks as the new fat kid before I came home one day and told my dad that they were having rugby try-outs, and that I didn't think I would sign up.

My dad is one of the most open-minded and supportive fathers anyone could ever hope for. I wouldn't be where I am today if both my parents hadn't let me follow everything I wanted to. Luckily for them, it paid off and I didn't have to sell a kidney – but I digress. My father was a boarder at St Andrew's School, Bloemfontein, from Standard 4 to matric and played a lot of rugby and swam for the Orange Free State. He is a solid, no-nonsense, generous man who is successful in business. Let's just say that, as a boy who liked painting and drawing rather than going for a leisurely cycle or casual sprint, I was wired slightly differently.

I think when he heard that I wasn't going to try out, my dad realised that what he had been waiting for as a parent wasn't going to materialise. I'm sure he had been counting the sleeps since I was born to when he could finally watch his son from the side of the field with all the other dads. I remember the moment very clearly, because his tone changed and he tried to reason with me in a soft and encouraging voice. He explained that rugby would be fun and that he would be at all the games.

I nearly shat myself. At age seven it suddenly dawned on me that this guy really wanted me to play. I didn't know what the benefits would be at that point, but I nervously said that I would at least try out. Even at that age, for me, trying out for anything was like I had the planet's future in my hands. Failure was not an option. The next day, I signed up.

A week later, I arrived at our first U9 rugby 'practice' as our poor coach, Mr Ward, looked us up and down and started trying to make sense of all the different shapes and sizes of kids who had never played rugby before. We had no idea of positions or how the game worked. We just stood in a row and waited to be told where to stand as he literally tried to assemble a team just by looking at us. Mr Ward told me I was a short, stocky guy with a strong neck and that I would make a good hooker. I could not know that from that moment I would be destined to scrum in the front row every Saturday, every season, until I left school. My entire rugby experience had been decided for me there and then.

We used to play barefoot in those days. Our first game was against an Afrikaans school called Hendrik Verwoerd Laerskool. These kids were tough. They looked like they ate a lot of meat. It was 9am, and my feet were freezing cold. Because my dad was there, I didn't want to screw up. I scrummed as hard as I could all game, hooking like a madman. Then my break came. I was waiting in front of an opposition line-out. I was facing the line-out with my back to the opposition hooker, just off the touchline. The ball bounced off their front jumper and literally fell into my hands.

Everything turned to slow motion and I ran. I just ran as fast as I could. I felt hands grabbing at my back and brushing off my feet, but I was too scared to turn around. I just kept running. After about 30m, a very tall, skinny boy took me down, 5m from the try line. I can't remember if we scored or if we even won (it was 28 years ago!). What I do remember is looking for my father to check if he had seen what had just happened. He was laughing and cheering. I felt an overwhelming sense of having done a good thing. I played it cool and smiled. I couldn't feel my feet.

That was the start of my school rugby career as a hooker. It's the only position I ever played, thanks to Mr Ward back in 1982 (I wonder if he even realises his influence). I played in the 'A' team every year, and when my family moved to Cape Town for my high school years I played first-team hooker in Standard 9 and matric. I had no interest in playing rugby at the age of seven; at that stage all I wanted to do was go to drama classes. Don't get me wrong; my dad didn't ever force me. I enjoyed playing, but I would never have got a taste for it if he hadn't introduced the game to me. I ended up doing both: drama classes and rugby.

Rugby gave me a sense of balance. It was something I did every winter. It was something I had started and was going to finish. This meant attending, without fail, practice days plus a game every weekend, all through the season. I dared not give up in case I missed out on something, even after those days where I was so tired and in so much pain and so hungry walking home from school. Rugby taught me about responsibility, teamwork, trust, discipline, motivation and the importance of routine. I committed to rugby, and I was going to see it through.

I learned that sometimes life isn't fair, and that if you want anything you have to fight for it. And, I will admit, I fought a lot. (Apologies to every opposing hooker who got a knee in the face every game.) I also had a couple of close calls collapsing face first in the middle of a scrum in the water and mud of a Cape Town winter. By the time I was in matric, I was playing my hardest rugby. Maybe I knew that this was going to be my last year and that I needed to make something of it before it was all over, forever. That year, I broke a finger, chipped a tooth (through a gum guard) and permanently damaged my left knee (although it's good for predicting rain now).

I was aggressive, big and had my head taped every game before hitting it against the wall a couple of times before going onto the field. For me, it was part of a ritual – from the first whiff of Deep Heat through pulling the laces tight on my boots, wrapping the bandage around my head to save my ears (I'm really glad I started wrapping them in Standard 6), meticulously placing colour-coded insulation tape over the bandages, and inserting the gum guard, which changed the shape of my face. It was a case of kill or be killed.

The psychological process I went through before each game is still with me. I go through the same process every time I step on stage as a stand-up comedian. Obviously I don't bang my head on things, but I work myself up to the same place where I'm ready to do battle with an audience. It's still a case of kill or be killed.

In my final year at school, I was the only player to be a member of the first team while also studying art as a matric subject. I was a walking dichotomy, to say the least, because my dress sense had been modelled off a clown. Literally. I was the arty-farty guy who had learned that rugby meant something to him, despite the sneers of the chino-wearing jock brigade.

There is one particular game that sticks in my mind. I was recovering from the broken finger and couldn't play. I was head boy of my school, a position that afforded a degree of respect from the pupils and teachers, except for narrow-minded Mr Durrheim, who taught us Physical Education. I arrived at the game to support the boys, wearing my first-team rugby jersey as well as red pants and gold shoes. Eccentric, I know, but it was 1993 (the 1980s were still lingering and I had already been working as a professional mime and clown for three years).

Durrheim instructed me to go home and change. I walked home, my broken middle finger throbbing, playing over in my mind all the different responses I could have made instead of just walking away and not saying a thing. I decided not to return to the game that day because I didn't even own a pair of jeans or any other pants which would have been acceptable. I knew that I had worked too hard for that team to stand on the sidelines and not feel that it was me standing there. I refused to meet the expectations of a teacher who didn't understand anything except sweat, Tee-savs and a whistle. Besides, he wasn't even our coach.

I learned that day how important it is to protect any sense of individualism, because it is so easy to disappear into obscurity while trying to comply with outdated ideals. It was only when I got to university the following year that I realised how many people there were like me. It was encouraging. I stopped playing rugby, but I didn't stop applying what I had learned. I became obsessed with training. I was training as a clown – trying new things, making sure I had every possible comedic movement timed and delivered with precision. I worked every day, training in the Drama department until all hours of the morning. I didn't touch a drop of alcohol until my third year.

Nowadays I shoot comedy-based TV commercials. I recently came out of performance retirement to play a character called Gary the Tooth Fairy in an ad I was commissioned to shoot. This is a character who was designed through the training processes I went through at university, which were in turn a result of what I learned during schoolboy rugby training. Gary has a fan page with in excess of 170 000 fans.

Playing rugby happened a long time ago for me, yet I watch the Springboks religiously. As a performer and comic, I enjoy all performance genres, but when all is said and done, the Springboks have a far bigger theatre and audience that any clown could ever hope for. I have great respect for them because I understand the mental and physical punishment they put themselves through – on and off the field. I'm not a Springbok, but I know what was required of me as a schoolboy hooker. I was hard on myself (and still am) and I hated losing (still do) . . .

This is some of the shit that rugby taught me.

BEVAN CULLINAN began his career as an actor and stand-up comedian, training as a clown at Rhodes University while completing his Honours in Drama. For ten years, he was one of South Africa's leading stand-up comedians, well known for his quirky take on the world. After retiring from the stand-up circuit, he became an award-winning director of TV commercials, specialising in comedy. The ingredients for successs – motivation, hard work, training and discipline – Bevan learned on the rugby pitch, every winter for eleven years.

WHERE WERE YOU?

FRED KHUMALO

Waiting for the Barbarians

My father is a mild-mannered man who hardly raises his voice regardless of how angry he is. In fact, when he does get angry – a rare occurrence – his voice ebbs to a hiss so soft that you have to lean forward if you want to hear what he is saying. But then the danger of leaning forward in that manner is that he will suddenly lash out with his open palm. Whack-whack! Always twice. Whack-whack!

Suddenly there's blood snaking out of your nostril, tears adorning your cheeks. I've seen him do this – not with us children, but with his comrades in the soccer fraternity. As an owner of a second division soccer club back in the late 1970s and early 1980s, he was always engaged in fights – if not with owners of other clubs who were trying to poach his charges, then among his players, using his hands to instil discipline. Running a soccer club is like owning a fleet of taxis; you have to be tough. If you're a sissy and you own taxis, your drivers will put you out of business before you can blink. They will rob you of your money, steal parts from your cars or run their own private enterprises using your vehicles.

In the soccer industry, other soccer bosses are always trying to steal your players. Players, too, take advantage of you if you are soft and unsophisticated. You missed soccer practice at your own peril if you were one of my father's charges at Silver Stars FC, which later metamorphosed into Crocodiles FC. But he treated his players like his own children, so much so that he used to pay school fees for some of them – to the outrage of my mother, who would shriek like a banshee: 'You are taking food from the mouths of my children and giving it away to these ungrateful, dagga-smoking urchins!'

Because there were no clubhouses in those days, players used to sleep at our house the night before a game. We used to call it 'doing camp'. And there would be all manner of odours in the house: there was the smell of cigarettes, the stench of unwashed armpits and the smell of an *umuthi* concoction that my father and his *inyanga* would spray in the room where the players would sleep. Some players smoked dagga openly, outside in our yard. My mother did not like this at all, but my father said the holy herb made his players more alert and potent. Anything to make the side stronger.

Whenever she was in a cheerful mood, my mother, who is more educated than my father, used to poke fun at him, saying that the school-going players were taking advantage of his ignorance in matters pertaining to education. 'I heard the other day that one of your players asked you to give him money so he could pay for chlorophyll at school. Of course you gave him the money because you don't know what chlorophyll is! These urchins of yours are going to pluck you like a chicken, I tell you.'

I used to love this joke. My father, who hardly laughs even if he is happy, would just shake his head and say, 'My father was right. Women are just like children. They laugh at things you don't understand.'

But why am I regaling you with soccer anecdotes when I should be telling you about my experiences of rugby? I suppose I want to show you how I crossed that 'sacred' divide between soccer and rugby, between black and white.

It was 1980, a Saturday, and my younger brothers and some of my father's players were moving about our yard, preparing kit for the following day's game. Instead of helping, I was sitting in the lounge reading a magazine. My father and I had been fighting over my refusal to go to soccer training during the week, and I was sometimes even boycotting soccer matches over the weekends. Soccer had been foisted upon me and my two younger brothers from the moment we learned to walk. Soccer was our religion. When my youngest brother, Thabo, was but a toddler, my father had a lightbulb moment. Thabo, who had been born a normal child, using his right hand to eat his food or tap his mother's face, was trained by my father to use his left hand instead. My father had ambitions: he wanted a strong left winger for his team! As he grew up, Thabo became ambidextrous. And he played good soccer to boot.

During the arguments with my father over my failure to turn up for soccer practice, I always told him that now that I was in high school I had to channel my intellectual and physical energies towards my studies instead. And my father – who drove his children hard to achieve educationally to somehow compensate for the fact that he had been unlucky enough to be taken out of school in Grade 2 – would grudgingly allow me to stay at home with my school books.

On this particular Saturday, I decided to defy him. Instead of pretending to read a school book, I sprawled on the sofa with *Bona* magazine. When he entered the room, I was engrossed in a story about Errol Tobias, a player from what was then called the Cape Province. My exposure to rugby at that stage was minimal. I knew that a game called rugby existed, but it existed in a world so remote it was almost mythical. I always saw it as a white man's sport – in fact, as an Afrikaner white man's sport. I didn't know who the leading sides were, nor did I even understand the rules of the game.

Over some weekends, I used to do odd jobs, cleaning white people's gardens to earn pocket money, and during those excursions into the white world I would see white boys playing rugby. I loved the speed of the game. I loved the energy. But the downside, always, was that rugby was for whites. In those days the battle lines were quite stark: everything was in black and white. We darkies had our own shit – soccer, soccer and more soccer. Some black elites – your teachers, lawyers and doctors (a minority of minorities in the black community) – played tennis, and a bit of golf. And whites had their rugby, cricket, tennis, golf and bowls.

There were some white people who played for the black soccer sides: Andy 'Jesus' Karajinsky, Phil 'Uyindoda' Venter, Basil Hollister, Noel 'Mzala' Cousens, the Tovey brothers – Neil and Mark – and many others. With the jackboot of apartheid firmly stamping down any pockets of rebellion, whether in the black or white community, whites who played for black teams were harassed by the police. They had to apply for special permission to play in the townships, thanks to the country's laws of segregation. Being white and playing for a black team was a drag. As a result, the whites who continued to play for black teams in the teeth of repression – and, sometimes, rejection from their communities – were embraced and regarded as heroes in the black community. But because a section of the white population loved soccer but couldn't be seen to be following existing soccer teams in the townships, they also created exclusively white soccer teams affiliated to an exclusively white soccer association.

On this particular Saturday afternoon, my father did a double take when his eyes fell on the story I was reading in the magazine, with a picture of Errol Tobias in rugby regalia in full view. 'Oh, I see it now,' my father hissed sarcastically. 'We are all busy preparing for tomorrow's game, and the boss is sitting here reading magazines. The boss says he can't join us for the real game, and the boss is reading about this white people's nonsense! Have you ever seen a black man playing rugby?'

Cheerfully, I rose from the sofa, and said, 'But here is a black man playing rugby! Errol Tobias is a black man who plays rugby. We should salute him, root for him!'

'Don't tell me about *amaboesman*! He is not black!'

Ah, he walked right into my trap. Just a few months previously, I had joined the Azanian Students Movement, the youth wing of the

Azanian People's Organisation (AZAPO), which was inspired by the Black Consciousness philosophy of Steve Biko. Now was my chance to try out my BC rhetoric on my father. Ahem, ahem . . . let's begin the salvos: 'But, Daddy, that's exactly what the white man has been doing: implementing his divide and rule tactics, encouraging the oppressed people to hate themselves and each other. According to the philosophy of Steve Biko, all those who are economically, socially and politically discriminated against are black, especially if they are not collaborating with the apartheid system in the oppression of their own people. As a result, Errol Tobias is black.'

My father blinked a number of times, and looked at me like a cat regarding a very-much-alive rat it thought it had already killed. 'But these Indians and coloureds live better lives than us Africans,' he said.

'Exactly the point of divide and rule. The white man introduces these cosmetic divisions between us and coloureds so that we can't unite against him . . .'

I wanted to remind him that I had 'coloured' cousins because my aunt – my father's own sister – was married to a non-black! But I thought that would be too much, so I decided to stick to the generalities of the race debate. The debate went on for some time, and he actually sat down to listen to what I was saying. The upshot of it was that it had taken a picture of a black man in rugby kit to get that conversation going between father and son. My exposure to that magazine feature about Errol Tobias and the South African Barbarians, who had toured Britain in 1979, sparked my interest in the game of rugby – not just the game itself, but the politics of it.

In 1981, Tobias became the first black person to be included in the Springbok side, when they faced Ireland at Newlands in Cape Town. Apartheid was at its most oppressive, and naturally there was opposition to Tobias's selection from both white and black communities. Blacks were of the opinion that he was legitimising apartheid and that he should not play as long as apartheid policies existed, while objections from the white community were inspired by sheer racial hatred. A black person couldn't, and shouldn't, compete against whites. Period.

Tobias was to say in a later interview: 'We had no say in politics. We didn't even have a vote, so all I knew at that stage was to play rugby. My goal was to show the country and the rest of the world that we had black players who were equally good, if not better, than the whites, and that if you are good enough, you should play.'

As I grew up and finally went to university, I became relatively well read in the history and politics of sport, thanks to the Black Consciousness teachings, which held that you couldn't separate sport from politics. Because you couldn't have normal sport in an abnormal society, you had to use all avenues – be they religious, cultural or otherwise – to strive for a society that was normal and egalitarian.

In my journalism class at varsity in the mid-1980s, our sporting horizons were further broadened when we could, for the first time for those of us who were black, learn and understand the history of sports that were hitherto the preserve of white people. We learned the rules of rugby and cricket and some of the history of those sporting codes.

It was also around this time that I discovered that in the Eastern Cape rugby was more popular than soccer among black people. That was quite a shocking revelation to a youngster who had grown up in a highly segregated society. The Eastern Cape black people's affinity for rugby suddenly explained the shortage of Xhosa-speaking soccer players. Amazing shit, this segregation.

The hoo-ha over Tobias's selection and subsequent astounding performances was to prove a major milestone in the development of rugby in this country as it gradually tried to shake off the yoke of apartheid. Tobias demystified the game and proved that colour had nothing to do with performance, and that the game could be used to transcend racial and cultural barriers in society. While some black people, including comrades of mine in **AZAPO**, thought he was collaborating with the enemy by playing in a whites-only team, in hindsight Tobias was ahead of his time, a trailblazer who opened the way for other players of colour. Many more were to follow: Chester Williams, Breyton Paulse, the Ndungane twins and the rest who to this day play professional rugby at national and provincial level.

That rugby administrators have had to impose racial quotas is sad. But it speaks volumes about the levels of resistance from many quarters that cannot countenance an increasing number of black players and fans 'usurping' the game from its rightful 'owners'. The mantra in the past was that you couldn't have normal sport in an abnormal society. From a very reasonable point of view, the urge to maintain rugby as a white sport – at both an administrative and a playing level – indicates that ours is still not a normal society.

Rugby has become the 'last outpost' of a sector of our society that is resisting change at its most basic level. They are refusing to put their shoulder to the wheel as we fashion an all-inclusive, non-racial society where we all enjoy equal access to existing cultural amenities. It's not going to be easy; it's not going to happen over-night. But, hell, something's gotta give. Defeating statutory apart-heid did not happen overnight, and it definitely wasn't easy. But you can't sit on top of the lid of a boiling pot forever, as the people's poet, Mzwakhe Mbuli, once said.

While the number of black people who follow and love rugby has increased, many of these fans still find it difficult to trek to a local rugby stadium to watch a game. The anger exhibited by some white fans at what they consider the encroachment of blacks into the 'white man's sport' leaves a sour taste. I don't think there is an agenda to 'usurp' rugby from white hands. People simply want to enjoy the game without having to endure racial insults at the stadium.

I go, and will continue to go, to great rugby matches, even though every time I do so I know that I am crossing the line. I first have to prepare and fortify myself psychologically for the taunts and insults that will unfailingly be thrown my way at a rugby game, simply because I am black. Sad.

But after all these years of reading up on rugby and garnering knowledge of the vibrant game, no fool is about to dampen my growing passion. I can hear the clamour of the barbarians at the gate, but I am ready for them. Rugby doesn't belong in any racial laager. At least, I don't think the Scots had any bigoted notions when they won the very first rugby Test match against England in 1871. I am waiting for the barbarians who need to learn that rugby, like any cultural pursuit, can be a powerful tool to help us transcend stupid, ignorance-inspired fears and misconceptions.

Let's celebrate the humility, the sporting gallantry and the visionary spirit of Errol Tobias, who shall forever be our reference point amid the growing pains of South African rugby. Let's play!

FRED KHUMALO is the editor of the Review section of the *Sunday Times*, where he also writes an award-winning socio-political column. His books *Bitches' Brew*, *Touch My Blood: The Early Years*, *Seven Steps To Heaven* and *Zulu Boy Gone Crazy* have won critical acclaim and rave reader reviews in equal measure. Fred has sat on the judges' panel for the Herman Charles Bosman Prize and the European Union Literary Award. He is currently writing an unauthorised biography of President Jacob Zuma.

INGE BECKMANN

Where I Come From

I come from a long line of jock. My father's father loved rugby and mastered the concertina; my old man played rugby for Western Province; and my big brother was good at all sports. My mother played excellent hockey during her university years but later decided ballet was more her thing. My uncle, Hein Schnell, was a South African javelin champion, and at least seven of my cousins represented our country in sport.

My brother was a supernaturally strong boy and he toughened me up quick-sticks with *lammies* (bruises), headlocks, slapping my forehead repeatedly, squeezing my little-girl knuckles until they popped and nearly breaking my back in a failed *Dirty Dancing* lift. I had to have my game face on back then. After I connected a brick with his head one afternoon, I guess he decided I was ready to handle a ball. I soon gained a skill not many ten-year-old girls dreamed of . . . I could spin a torpedo pass like a man.

However, what I remember most about rugby games as a child was what came with them: my dad's hand, which would instinctively shield his beer when I waltzed into the lounge; his brown paper bag filled with *droëwors* and biltong that I pilfered over the first half of the game and chased down with the dregs of his shandy (which, strangely, was allowed back then); and, last but not least, feeling totally invisible. My head could have fallen off and it would not have produced even the slightest reaction from Pa during a match.

Watching rugby indoors was never much fun for me, but I must say I did enjoy being at a game because there were actual people walking around and I could go exploring. I also loved watching my brother play scrumhalf against other schools and fight his way through the scrum. Even though he was a lot shorter than the other boys, he was a good strategist and quite a nimble lad. I remember the wet, silty patches on the field, pitching my dad's nifty golf umbrella, which doubled as a little seat, and inhaling the glorious smells of boerewors and pancakes. It filled me with such glee. But as I got a little older I started to notice the sports-obsessed mothers cheering for their mini-husbands, and found myself silently praying, 'Oh Lord, save me from the clutches of this leviathan, this sick, sick obsession they call rugby!'

My dad grew up in Piketberg during the Great Depression in the 1930s. He went to a tiny *plaasskooltjie* (farm school) in Broodkraal, played *kleilat* (clay-sticks) and learned to kick a ball while his father worked for the railways. Being the eldest of seven, my dad was *ouboet* – the protector and leader of the pack. He once wee'd on the stationmaster's bratty son for constantly picking on his baby sister, Baba. My oupa taught his offspring not to indulge in physical fights with other children, so it seems my dad learned at a young age how to play the game without breaking the rules.

My father ended up playing in the backline for Western Province, Griquas and Boland. My grandmother Breggie told us how Oupa listened to the radio when my dad played and how he would get up and hug it when my father scored a try. Oupa died in 1959, and my dad finished his degree the same year. My dad eventually stopped playing rugby, but he continued coaching and reffing. We have beautiful black and white photographs and newspaper clippings from his days as a player. I can just picture his strong, young body; he still has the best pair of legs I have ever seen on a 76-year-old. I remember hugging Pa when he came back from Gardens Rugby Club and smelling a combination of *braaivleis*, brandy, second-hand cigarette smoke and Old Spice. If I learned to love anything about the game back then, it was simply what came along with it.

My father, Frans Schreuder, in his rugby prime during the 1960s.

During my matric year in 1995, I was asked – via my modelling agent – to be part of the Rugby World Cup opening ceremony at Newlands in Cape Town. A few other girls and I were to represent the different countries participating in the tournament. I was chosen as Miss Argentina, and was asked to lead the parade! I realised that day that a rugby game can unite all types of people. Who would have thought that I of all teenagers – the complete opposite of a rugby-watching, jock-dating girl – would be picked for such a task? As I entered the stadium during our dress rehearsal, passing the dancing girls, I promised myself that this would be the first and last time I would ever do this sort of thing. I shivered at the thought of ending up with flat, ironed hair, prancing around in a pair of those – well, what shall we call them . . . *poeslappies*? – hotpants and bikini top, and answering to a name like Abigail, Jessica or even Mandy.

What impressed me the most at that point were the acoustics inside the stadium. I can't remember who sang the anthems that day, but knowing what I know now they should have had me sing rather than walk and wave. I must say the moment Newlands filled up, I felt the rugby *gees* come over me in a big way. Four weeks I watched the final between New Zealand and South Africa on TV with my mom (my dad was at the game) and felt very proud of our players.

Rugby can be a delicate science: it is a fierce display of power and strength, and when played with heart it is certainly one of the most engaging games on the planet. That said, it is incredible how the love of a game can transform ordinary folk into complete nutters. I was watching a game at a bar not so long ago and ended up sitting behind a table of keen female Stormers supporters. It was totally surreal. These ladies, sporting team jerseys and war paint, were just about smashing bar stools over people's heads in their drunken over-excitement. It was beautiful. I made friends with a sports writer sitting next to me and he told me that he lurks behind them every weekend because they always provide the best scoops.

Similarly, I drove through Paarl one balmy summer afternoon, admiring gardens, when I passed a house where a father and his six-year-old son were posing for a photograph on their stoep. They were dressed from head to toe in identical Blue Bulls kit, complete with horns, face paint, socks, boots and one oversized flag billowing at their side. It was like something out of *The Shining*, only creepier. The wife taking the photograph had no expression on her face, and seemed more like a ghost than a mother. I felt sorry for the boy. I think some people, especially up north, get a little bit carried away. I can just picture a crazed Bulls supporter at Loftus in full regalia, bellowing something along the lines of, '*Ja-nee, ek sê julle mense nou. God is 'n Blou Bul! Vandag kan ons nie verloor nie!*' (Let me tell you: God is a Blue Bull! Today we cannot be defeated!).

So, am I a real rugby fan, or am I perhaps desensitised to the thrill of the game due to my overexposure to rugby culture as a child? Is there any true love for the sport left in my heart? I have to say that when the stakes are high, I truly am a rugby supporter. Bokke games always seem worth it to me . . . especially when there is talk of a braai or the promise of a half pint of Guinness at my local Irish bar.

––––––––––––––––––––

INGE BECKMANN is an award-winning singer-songwriter and consummate creative from Cape Town. She is best known as lead vocalist for indie band Lark, and has performed, recorded and toured both in South Africa and abroad. Lark's third album is due out this year as Inge continues to successfully juggle parallel acting and modelling careers. With a father who played for Western Province, Inge has never been able to totally escape the pull of rugby . . . and that's the way she likes it.

ANTON FERREIRA

The Tao of Rugby

The seeker after enlightenment who wishes to delve below the surface of things, whose soul cries out for meaning, and whose heart yearns for eternal verities, must subject himself to long, arduous years of fasting and celibacy in a Zen monastery.

Or, he could just watch a lot of rugby.

That has been my strategy, and although full sainthood has so far eluded me, I have at least gained some modest insights into the meaning of life. And what's more, I have done so while greedily stuffing myself with braai chops and beer. Indeed, there has even been the occasional, thoroughly enjoyable lustful thought.

Here is perhaps my most important rugby insight: if you're ever in a fistfight with a visually challenged opponent, make sure your first blow knocks his or her glasses to the ground. Your adversary will immediately drop to his or her knees to retrieve them, and you can thereupon put the boot in to your heart's content, safe in the knowledge that he or she will never be able to pick you out in a line-up.

This is a lesson I learned one bleak winter evening outside Ellis Park. Unfortunately, I was the one wearing the glasses.

The year was 1992, and the Springboks had just returned to international competition after spending a decade or so out in the cold. Nelson Mandela was out of jail, sanctions had been lifted, Calvinism was in retreat and there were even rumours that McDonald's might open a branch in Joburg. In those exhilarating days of heady promise, all we needed to make our joy complete were crushing victories over the All Blacks and Wallabies as we made our grand re-entry onto the world rugby stage.

We know now that it was not to be. Like an inbred family on a junk-strewn West Rand plot, our rugby players had in the years of isolation become weak, pallid and dysfunctional, their spasmodically twitching hands incapable of holding onto passes. They hobbled around the pitch without a plan, back-pedalling in constant retreat, pain-crazed eyes rolling wildly like cattle in the abattoir chute. Even our national hero, Naas Botha, was shown to be several seasons past his sell-by date.

It shouldn't have mattered to me. But it did, and that was another insight from the school of rugby: I was no longer a rootless white liberal exile.

For that is what I had become, thanks largely to the South African Defence Force (SADF). I knew when I was called up for service in the apartheid infantry all those years ago that I didn't like physical exertion. How did I know? Rugby had shown me, of course. It was a compulsory activity at Roosevelt High School, where I spent some of my formative years. Twice a week we had to go to rugby practice when the final bell rang, and those two days – Tuesdays and Thursdays – are imprinted in my memory as the days from hell.

The men who taught us industrial arts, Attie Swart and Flippie Nel, were also our rugby coaches. (Flippie, by the way, got his name from his habit of 'flipping', or beating with a ruler, those who failed adequately to master the secrets of Welding 101 and such like.) Every Tuesday and Thursday they made us run till we dropped in a vain bid to get us fit enough to beat real rugby schools like Krugersdorp High and Linden Hoër and the dreaded Jeppe Boys from the wrong side of town.

What I discovered on those two afternoons a week was that my lungs were tiny and weak, that my leg muscles were those of a consumptive poet, and that rugby was a sport best enjoyed from the sidelines. So yes, on being called up to fight terrorists only weeks after finishing matric, it didn't take long to realise that the life of a tough, tautly muscled bush fighter was not for me. To become such a warrior, you have to run and run and run in the blistering heat, carrying extremely heavy loads.

To escape further torture at the hands of sadistic SADF physical training instructors I went overseas, for years and years and years. I stayed away so long that I lost interest in rugby. Indeed, I became one of those pathetic figures, a South African who supports Liverpool, even though buying a Beatles record is the closest he has ever come to the city. I knew the English football league standings; I could make convincing comments in the pub about Kenny Dalglish and John Barnes and Peter Beardsley and who knows who else. But once annual army camps were scrapped, along with the pass laws and whites-only park benches, I rushed back home. I lost my faux English accent within days, and my interest in soccer evaporated.

Suddenly it was cool to be South African. Biltong, Klipdrift, snoek braais – I couldn't get enough of it. I drew the line only at drinking Castle. I revelled in this strange new world where you could be proud of your Transvaal vowels. Then the sports boycott was lifted, the All Blacks and Wallabies were on the way, and my reversion to type was complete.

In the bad old days of Attie Swart and Flippie Nel, I had always supported whoever was playing against the Springboks. I wanted Benoit Dauga's autograph, not Frik du Preez's; I yelled for Wales at King's Park stadium; and I jumped up and down on the cheap seats at Ellis Park when the British and Irish Lions scored a rare victory. But now I wanted the Boks to win.

Perhaps it was because I had spent so long betraying my ancestors by laughing at the snide anti-Boer jokes of foreigners that I embraced the green and gold with the fervour that I did. I had no idea who James Small was, had never heard of Pieter Hendriks, but I was confident Naas would kick us to victory. And so what if Danie Gerber had a paunch? He was still a legend.

I watched our 27-24 defeat to the All Blacks from an Ellis Park hospitality suite, so at least I could drink a beer afterwards while trying to fool myself that rugby was only a game and it didn't really matter if we lost.

By the time I walked out of the stadium, the crowds had dispersed. A black man pushing a bicycle was still trying to sell ice creams in the gathering gloom. A big white rugby fan staggered up to him, but not to buy an ice cream. The ice-cream seller represented all that was wrong with the new South Africa, judging by the way the fan laid into him with the angry hatred that only a drunken Springbok supporter whose team has been humiliated by the All Blacks can muster.

I hurried over and shouted at the fan to stop. He paused long enough to pick up an empty beer bottle and smash it against a tree. Jagged weapon in hand, he headed back towards the ice-cream seller, who, instead of running for his life, was standing his ground and yelling that apartheid was over and whites were no longer allowed to beat up blacks at random.

I stepped in front of the bottle-wielding fan. 'Don't do it,' I said in Afrikaans. 'There are too many witnesses.' I tried to sound like a savvy fellow-racist who was just giving him some friendly advice to save him from long years of being heavily outnumbered by blacks in a filthy jail cell.

It worked, up to a point. Instead of murdering the ice-cream seller, he swung at me, and knocked off my glasses. I would have kicked him in the balls, but I couldn't see where they were. As I scrabbled about on the tarmac, the drunk's slightly more sober friend grabbed his arm and led him away.

Ah well, I thought. It's only just over a year since FW scrapped apartheid – you have to accept that some whiteys are going to be a bit slow to catch on.

Fast forward three years to the World Cup. The important one, not the dismal cricket affair or the over-hyped FIFA pageant. We had a new coach in Kitch Christie, but by the time he arrived the Springboks were still losing more often than they won. Optimists believed we could finish second in our group, behind Australia, and go through to the knockout stages. And that's exactly what would happen next – we would be knocked out.

I was working for Reuters at the time. On the eve of the opening match – South Africa vs Australia at Newlands – I heard that Nelson Mandela was going to visit the Springbok team at their secret training venue at the Silvermine military base.

If rugby today is regarded as untransformed, in those days it was positively Neanderthal. Fans waved the old South African flag in the stands, raucously sang '*Die Stem*', and generally acted like Test matches were AWB political rallies. Not surprisingly, the ANC were highly suspicious of the white rugby supporter demographic, periodically muttering grim threats to reinstate the international sports boycott.

That Mandela himself was going to meet the team, and publicly embrace the icon of white South Africa, was astounding. I hurried up to Silvermine, just in time to catch the world's favourite president as he shook hands with Francois Pienaar before climbing stiffly back into the helicopter that would bear him away to the city. Two words that Mandela said after the handshake with Pienaar still stick in my mind today: 'our boys'. The Springbok rugby players were 'our boys', and the whole country should get behind them.

The Springboks, in their wildest dreams, could not have hoped for a more important endorsement. And it was incredible to watch these grown-up men in the aftermath of Mandela's visit – they were as gleeful as schoolboys who had just broken up for the Christmas holidays. James Dalton and Joel Stransky, Francois Pienaar and Balie Swart . . . written off as no-hopers by the world's rugby media, they should have been dour, irritable and defensive. But here they were laughing, joking, having fun, as if Mandela had promised them highly paid Cabinet posts with a chauffeur-driven 7-series BMW each. I couldn't figure it out.

Still marvelling at the day's events, I went to a braai in Camps Bay that evening, attended by a dozen lawyers from Gauteng who had come down to watch the opening match against the Wallabies. 'You won't believe it,' I told them. 'Nelson Mandela just visited the Bok training camp!'

I assumed they would be as excited as I was and that they would immediately grasp the nation-building significance. 'Fucking k****r,' one said. 'What does he know about rugby?'

I made my excuses and left, thoroughly deflated. When educated white men, presumably well-versed in the principles of justice, re-acted like this, what hope was there for the country?

I remained depressed until the next day, when the whistle blew to start the first match of the World Cup.

Then a strange thing happened: the Springboks started domina-ting the game. The world champions, Australia, were supposed to crush the life out of the hosts, but here was Pieter Hendriks pump-ing the air with his fist as he effortlessly rounded the man who up until then had thought he was the world's best player, David Campese. How absolutely delicious.

We won, and Pienaar attributed the team's sudden discovery of skill and conviction to that Silvermine pep talk from Mandela.

After that, it was pretty much plain sailing until the semifinal, when we beat France thanks to a bad refereeing decision that robbed the French of a try. Anyway. That bit of injustice was a necessary evil, because without it we would never have made it to the final against the All Blacks at Ellis Park.

How wonderful that we've made it this far, we Springbok fans told ourselves as we sat down for the final. We may not win the World Cup – the All Blacks will take it, of course – but at least we've done a lot better than those insufferable Brit rugby correspondents ever thought we would.

I sat in the press benches, psychologically prepared for the inevitable Springbok defeat. It was the final, neither side would take chances, the rugby would be dull. My expectations could hardly have been lower.

Then that jumbo jet flew over at roof height. It came out of nowhere. It was not on the programme. It was as if the lumbering aircraft had sucked the oxygen out of the stadium as it cruised past – suddenly I was struggling to breathe, my heart was palpitating, and the final shreds of my journalistic objectivity were dissolving in the acrid fumes of burned jet fuel.

It was minutes before kickoff and the crowd's hysteria was peaking. This is arguably the best moment in a rugby match; nothing has happened on the pitch yet, so it's possible to believe that your team are going to play like supermen, destroy the opposition, and win handsomely. Everybody in the crucible of Ellis Park was gripped by this optimism.

It doesn't get better than this, I told myself.

But of course it did.

Mandela walked out onto the pitch wearing the No. 6 Springbok jersey, waving at the crowd.

There was a stunned pause; we all looked at the elderly black gent in the rugby jersey and cap for a second and wondered who the hell he was. A stray groundsman perhaps? Then the truth dawned on us.

There must have been one person, somewhere in the 62 000-strong crowd, who was the first to rise to his feet and start chanting 'Nelson! Nel-son!' Who was that person? We will probably never know. But within seconds the entire stadium was chanting. Mandela beamed and waved up at the crowd, and from that moment the fate of the All Blacks was sealed.

So rugby had taught me another lesson – that we never see the most important events in the universe coming. We learned the same kind of lesson on 11 September 2001.

I thought I knew what was predictable – that the All Blacks would win the 1995 Rugby World Cup, that South Africa was teetering on the brink of civil war, that white male Springbok rugby fans thought of blacks as grossly inferior.

Then Mandela did what he did, possibly without having any idea what reaction he would get. If he had asked my advice beforehand, I would have said, 'No, don't even think about it. Some drunken idiot is going to leap the crowd barrier and come at you with a broken beer bottle.'

That's the enduring lesson of rugby – miracles do happen, and more frequently than we expect. So don't rule out another Springbok World Cup triumph.

ANTON FERREIRA is a journalist and author who admits to being old enough to have once watched Keith Oxlee play flyhalf for the Springboks. He believes it is best to be on the losing side in a rugby match; that way, you get to tackle other players more often than other players tackle you.

RYK NEETHLING

Vrystaat!

I grew up with Wouter Hugo giving me scrumming tips. Wouter was one of my father's best friends, but more importantly he was the captain of Free State when they won their first-ever Currie Cup in 1976.

Gerrie Germishuys and my mom were also great friends (in fact, they still are), and guys like Gerrie Sonnekus and Free State sports legends Steve Strydom and Ewie Cronjé (Hansie's father) would often visit our home in Bloemfontein. I spent a lot of time in their company as a boy, and listening to their stories is where my swimming dreams began. Once I had started to show some promise, the conversation would often turn to swimming. This exposure to top sportsmen fuelled my desire and ambition to become part of that world.

At first, my involvement took the form of watching rugby from the roof of the Free State Stadium, years before Rassie Erasmus ever dreamed of doing so. My dad's company had a box at the stadium, so every weekend we would get to the rugby at about midday. I was still in primary school, so I'd spend the next couple of hours messing around until the main match started. This was the old Free State Stadium, which had both a cycling and an athletics track around the pitch, so there were plenty of alleys and hallways to explore. At some point, I found the door to the roof, and for a couple of seasons I watched all the Cheetahs' matches from the roof. I had it all to myself, and, as Rassie will tell you, the view is awesome.

After every match, my friends and I would wait outside the teams' change rooms and ask for the players' socks. There were about ten of us regulars, but when a big team visited, like Western Province or

Northern Transvaal, there'd be about 50 kids. *'Oom, kan ons Oom se kouse kry?'* (Uncle, may we have your socks?). When the players had left, we'd scuttle into the change room to see what we could salvage. Every once in a while a torn jersey or a discarded boot would end up as some boy's prize.

Free State didn't have many Currie Cup finals to celebrate, so when we won a game against a major team – one game in 1987 against Northern Transvaal was made memorable by Jan Els klapping Naas Botha – people would be allowed into the change rooms. As a kid, you could sneak in and see these huge men walking around naked, drinking beer. As a young fly on the wall, it was another world.

Free State centre Helgard Muller would always go out of his way to get me a sock or two. He once gave me a pair of Shimlas socks when he was playing at the University of the Orange Free State, and those socks were really hard to come by. Gerrie Sonnekus gave me a jersey, which was my pride and joy. I still have it, along with my sock collection: probably about 35 pairs, from Western Province, Natal, Transvaal, Northern Transvaal. You name it, I've got it.

I've even got a pair of South West Africa socks. André Joubert organised them for me from Gerhard Mans, who was a big player in South West, after we sat next to each other on a flight to Windhoek. I was on my way to a swimming camp, and André and the rest of the Free State team were flying to their season-ending match against South West Africa.

For a boy in Bloemfontein, which was not exactly a bustling metropolis, things like socks and jerseys were a pretty big deal. I wanted to be like these top sportsmen, and once I achieved my success in swimming, I remembered people like Helgard taking time out for a young kid, which is why I make a point of never turning down autograph or photograph requests.

I played for Free State at Craven Week in primary school. I had started off as prop for my first couple of years of rugby. I wasn't big, but I was strong. Then I switched to flank. I was a down-and-dirty fetcher, not a ball-carrier. When I got to high school at Grey College, my senior was Ollie le Roux. I would have to fetch and carry his book bag from the hostel, and run other errands for him. He was as big then as he is now, and he would pick me up in the air, hold me against the wall and demand, '*Spel my naam!*' (Spell my name!). His full name was André-Henri le Roux, and I had a bit of a stutter, so it was quite an ordeal. I would stutter and call him Henri and end up completely terrified.

Every boy at Grey College had to play rugby at some point. I played U14A and a couple of games for the U16A team, which was not bad. Then, halfway through the season I was chosen for the South African swim team going to the Commonwealth Games in Victoria, Canada, so I quit rugby. The only other time I played was in matric, when I turned out for a couple of games with the seventh team, and played every position in the backline. We had Boeta Dippenaar at flyhalf (who was a superb athlete and had started playing provincial cricket in Standard 9), a bunch of other sportsmen who used to play good rugby, plus some smokers and drinkers – it was a great team. The opposition used to protest that we were way too strong to be called sevenths, but we just pulverised them.

From then on, I focused on my swimming, but I remained a serious rugby fan. In fact, a serious Cheetahs fan. That was be expected given the amount of time I spent at Free State Stadium and after representing the province at rugby, but I was also addicted to the exhilarating way Free State played the game. The Bester brothers, Dawie Theron, Johan Styger, Vleis Visagie, Ryno Opperman, Cheese van Tonder, Pote Human (captain), Stompie Fourie, Henry Honiball, Helgard and Pieter Muller, Brendan Venter, Eben Scheepers, Chris Badenhorst, Hendrick Truter . . . those names define an era for me.

In 1996, I left South Africa to swim in the United States, and only returned on a permanent basis twelve years later. Living in the States, I didn't watch much rugby. It would be mentioned in the papers and obviously on the internet, but we had to wait until 2002 before a TV station called Setanta started showing the Tri-Nations. At the University of Arizona, in Tucson, there were a bunch of us South Africans (including our Olympic team: Lyndon Ferns, Roland Schoeman, Darien Townsend and myself). One guy would sign up with Setanta, and the rest of us would go over on Saturdays after training and watch a delayed broadcast of the game.

I actually went to watch a couple of rugby matches at the university, but I think the Grey U13C team would have beaten those guys. More worthwhile was travelling to see the Springboks play in Houston, which was coach Harry Viljoen's last game in charge. At Tucson airport, I spotted one guy who looked like he could be a *boertjie*, but by Denver there were about ten guys on the plane, all talking Afrikaans. The whole experience of watching the Springboks play in America in front of a crowd of 10 000 people was quite surreal. I met up with Ollie and the rest of the Boks afterwards, and we all went out and, *ja* . . . Herschelle would have been proud.

I've seen a couple of other big games, too: for instance, when the Cheetahs beat the Lions in the last minute of the Currie Cup final at the Free State Stadium in 2007. I also flew to Paris to watch the World Cup final that year because I was injured at the time and couldn't swim. I was at the Currie Cup final when the Sharks beat the Bulls in 2008, and I watched the Springboks beat the British and Irish Lions at Loftus with the last kick of the match in 2009.

But I think the biggest game I've ever experienced was the Cheetahs winning the Currie Cup for the first time in 29 years, in 2005. It was certainly the first time they had won it in my lifetime, because I was born in 1977, the year after Wouter Hugo lifted the trophy. The Bulls were leading 25-15 with nine minutes to go, and you know how it is at Loftus . . . you proudly wear your Cheetahs jersey and wave your flag, but you need a thick skin to take all the taunting. Then Bryan Habana was sin-binned, and the Cheetahs scored a converted try to make it 25-22. In the next move, Noel Oelschig (who I'd played with since U9) kicked ahead, the ball bounced straight into Meyer Bosman's hands, and over he went. Willem de Waal converted, and the rest is history.

The Cheetahs fans were totally outnumbered, but the rest of Loftus was shocked into silence. They couldn't believe it.

Now *that* was a great day in my life.

——— *As told to Angus Powers*

RYK NEETHLING is South Africa's most experienced Olympic athlete, with four consecutive Games and a gold-medal, world-record performance in the 4x100m freestyle relay in Athens 2004 to his name. He is the third-most successful swimmer in US college history; a three-time short course world champion; and a multiple South African, African and world record holder. Ryk currently runs a swimming academy in Pretoria, and although he is good friends with many of the Bulls players, his true rugby loyalties lie elsewhere.

CLAIRE MATHONSI

Newlands Pilgrim

I am a black, female All Blacks supporter who has chosen to live as close to Newlands rugby stadium as possible. This is my story.

I was born and raised in Zimbabwe. Rugby was a core part of our upbringing; we grew up watching New Zealand teams on TV, and automatically became fans. Many Zimbabweans are staunch supporters of New Zealand, but it is difficult to say exactly why. Maybe it's because South Africa was not accessible and there was never really an opportunity to watch and follow the Springboks. Rather than enrolling at Rhodes University in Grahamstown, Zimbabweans' usual choice of university, I decided to study in Cape Town instead, mainly so that I could watch rugby live at Newlands. For the past ten years, Newlands has been my life.

In our early years at university, my rugby-mad friends and I never had the cash to attend many matches at Newlands, nor enough to install DStv. We saved our pennies to have the cheap breakfast at Wimpy so we could watch matches on their TV, or pretended to work out at the gym while keeping an eye on the score. We devised as many ways as we could to take in games.

Watching in pubs was often the easiest option, but we usually stuck out because we were a gang of black people who were always supporting New Zealand or Australia. All of us were aware of the tensions surrounding our support for the Boks' opposition, except for my friend Tinashe, who was always a very vocal (and inappropriate) supporter of the Wallabies. Tinashe was 'special' in that he could never pick up on the vibe of a room, and his amazingly misplaced bravado often got us into trouble.

Once we were seated at a table in the middle of a pub, watching the Springboks get off to a flyer. They scored two tries against the Aussies, before Australia retaliated with a try of their own, which silenced the room. Tinashe jumped up and started screaming, 'Yeah, yeah, yeah! Fuck you! Fuck you!' The whole pub stayed very quiet. Tinashe was the only one standing up. We tried to pull him down, but eventually he just started laughing and sat down himself. Needless to say, we were glared at for the rest of the game.

Eventually we could regularly afford tickets to games at Newlands. Our match-day tradition involved parking at a mate's house near the Rondebosch railway station, and walking rather timidly to the stadium wearing our Crusaders, Blues or Hurricanes rugby jerseys to show our support for the visiting New Zealand (or Australian) teams. We soon got used to the negative attitudes we sometimes encountered. Although there were very few black faces in the crowd in general, we knew we could look forward to bumping into more Zimbabweans in the lower Grandstand section, especially when it was still standing room only. Being so close to the field was an added bonus. We always treated our mishaps with humour, as it disguised our fear and the fact that the lads I was with were too chicken to get into any physical tussles.

When seats were installed in the lower Grandstand, we moved up in the world, but were still referred to as 'k*****s', and told to go back to Soweto. One individual informed me that it did not matter if I was female, he would *donner* the hell out of me anyway. According to this chap, the new South Africa did not exist in the stadium. In fact, no space inside Newlands was devoid of racist drama. Even in the toilets I had women yelling at me for using the toilet because 'toilet cleaners were supposed to clean and not use the facilities!'

But nothing could keep us away from Newlands and the thrill of watching wonderful players (on both sides) and being part of the multitude of Cape Town fans who, for some strange reason, turned out to welcome and support the New Zealand Super Rugby teams. We took our rugby supporting pretty seriously. We once walked in the rain to Rondebosch Boys' High to watch the Auckland Blues train, and on another occasion my friend Wayne refused to wash his jacket because Wallaby players Stirling Mortlock and Julian Huxley had touched his shoulder.

Not surprisingly, Tinashe was the source of our most dramatic encounter at Newlands, which occurred after a hard-fought Tri-Nations match. For once, I had managed to secure fantastic seats in the Grandstand, on the halfway line and close to the action. Unfortunately, the All Blacks ended up losing to South Africa, but the defeat was mellowed by the large amount of alcohol we had managed to imbibe (we had joined a drink-all-you-can ticket system with our mates). Afterwards we stood behind the stands finishing our drinks, and good old Tinashe was celebrating because the Wallabies were still in with a chance in the Tri-Nations after New Zealand's defeat.

We got chatting to a young man at the top of a flight of stairs, and began explaining why we didn't support the Springboks. Somehow the lad's father thought we were fighting with his son and came charging up the stairs with the sharp end of his flagpole pointing directly at us. Tinashe was standing behind me and a friend, but we all somehow managed get out the way. We tried explaining to the man that we were just chatting, but he was yelling, 'Fucking k*****' over and over again, and shouting that we had no business being at the game.

Unexpectedly, Tinashe started giggling and yelling back, 'Fuck you! Fuck you!' The man went ballistic and started pushing us. We were wedged in at the top of the stairs, with nowhere to go, and nearly falling over the edge trying to dodge him. The youngster begged his dad to stop, which eventually he did. It was really frightening. The young man got rid of his dad, came back and apologised so kindly to us. I remember he had tears in his eyes.

We left very quickly after that, but none of these unsettling incidents have ever dampened our enthusiasm for the game of rugby, for Newlands as a stadium, or for sharing the rugby-watching rituals that so many South Africans enjoy every Saturday afternoon during rugby season.

As an All Blacks fan, I have to admit that my relationship with South African rugby is complex. I'm wary of the Springboks because they are always worthy opponents, with exceptional skill. But I also get caught up in the rivalry between local teams, and I love seeing exciting new talent surface for the Boks. My friends and I regard the Blue Bulls with awe and respect for the strong traditions at Loftus Versfeld, and I'm also partial to the Sharks and the Cheetahs at times. But I very rarely support the Stormers or Western Province.

Over time, the atmosphere at Newlands has changed, with fewer altercations taking place. My gang of Zim ex-pats are still All Blacks supporters, but our experience of watching rugby has been enriched by the drama and dynamics of South African rugby crowds. I've mingled with fans of teams from all over the world, had heated rugby debates, and witnessed the passion that drives the Springboks and their supporters, which always leaves fear in the hearts of their opponents until the final whistle blows. It's been awesome to participate in a living, breathing tradition of rugby that is committed to making the game exciting and accessible, and I'm proud to have seen the work that has gone into transforming the game, although there is still more to be done.

I am now able to afford season tickets to Newlands, and I ensure that my seat is ready for me, year after year. Being black and female at a rugby match is no longer a novelty, and through rain, cold, wind and some stunning sunny days, Newlands stadium remains a major part of my life. South Africa has deepened my passion for rugby, and Newlands will always represent that for me.

CLAIRE MATHONSI has been an activist in the development sector for the past eight years, working to improve women's rights locally, regionally and globally. She played rugby and cricket at junior school, but finally settled on the more sedate sport of swimming. Rugby's combination of teamwork, individual brilliance, subtle tactics and brute power made her an instant devotee. Claire is an avid supporter of women's sport (especially the Black Ferns) and the All Blacks.

Memories at Piet se Gat

There really is a place called Piet se Gat. It's somewhere in southern Damaraland. All that's left there now are a couple of broken houses and a hole in the ground that I guess was once a spring. Piet has long since buggered off. Piet se Gat remains important to me as it is the only place where I ever think back, very briefly, on my rugby career.

I played wing for Northern Transvaal Schools in the *first* game of the *first* Craven Week tournament in 1964. The night before, I had met Anne Ballantyne. She was even lovelier than her name. So, in that first game of the very first Craven Week, I had one eye on her and the other on the ball. When they finally passed the ball to me in the last minute of the first game, I dropped it, and my opposite wing scooped it up and scored a try. It was a sin against Afrikaner humanity (all the other players in my team came from Afrikaans schools). That was that – my rugby dream lay in tatters. What made it worse was that Anne also buggered off shortly after the game – just like Piet from Piet se Gat.

Trauma on the rugby field was followed by the traumas of the army and love, after which I entered academia at the University of Stellenbosch. The word 'academia' was soon to be forgotten, just like Piet se Gat. I was, however, most fortunate to be thrown into Wilgenhof hostel with a whole lot of other reprobates. Most of us were an unruly law unto ourselves. Many of my peers, more attentive to the rule of law and Danie Craven, became Springbok rugby players: Gert Muller ran over his opponents; Jannie Engelbrecht swerved past them; Andy van der Watt ran around them; Morné du

Plessis ran the right lines at them; Boland Coetzee ran under them; Johan van der Merwe glided through them; Eben Olivier ran between them; Jackie and Dawie Snyman stepped past them; Hannes Marais *drukked* them; Andre de Wet jumped them; and Albie de Waal had a politically incorrect nickname and also ran around a bit. The most famous of them all chased my pet squirrel around my room in a state of 'in-Tassie-cation', with murderous intent, after losing some intervarsity game. This hero, now a respected citizen and Springbok legend, wanted to see if he could chop the poor animal in half with somebody's panga. Luckily he was quite a slow Springbok. Tall and lanky and mean, but very slow. The animal got such a fright that he died the next day. There were three Springboks at my squirrel's funeral. (The mean killer Springbok wasn't invited.) I could tell many other such stories, but unfortunately they could not be published in any book, anywhere, any time. What happens in Willows stays in Willows.

Another strange, if not embarrassing, Springbok experience happened years later in Madrid. It was 2001, and the Springboks were due to play the French in Paris. Trying to find a TV channel that would broadcast a rugby Test was like trying to find a Woolworths in Piet se Gat. Finally, after a desperate search, I found a French bar in the *gat* end of Madrid. There were many small bars along this road to the *gat* end of the city, so to gather some *gees* for the game against the Frogs I had a drink in each of them. Well, actually, I had to check whether or not the bar I was in was the one that I was supposed to be looking for.

When I finally reached the French bar, it looked just like all the Spanish ones. This was quite a disappointment. French rugby supporters had packed the place to the rafters – where all the Spanish hams were hanging. My *gat* was *stamping* a bit, so I didn't mind that my head was wedged between a cured hind leg and a French armpit. The small TV screen flickered blue and green. My 13 words of fluent

French soon returned as I screamed my support for the Bokke. Dozens of French eyes turned my way with Guillotine hate. Then the French scored, they cheered and my eyes watered. The TV screen started to flicker more blue than green. They scored again and the room burst into such celebrations that the cured pigs hanging from the ceiling started to dance. Shit, they must have been French pigs. The TV screen was flickering almost only blue now. Damn blue cocks playing great rugby. We lost, and the Springboks slouched out of the Stade de France, leaving me alone between the smoked pigs and 60 cheering Frenchmen at the *gat* end of town. *Gatslag*. You would have thought that Napoleon or Charles De Gaulle had returned from the dead.

A few years later, I returned to Piet se Gat in the most distant corner of Damaraland. The broken buildings had become ruins and the hole that was once a spring, in the days when Piet still lived there, had now grown over with weeds. It was here that I once again remembered the curious story of the rotten ladder. The pinnacle of loneliness is sitting at Piet se Gat and thinking about rugby. I called out for the spirit of Piet, but the only reply came in the sad monotonous swish of the *bossies* between the rocks.

In 2007 I was asked by Justin Nurse to take photographs for his business, Laugh it Off, which was publishing a youth calendar. I should have known then that anything to do with youth should be laughed off immediately. The Springbok rugby team was about to leave for the Rugby World Cup in France. It was a beautiful spring day in Cape Town when the Springboks gathered at the Southern Sun Hotel for their official team photographs. By some unknown and devious method, Justin had arranged with the Springbok management that we could take a team portrait of the Bokke in their school jerseys. I should have smelt the rotten wood then already. Once the official photographs were over, they all gathered in a special room and changed into their school jerseys. Their manner and

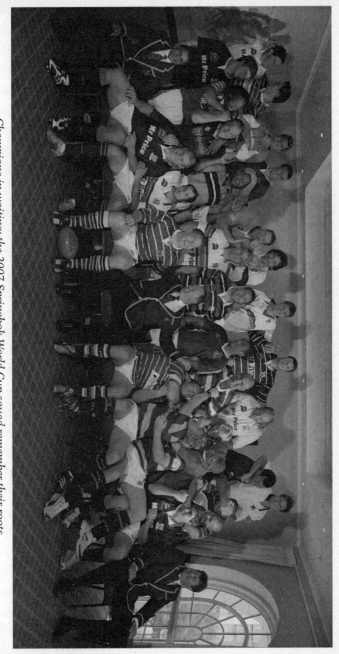

Champions in waiting: the 2007 Springbok World Cup squad remember their roots.

Photograph by Obie Oberholzer

expression were suddenly transformed, as if they had become boys again. Os and Victor and Habana were pushing and pulling at each other with schoolboy exuberance. Bobby was klapping Bismarck. Bakkies Botha wanted to sit at the back of the class so that he could have a *skelm* smoke. Francois Steyn didn't really know what to do as he was barely out of school anyway. Only Jake White seemed relaxed and happy, but then he was an old schoolteacher.

I finally managed to get this lot of rugby hooligans into some kind of formation, and by using the wooden ladder brought along by Nurse, I could get an elevated angle. 'OK, boys!' I shouted, climbing higher and higher up the ladder. 'Calm down, calm down! Look at me and be happy!' Never mind smiling, they were all laughing and *gaaning-aan*. Little did I know, while balancing on top of the ladder with my camera, that I was looking down at the future 2007 world champions. Little did I know that Justin Nurse's ladder had a rotten leg. Suddenly, among all the lekker and happy Springbok camaraderie, the rotten part of the ladder gave way and the uncle with the camera came crashing down to earth.

Two and a half metres is a long way for an old oke to fall. *Gatslag.* Boom, crash, bang, followed by a long, dark silence. When I looked up from the floor, at first I saw only vague and blurred shapes . . . strange faces peering down at me. Then the faces slowly came into focus and became John Smit, Victor Matfield, Os du Randt, Bakkies Botha and the rest of them, looking down at me with great concern.

'*Jis, Oom,*' Bakkies said slowly. '*Lewe Oom nog? Jislaaik, maar Oom het jou gat af geval!*' (Are you still in one piece, Uncle? Jeez, but you really came crashing down!)

Then I slowly got up, and, as I checked my body for any protruding bones, the Bokke all started to clap . . . and for just a few seconds, I felt like I was one of them, a Bok, a Springbok. A wonderful thought, short and sweet. Lekker. *Windgat.* Someday soon I will go back to Piet se Gat and tell Piet's spirit the story of the Bokke and the rotten ladder.

OBIE OBERHOLZER has always thought of himself as a visual thug. He takes and makes pictures of unusual and interesting people, landscapes and things. As a boy, the happiest times were spent with his father, a Tukkies-Blue-Bulls-Bok fanatic and academic scientist. In high school, Obie played on the wing for then-Northern Transvaal Schools in the first ever Craven Week in 1964. Stellenbosch University saw him concentrating on athletics, but befriending many future Bokke of that time between 1967 and 1970. With Danie Craven as his *koshuisvader* (housemaster), he was nurtured in the cradle of rugby, which consumed them all in those days.

DREAMS DIE HARD

JOHN VAN DE RUIT

The Beautiful Violence

I am not a violent man. Or at least no evidence pointing toward such a statement has ever successfully emerged.

Aside from the odd schoolboy fracas, I can solemnly and proudly declare that I am yet to shoot, stab or punch anybody in the eye, throat or groin. I have never suffered from road rage, despite suspecting that for most of my adult life I have been followed by a canary yellow Toyota Corolla manned by a woman who looks like the unlikely combination of Debora Patta and Bjorn Borg. As Retief Goosen will tell you, lightning should never strike the same place twice.

However, in the passage of a single year I demonstrated two separate acts of thuggish violence that led to months of soul-searching, a mostly appalled girlfriend and gradual acceptance of the fact that, despite being born with a gentle disposition, I had one fatal and violent flaw.

Rugby.

The year was 2007, and for any semi-committed rugby supporter it appeared to be a year like any other. Yes, there was a Rugby World Cup but it was (erroneously) presumed as always that the time had finally arrived for the All Blacks. But 2007 had its own grand plans for South African rugby, plans that included the Super 14 and which were obviously drafted in Pretoria. Just as the usual sequence of Super 14 hope-giving-way-to-failure seemed destined to be realised, the Sharks did the unthinkable by topping the log. The fact that the Bulls finished second and the final was contested between two South African teams was far in excess of any village idiot's prediction.

I have witnessed galling climaxes to sporting spectacles before (most of them involving the Proteas), but somehow the catastrophic events that led to that Bryan Habana try after the hooter rendered me temporarily insane. My violent reaction didn't happen quickly, as it would six months later during the World Cup quarterfinal, but simmered ominously under the surface, like a psychopath biding its time.

After a suitable period of silence, I excused myself from the gathering and drove home erratically. Upon reaching base camp I strode down the passage and paused momentarily outside the bathroom, contemplating relief on a grand scale. I then drove my heel through the bathroom door with a satisfying crack. Achilles himself would have glowed after the unleashing of such cave-manly force. After surveying the extensive damage for some time, I gradually felt a needle of shame for my senseless act of thuggery. Mostly, though, I was thrilled to have simultaneously broken the door and terrified the blazes out of the caretaker's cat.

Months of sterile calmness passed by. The Rugby World Cup began with a series of ridiculous upsets that made the Republic compulsively insecure. Remote tropical islands with the population of a small primary school suddenly loomed as possible land mines lying in wait for the beloved Springboks on their quest for world domination. These were jittery times, and there was a countrywide spike in the sale of painkillers and cheap brandy.

And then, of course, there was Tonga. Or whoever it was who disguised themselves as Tonga that day. Alf, the guy who comes round occasionally to drink my beer and check my water meter, threw about a rumour that Tonga was in fact the All Black 'B' team in some typically cunning form of disguise. I laughed loudly at the time, but against the run of play the rumour gained some traction at Collegians Rugby Club in Durban, where an undercover international investigation into the matter was launched, and later aborted, one Friday night in the clubhouse bar. They always did say College boys were gullible.

By hook or by crook, Tonga/New Zealand B contrived to launch a blistering attack on the Boks that left Tonga/New Zealand B on the verge of a life-changing upset with only 20 minutes left on the clock. An appalled John Smit called his team into a huddle and commenced shouting. I stood up decisively from my rocking chair and calmly made my way to the window for a breath of fresh air. And then, for no apparent reason, I lunged at the window bar and snapped it clean off. It was all over in less than a second, but it was obvious that the plague of senseless violence had returned. It was also at that moment that I realised that I had a major problem with my security. Let's face it, if a 73kg former actor could so easily breach the last line of his own defence, how would I ever keep out the contract killers sent round by Debora Patta/Bjorn Borg?

Perhaps at this juncture it would be wise to point out that I've never been one of those 'shout-at-the-screen-lash-out-at-the-cat' brands of rugby couch potato. My explosions require a sequence of events so unforeseen and gutting that the ability for logical thought is instantly removed as I enter the eerie white world of unrestrained irrationality. Sanjay, my local electrician and Nostradamus, ventured that I might have a serious problem upstairs. He euphemistically called it a loose wire, before confidently foreseeing a Manchester United bloodbath at Stamford Bridge that Sunday.

Short circuits aside, perhaps a brief and sepia-toned chip-and-chase down memory lane to the days of freshly mowed fields and ill-fitting gum guards would be in some way revealing. My initial foray into the sport was brief. My father drove me off to Glenwood Old Boys club in Durban North one sunny Saturday morning. Here, barefoot mini-rugby games were played out as far as the eye could see. Having been brought up on a diet of my father's stories of playing hooker for Queens College's Fifths, I informed the man with the clipboard that I too would be a hooker, despite my drastically small size and starving-dog appearance.

At the next break in play, I replaced the current hooker and tore out into the middle with some intensity. Two sweaty fat boys put their arms around me and squeezed me into a contorted shape. It was a little like being a small piece of Masonite at the mercy of an unforgiving vice grip. Further bad news was that two long bony hands appeared between the fat boys' legs and gripped handfuls of their jerseys alarmingly close to their nethers. These sudden actions meant that I was pulled down into a crouch, and that's when I laid eyes on the large and unfriendly boy facing me in an identical position. Somebody shouted something and there was the crunch of shoulder on shoulder. I was now in the centre of a terrifying scrum, and such was the pain in my neck that I forgot all about hooking the ball back and suffered the great shame of all hookers – a tighthead.

The referee broke the scrum apart with an urgent blast of his whistle because some maniac was shrieking and screaming like he was being tortured by a man with beady eyes and a neatly clipped moustache. The screaming child turned out to be me. The coach immediately stepped in and suggested that I should take up the vital position of reserve scrumhalf instead. It was a terrible effort, and despite being just nine years old I felt like I had let my father and Queens College down. My disappointment aside, those first ten seconds on the field established an inescapable truth about the sport. Rugby is for the tough, and frequent intense pain is very much a part of the deal. Being a born masochist, I fell in love with it instantly.

My passion for the sport grew exponentially, and after an extended period of targeted and systematic nagging my father dragged his now ten-year-old son off to the cauldron of King's Park to witness his first-ever Currie Cup match. The fact that the Banana Boys, as the Sharks used to be known, were languishing in the B-section didn't dampen my spirits, and I sat enthralled as the might of Natal singlehandedly took on an entire country. Sure, it might have been the mostly uninhabitable South West Africa, but it was a country nonetheless.

Scanning the match-day programme, I was entranced by the names of the players. There was Hugh Reece-Edwards, whose thumping right boot echoed around the stadium like a bass drum. (Unlike the incensed men in the stands around me, I didn't mind that he never seemed to find touch with his long-range punts, I just enjoyed watching that brown torpedo scything through the air in perfect rotation like it might never return to earth.) Then there was the bullish Henry Coxwell, the elusive Neil Penrose and the dogged Rob Hankinson. It didn't matter that we lost via a few penalty kicks to the future Namibians. A small province had nearly beaten a whole country that day, and I was damned proud of my defeated heroes. One match is sometimes all it takes to connect you to a sport for life, and, bizarrely, a try-less kick-athon in Durban is what fired the rugby furnace within.

As a junior I scaled the low fence of rugby mediocrity, and as a senior I vice-captained the Michaelhouse eighth XV to a narrow victory over Hilton and a succession of embarrassing defeats to just about everybody else thereafter. These were tremendous times. I vividly recall hoarse-throated war cries, Tiger Balm, orange quarters and good old rugby the way it should be played – badly.

But back to the violence. It is clear that my brief and forgettable rugby playing days shed no light on any future loose wires or rugby-rage vandalism. It would be fair to say that my rugby days shed no light at all. While chatting to Big Garth, my psychologist and motor mechanic some months later, he observed that my two moments of destruction and rage could in fact be connected to highly anticipated and lengthy rugby competitions where one's level of investment is raised together with one's expectation of success. This made no sense to me. I know pseudo-speak when I hear it and this was straight off the back of a sugar sachet. It's just the kind of nonsense that leads to warped rugby logic like 'Whichever team wins the collisions, will win.' Or 'The team that wants it enough will take home the cup.' Nonsense. Everybody knows the side that kicks off first in the second half wins.

Then, with his hands covered in stubborn grease and his right foot raised and resting on the bumper of a Fiat Panda, Big Garth had an epiphany. After a few seconds of solemn pause, during which he gazed intently into the zinc ceiling of his workshop, he nodded slowly to himself as the full stature of his thoughts gained resonance in his mind.

'There's only one way to understand rugby,' Big Garth said, nodding sagely at the roof once more. 'We live our lives under blue skies and sometimes cloudy skies. But every now and again a bank of black clouds builds up on the horizon and comes slowly towards us.'

I had no idea where the man was heading with all this talk of weather but I couldn't deny that it was a compelling start to his epiphany. 'Now, think of those thunderclouds as a looming Test match,' he said, becoming positively inspired. 'It's impossible to predict what might happen.'

'Impossible,' I replied softly, lost in the mechanic's climatic metaphor.

'Inside those clouds,' he continued, 'are beauty and destruction in equal measure. And what might befall each and every one of us when those clouds collide overhead and explode into lightning, only God and Hugh Bladen will ever know.'

Big Garth may never have found the rattle in my dashboard, but on that sweltering day in his workshop, with a few powerful words about weather, he simultaneously explained the periodic madness in my head and perfectly defined the beautiful violence of rugby union.

JOHN VAN DE RUIT made a living as a moderately successful actor and playwright before confounding himself and others in achieving overnight success with his bestselling debut novel *Spud*, which has subsequently spawned a film starring John Cleese and Troye Sivan. During his recently deceased youth, he was a prominent member of the Michaelhouse eighth XV, where he made the position of fullback his own despite his small frame and ill-fitting rugby boots. John is prone to suffering bouts of uncontrolled swearing and violence when viewing rugby on television, a disease which he inherited from his father.

GAYTON MCKENZIE

The Flag

Before going to prison, I cared for rugby about as much as I cared for the law; it was something that mattered only to white people. It was the same when I sat behind bars, after emptying a number of bank vaults and earning a lengthy prison sentence: if anyone dared to watch the rugby while the soccer was on a different channel, they were assured of an unpleasant encounter with me.

I wasn't one of those people that Clint Eastwood made a rugby movie about. I was an angry young black man who wanted war, whether Madiba wore a Springbok jersey or not. This kind of attitude didn't help much to prevent my fifteen-year residence in Grootvlei Maximum Security Prison outside Bloemfontein.

What prison taught me, as the years passed, was that South Africa was changing. When I was released in 2003, it was with the attitude that everything about me also had to be about change. I was determined to prove to the world that I *could* change, and that I was worthy of my freedom. That a friend of mine, Ashwin Willemse, was playing rugby as a Springbok that same year made it easier for me to develop an interest in the sport. I told myself that if a strong, talented coloured boy from the Cape Flats could play in a team previously the jealous preserve of whites – well, then, anything was possible and perhaps the new South Africa was real and worth believing in after all.

That was until the day an old South African flag blocked my way.

I still look back on that day as the greatest test I have had to face since leaving prison. Reflecting on it now, I'm glad it happened, but I shudder to think where I might be today if I had failed this test.

Anyone who knows me will tell you that my greatest flaw is my short temper, which can be a problem in someone who is 1.87m tall and weighs over 120kg, with hands the size of frying pans, a head like a bowling ball and a long police record of violence. When I say 'problem', I mean it was normally always the other guy's problem. But by this time I was trying to be good.

My wife and I were trying to leave Vodacom Park in Bloemfontein after the Springboks' brilliant win over Ireland in their opening Test of the 2004 season. Two drunken Afrikaners probably thought it would be funny to drape the old South African flag over my car's windscreen. I was in good spirits, feeling elated after watching the Boks' first win since the disastrous 2003 Rugby World Cup, so I didn't take it badly, actually laughing it off and waiting for these guys to just lift the flag and allow us to go on our way.

Aside from the Test match win, I had a lot more to feel happy about: I had a sponsorship from security company Chubb to fight crime by telling my story to the youth, and I was becoming increasingly popular as a corporate motivational speaker. Being the best motivational speaker in the country was my dream, despite people telling me that no one was interested in listening to an ex-con. Nowadays, just about every prisoner who leaves jail wants to be a public speaker, but back then I was breaking new ground.

I knew all eyes were on me, so I just rolled down my window and asked the guys to remove their flag. 'Let me go home,' I said.

They just stood there, staring at me, holding the flag in place, challenging me to do something about it. I still didn't think anything serious would come of this, even as I got out of the car – normally just standing up is enough to make most men back down from a fight with me, but these two guys were already too worked up to think clearly. The one nearest me gave me a shove and said, 'Why are you wearing this shirt, huh? You are not a white man who can play rugby.'

Ashwin had given me the shirt. I immediately thought about my friend and everything he had gone through to become a Springbok. It occurred to me that perhaps they wouldn't cheer him, regardless of his talent, and never would, even if he scored a hundred tries. So I told them, 'It's none of your damn business where I got this shirt.'

I grabbed the flag from the windscreen and tossed it to the ground. Before I could say any more, though, a bakkie pulled up and another eight men piled out. One took a swipe at me, and I was quickly overwhelmed. I could hear my wife screaming, followed by one of the men hurling abuse at her. To them, she was just another 'kaffirmeid' – not an advocate, not a woman, perhaps not even a human being.

No man wants the indignity of being beaten in front of his wife. No man can stand idly by and listen to his wife being insulted. So I fought back like a berserker until I was free of them and they were more wary of me. There was another coloured guy watching the whole scene, and he was cheering. He handed me a glass bottle and spurred me on: 'Go donner them, Gayton!'

As I had done a thousand times before, I broke the bottle on the pavement and went for the men. They could see the doom bubbling in my eyes and tried to run away, but I tripped one, rolled him over and brought the jagged edge of the glass to his neck. I could see the veins and tendons straining against his skin. His eyes were bulging in terror. He begged, but then looked at my face and closed his eyes, knowing he was about to die.

I don't know how I managed to, but somehow, through the rage, I saw my life and all the tough choices I had made to get this far. I'd already told my life story, with its lessons, to tens of thousands of schoolkids, and I had read letters from them saying that because of me they had walked away from petty fights and other mistakes that could lead to crime. What would they think if they came across tomorrow's headlines, with a photograph of me in handcuffs being led away from a body bag?

I could so easily have driven the bottle into this man's jugular, but I would have been killing myself too. So I dropped the bottle and stepped away.

The front page of next day's newspaper had a minor article that featured my bruised face. The messages of support that started pouring in made one thing clear: those guys still hanging on to their old apartheid flag as if it were a security blanket were a tiny minority. The South African Rugby Union (SARU) apologised for the incident, and requested that I not see all rugby fans the same way. Decent, forward-thinking white people made clear their disgust, and I soon learned that the incident had won me more friends than I could ever have imagined. I even got a few more motivational talks out of it.

Fortunately, I didn't blame rugby for what happened, or seek to cast all rugby fans in the same ugly mould. Rugby has given me so much since then. Those idiots could have robbed me of it all – if I had let them. But because I didn't, I got to drive around five European countries – France, Germany, Austria, Italy and Switzerland – between South Africa's 2007 Rugby World Cup semifinal match against Argentina and the final against England. It was the greatest road trip of my life, with two of the best friends a guy could ask for. All through that week, we knew that South Africa would beat England. They'd already beaten the title-holders once during the tournament. We were so proud to walk the streets of Europe telling everyone we were South African. If they looked confused, I just said, 'Nelson Mandela!' and the smiles would beam back at us.

Walking along the Champs-Elysées in Paris, my friend Kenny, also a reformed ex-convict, passed another *stoere* (staunch) Boer, so clearly an Afrikaner farmer that even here, in one of the world's fashion capitals, in cold weather, he was wearing his khaki shorts, his long khaki socks, his *veldskoene* and his leather hat. When he saw Kenny, covered head to toe in Springbok colours, he beamed with joy and said: 'My boet!'

The two of them started hugging. I could barely believe my eyes, and I wondered if this would ever have happened in South Africa, a place where we can sometimes forget that, at heart, we are just South Africans – not black or white.

On the day of the final, while everyone was standing outside the Stade de France waiting for the kickoff, drinking beers and enjoying the banter between the barmy English fans and the slightly more reserved South Africans (despite some guy who painted himself green and ran around yelling 'the Incredible Schalk!'), I noticed someone being pickpocketed. When you live in South Africa, it's easy to start thinking that ours is the only place in the world with crime; it must have come as a big shock to this Afrikaans businessman when I handed his wallet back to him and explained that I'd just had to bash two French thieves' heads together before they gave it up.

'I can't believe it!' he said. 'I have to come to a rugby game in France to have a black South African save me from crime!' He gave me a big hug and said, 'When you're back in South Africa I want you to come to my shop and pick out a flatscreen TV for yourself. I insist.' It turned out that he owned a big electronics chain.

I laughed later when the story of the foiled crime had been passed around enough that people started trying to find out who the black man was who had caught the thieves, only for Kenny to start telling whoever asked him that, yes, indeed, he was the hero! I had earlier told him I didn't want anyone hanging on to me, so we should pretend not to know anything about the incident, but Kenny had decided that if I wasn't interested in taking the credit, it was far too good a story to waste. By the time the final started, he had built up quite a fan-base; for the rest of us who knew him, it just added to the tremendous sense of fun we were having.

The final of the 2007 Rugby World Cup was special for so many different reasons. The Wallaby and All Black supporters who hadn't sold their tickets after their teams were knocked out of the tournament were there to support South Africa. My friend Charles, a young white guy, spent an hour teaching a whole group of Aussies and Kiwis how to sing 'Nkosi Sikelel' iAfrika', and they were all really into it.

But the thing I remember most, and I'm still amazed that I seemed to be the only one who noticed it, was yet another of those staunch Afrikaners, standing there on that chilly October evening, in his khakis sure enough, but covered in the flag of the new South Africa, his head thrown back in rapture, his fist clenched over his heart, and big tears of unbridled emotion streaming down his cheeks and into his beard as he sang words he probably didn't even fully understand but which he knew were 100% South African and which he was completely proud of. In that moment, he would have gone to war alongside Kenny and me against anyone who dared to say anything against our fatherland.

South Africans were by far the minority in the stadium that day. For the Brits, getting to the game was a simple matter of a train ride under the English Channel. For South Africans, it was a whole lot further and much more expensive. I can only imagine it hadn't been easy for this Afrikaner to stand where he was, but for him nothing on earth could have been more worthwhile. And I don't think anyone has ever sung 'God Bless Africa' with more sincerity.

Almost all of us want the legacy of Madiba wearing Francois Pienaar's jersey to last for the rest of our lives, and for us to build on it – but not everyone really understands what has to be done. A group like the South African Rugby Legends Association (SARLA) – through their efforts to develop school and club rugby – understand what the new spirit of rugby is, but SARU sometimes miss opportunities to bridge the old divides. Although SARU have the best of intentions, they can occasionally be their own worst enemy.

I wasn't thinking of any of that, though, while listening to the anthem play in the Stade de France that day. There wasn't a single old

South African flag in sight. Perhaps that was because there's a Union Jack snuggled into the heart of the old SA flag, and even that small sign of support for the opposition would have been treasonous, but really I think it's because the new South Africa is growing up and doesn't need its old security blanket any more. We can wear the flag of a true, grown-up democracy without being afraid. We can pull our thumbs out of our mouths and sing our anthem like real men and women, not parroting the sound of it like children who don't know any better.

Rugby has been at the heart of our development as an integrated nation. It's taught us to do less crouching, less pausing and more engaging. Long may our scrum endure.

GAYTON MCKENZIE came to public attention when he and a group of fellow inmates filmed warder corruption in Grootvlei Prison using cameras smuggled into their cells. After serving time for bank robbery (and securing an early release), he became one of South Africa's most sought-after public speakers, starting with school tours and then finding success in the corporate world. Today he is a successful entrepreneur, with business interests in mining, lounge bars and entertainment.

JOOST VAN DER WESTHUIZEN

In Retrospect

A lot of people won't understand this, but the Blue Bulls' Currie Cup win in 1998 was my best moment on a rugby field. Most people would think that it would be the Springboks' Rugby World Cup win in 1995, but they'd be wrong. I'll tell you why.

It took me six months to win the World Cup, but six years to win the Currie Cup. Those are two completely different sets of goals, and when we lifted the Currie Cup after beating Western Province 24-20 in 1998, I thought, 'At last!'

Conversely, my worst moments were when I tore my knee ligaments, in 1999, at the end of 2000 and again in 2001. Three major knee operations. That was hard.

I played rugby in both the amateur and professional eras. When I started playing senior rugby in 1992, we were all amateurs: you played, you enjoyed, you studied and you were a person. In 1996, rugby turned professional and things changed. By the time I retired, in 2003, I wasn't playing my natural game any more. The game plan stated that I had to be a link, to get the ball from A to B, and that was it. I wasn't allowed to break, because I was running away from my support. It's almost as though you lose some of your character.

I didn't enjoy my last two years of rugby, but when I look back, I'd do it all again. I made a lot of friends, I met many good people, and I learned a hell of a lot. Take a guy like Ruben Kruger. Although I had my shit in 2009, he was battling a brain tumour and fighting for his life. But he still phoned me every month to find out how I was. Ruben and I went back to school days – not the same school but we'd play against each other, and then we played with each other at Craven Week and at the Bulls. He was just a phenomenal person. So is Gary Teichmann. Probably the best captain I've played under. An unbelievable leader: always honest, always cares about you, knows exactly when to lead by example, when to talk to you and when not to.

Even Jonah Lomu – we're good mates. He sent me his book, autographed with 'Good to be your friend!' Nick Farr-Jones and Gareth Edwards, too. And I've had a good relationship with George Gregan, who's a very nice guy. You'll notice that most of my international friends are scrumhalves. What can I say? We're good guys!

I think the most humble rugby nation is New Zealand. They are the most down-to-earth people I've ever met, especially the players. That didn't make beating the All Blacks in Wellington in 1998 any less sweet, though. That was a phenomenal victory because of the tradition between our two countries. Just to run onto the field, sing the national anthem and face the haka . . . as a little boy, that's what you see, that's what you want.

I always turned the haka into motivation. I would look the opposing scrumhalf in the eye while he was doing the haka, and the moment he looked away I knew I had him. So it wasn't scary, it was a huge privilege. I was proud to stand there.

I believe New Zealand played the wrong game plan in the 1995 World Cup final. During the tournament, Lomu became a superstar and everyone was obsessed with the threat he posed. But the Boks would have tackled each other to get to him! We knew they were going to play him. Can you imagine if he came through that gap and Andrew Mehrtens had dummied him? We all tackled Lomu and they actually had a double overlap on the outside. I believe if they had used Lomu as a decoy in that game, we would have lost. They should have gone dummy, dummy, then swung it wide. Wrong game plan!

Were we worried about tackling Lomu? No. Kitch Christie said we were going to win the World Cup not by being the best team but by being the fittest. And look at what happened: extra time and survival of the fittest. We were super-fit. And when your confidence is so high, there is no way anyone can run over you . . . because you know what your buddy can do if you need him. We were super-fit, well prepared and scared of nothing. There was no way Lomu could run through us. No way.

As players who were incredibly focused, we saw the moment of winning the World Cup simply as part of a rugby event. But afterwards, when you look back, you go, 'Man, I was part of a team that really did something for this country.' Then you feel proud, but only afterwards. And thankful, because in the end it's the people, the supporters, who carried us. So it's for us to say thank you to them.

The reality is that rugby was the only life I knew. When you first start out, you're playing with your heroes; you become part of a team, and for the next ten or twelve years all you know is how to be a sportsman. You do what the senior players do. When they go out, you go out. And you think that's life. But looking back from where I am now . . . that's not life.

Although I appreciated every second of playing rugby, I thought being a successful sportsman was all there was: everybody wanted your autograph, your picture, your attention. It was all about you. Even when I stopped playing, even when I got married, all I knew was how to get away with it. I stuffed up, and when I think back, I wish other players could learn from my mistakes. Because I fell on my ass. Hard.

When you become famous, you basically lose your privacy. The sooner you learn to cope with it, the better. I can actually remember when I became an ass. I thought I could get away with everything. I spoke before I thought. Now I've lost my job, I've lost my wife and I've lost my family. But everything that happened to me was my choice, my decision. The only person I can blame is my-self.

I was an idiot; I got caught and it stayed in the media for 20 months. I went to hell and back. I lost 14kg. The video scenario happened years ago, but it came back to bite me on 13 February 2009 when the journalist phoned me. I had started to fix my life from the end of 2006, and Amor and I were actually in a really close relationship when it came back to haunt me.

Yes, there was one very big disappointment in my life in early 2005 and that helped push me off the rails. Instead of trying to fix it, I decided that if *that's* going to happen, then I'm going to do *this*. It was a decision I made when I was too emotional. You think some things are really important, but when you look back, you realise those things aren't important at all, and you think: who cares?

The biggest mistake I made was to deny everything instead of just owning up and saying, 'I fucked up.' It's questionable whether Amor and I would still have been together if I had owned up. But that's the hard part: to know that I had fixed my life when everything fell apart.

I don't come from a wealthy home. I always had to fight for every single thing I wanted. I always wanted to be the best and to play for the Boks. That's what my mom taught me. Even though I'm 39, she said to me, 'You know what, son? I know you're hurting, but use that same fighting spirit to stay positive. Whatever you think and do, do it positively.' And that's what I've learned from Gavin Varejes at the South African Rugby Legends Association as well: stay positive, achieve what you can and give something back.

Maybe there's a bigger picture to consider, too. I think fans should support rugby and support the players, but without idolising them. If you start to prepare at 9am on Saturday and you put on your horns and your Blue Bulls shirt to go and sit at Loftus from 10am and you only get back home at 1am the next morning and you're too tired to go church at 9am on Sunday morning, there's a problem. If you spend every Saturday at Loftus, but you don't have one Saturday to kick a ball with your son, there's a problem. If nobody can touch you because you're going to Loftus, you tell me where the problem is.

I was 33 when I found out what a litre of milk and a loaf of bread cost. As a player, you're away seven months a year. Even if you tour in South Africa, you're away from home. The team becomes your family. It's a different perspective. The moment I held my first child, I thought, 'OK, what do I do with this?' Only then do you realise there are actually other people in this world too. My kids were born on 16 January 2004 and 7 March 2006. That's when I went, 'Wow, this is what life is actually about. Not rugby.'

Now I surround myself with positive, successful people. And that's what I want, because you become like the people around you. I used to have a lot of friends, but now I can count my friends on one hand. It's much better, because for once in my life I actually care about other people. But I've had a lot of other support too. So far, I haven't had one negative person talk to me. I've had many emails from people wanting to commit suicide, but they read my book and realised that there's life after making a big mistake. People still recognise me and come up to greet me. A lot. It's unbelievable how that builds your spirit. But my smile is different nowadays from what it was before.

All I can do now is apologise for my behaviour, because there were a lot of people who looked up to me and I disappointed them. I just want to live my life in such a way that people can see that I've stood up, I've fixed my life and this is the real Joost. If you constantly worry about what people think, you're not going to have a life. I can do nothing about the past, but I can do a lot about the future.

——— *As told to Angus Powers*

JOOST VAN DER WESTHUIZEN is is one of the most decorated players in Springbok history: most capped scrumhalf (87 Tests); top try scorer (56; 38 in Tests); and an 80% win rate as Springbok captain. He has won two Currie Cups, a Tri-Nations trophy and the 1995 Rugby World Cup. Joost was nominated as South African rugby player of the year in every year bar one from 1993 to 1999, and is (so far) the only Springbok to have played in three Rugby World Cup tournaments.

The Parliamentary Try-Scoring Machine

I didn't want *any* contact. The important thing for me was speed. I played wing or fullback, occasionally flyhalf. But I didn't want to be tackled. If I got the ball in time – and leaving me with five metres to work with was fine – then I could negotiate my way forward. I would apply some CODESA skills to my opponents: swerve or put the ball on the boot. What I didn't want was a hospital pass, when I got man and ball at the same time. We used to say, 'You're selling me out!'

I played rugby at school, and then for Orientals rugby club in Umtata. I was working for the Post Office when I was recruited by my former high school friends. They said that joining the Transkei Defence Force would mean I'd be better paid, I'd get fit, and I'd have a chance to achieve Transkei rugby colours. They dangled that carrot, and they were right. In 1976 I joined the army and I played Transkei Defence Force rugby for two years before retiring with an injury. Thereafter I became involved in the administration of the game as secretary of the Transkei Rugby Board.

As secretary of the Board, I often dealt with Danie Craven. *Die madala*. Meetings with Dr Craven never took long. He just issued instructions and then held a press conference. 'We have just had a successful meeting,' he'd say, 'and we discussed the following . . .' Then you'd know that there had been no discussions. In his old age he had to be content with mentoring the up-and-coming provincial administrators, but Dr Craven was highly respected and was always ready with advice or solutions. He was a good man who built rugby in this country, a simple person with a good sense of humour.

When I was elected to Parliament, I continued with my try-scoring ways. We had a parliamentary team who would play match-es against the parliaments of foreign countries. One of the best games in my parliamentary rugby career (1994 to 1996) came against the Irish parliament. It was an evening match, and they were leading when I got the ball on our 22m line. I dashed all the way through, along the touchline, beating all those *madalas*. When I returned to my position after scoring, I could hear Irish spectators and their wives saying that there was no way a Member of Parliament could run like that. He had to be a schoolboy; the South Africans were cheating!

At the post-match function I was introduced as the vice-captain of the South African parliamentary rugby side, Deputy Minister of Environment and Tourism, and a Member of Parliament. I looked across at the Irishmen, and they were shaking their heads with dis-belief. I went over to chat to them afterwards, and they asked a lot of probing questions, trying to establish when I joined Parliament and what my background was. They were definitely surprised by this MP who could run like a young man!

The South African Parliamentary side was very good, and we won most of our games. The only team that gave us trouble were New Zealand. Christopher Laidlaw was the scrumhalf. That veteran All Black was still providing a great service from the back of the scrum. I don't remember our Parliament ever beating New Zealand.

Our side was a good mix of cultures: Afrikaners, Africans, English-men and more. Because I was one of the few MPs who was known for having played and administered rugby at a top level, rugby helped me enjoy a good understanding with the Afrikaans community. But what we had even more in common, I think, was the military. At that time, virtually every Afrikaner male had passed through mili-tary training. I had completed my senior staff officer course at the Army College in Pretoria, so I had a fair idea of how to approach the Afrikaner people.

Afrikaners are often very straightforward. They don't like decep-tion, and if you're honest with them you will win their friendship. I have a lot of respect for Afrikaans culture, which helped during our constitutional negotiations with the Conservative and National par-ties. *'Generaal, hoe gaan dit?'* (General, how are you?) they'd say. I'd reply, *'Ja, ons sal jou donner vandag.'* (Today we're going to work you over.) You have no chance. We're not going to accept your recom-mendation.' Rugby and the military helped me speak their language.

Nowadays I support the Blue Bulls. I live in Pretoria and I'm happy to see a rugby team who are consistent. They're bringing through players of colour and they play with an element of running rugby. But when Fourie du Preez is injured, the void in the team is unfortu-nately there for all to see. What I like about the Bulls is the way they manage to use the *krag* (strength) they have in the forwards before they spin the ball to the backline so that their wings can score.

My own experience of being a team manager was that it was a challenge to console my players after we had been beaten. I ima-gine it is the same today, but when I was involved there was no video analysis to fall back on. When we reassembled for training, we would do a debrief about our defeat. Why did we allow our oppo-nents' backline to toss us around, for instance? Or, how should we defend against fast wings, or a kicking flyhalf? It was a team process, and it emphasised that in sport there will always be winners and losers. No one was to blame. This is 15-man rugby, let's move on. I would remind the team of the glory which they had enjoyed a few weeks ago and underline that the next game was not a foregone conclusion.

Nowadays rugby is a tool that has many uses. Many businessmen travel on their own initiative to Europe in November to do business, but also to watch rugby. The Springboks, All Blacks, Wallabies and the Pumas are all in action against the Six Nations teams, so there are four or five weeks of high-quality Tests. I've always thought that the major sponsors, or for that matter the governments, should arrange business conferences over that period so that people can talk business but also watch rugby.

Rugby's role in transformation is also coming to be understood by all South Africans. I think the black community recognises that playing rugby is often a new experience for them. Apart from the Eastern Cape, most other provinces previously played soccer. People are patriotic and have always supported the national team, but now they are embracing the sport itself. On the other hand, transformation is not about finding any black person and giving him a jersey to wear. It's going to take time.

Discipline is going to be the key if we want to maintain the high standards of the Springboks. There are challenges, but I think the coach has tried to give every player – black or white – an opportunity to prove himself. But sometimes I wish we could change our style slightly, and focus a little more on skill and letting the ball flow through the team. That is where black players will often be best accommodated, but if we are going to expect that a centre weighs 120kg, it will be a backline of hippos instead of skilful runners who can entertain the crowd. Watch the Australian backs play . . . it is a joy.

My favourite player was Dr Divan Serfontein. What a scrumhalf – always at the breakdown ready to distribute the ball. Another player I admire was the former British and Irish Lions fullback, JPR Williams – so strong, aggressive and skilful. But one of the best players I've ever played with was the great French fullback, Serge Blanco. It was during a festival game in Port Elizabeth, and there were a number of former Springboks playing, too. Rob Louw was playing No. 8. That guy gave me a tough time! But I managed to beat him to score a try. I broke from the centre and Rob Louw and Carel du Plessis chased me all the way to the try line. I've never run like that. By the time I dived over, I was having difficulty breathing. I boasted to my teammates at half-time, 'Guys, I've beaten two Springboks already today!' Hopefully it was a run worthy of Blanco himself.

I've always found the braai before the game one of the most enjoyable experiences at a rugby match. These days I'm in the suites, so I no longer join the fellows outside the stadium, many of whom arrive early – depending on how far they've travelled – to enjoy a braai and a beer before shouting for the Springboks from the open stands.

It's different when you are in the suites. You need to maintain your discipline because the person sitting next to you could be the president of New Zealand rugby! It's too formal. I miss the freedom of just being a fan.

———— *As told to Angus Powers*

BANTU HOLOMISA played both wing and fullback in school and club rugby. Injury in his mid-twenties forced his retirement from the game, but he promptly made the transition to sports administrator. After that, politics seemed relatively straightforward. He ruled the former Transkei and helped to ensure a peaceful reintegration of that homeland with the new, democratic South Africa. He served in Nelson Mandela's first Cabinet, but left the ANC in 1997 to form the United Democratic Movement.

FRASER THOMSON

Bittersoet

There are a few rare moments from childhood that stay with you always. Moments when some magical confluence of sense, place and activity conspire to enter so deeply into memory that they are never forgotten. Of course, as with all things magical, there's the chance that things may not turn out quite as you'd like them or that things may not have been quite as they seemed.

One of my magic moments happened nearly 30 years ago. I stood on a field of manicured turf beneath a sun-shot Cape sky of deepest autumn blue, surrounded by my closest friends and comrades. I was 15 years old, physically and mentally fitter than I'd ever be again, a glowing crucible of incipient acne and overwhelming confidence. The great smooth-sided bulk of Paarl Rock gleamed high above us, veiled in the light morning mist. The eucalyptus trees surrounding the field released their scent to lazy bees. I should have been in heaven.

And I would have been, had it not been for the fact that, 20m away across that immaculate expanse of green, the massed ranks of the Paarl Boys High U15D rugby team were waiting for the referee to blow his whistle. Crouched and coiled, a human panzer brigade of *boere*-muscle and pure white bone, they were more than ready – they were *paraat* (poised to strike). The *rooinekke* stood on the other side of the field of battle, and their Voortrekker ancestors stood at their sides, whispering tales of concentration camps and scorched earth. Their parents and schoolmates crowded the sidelines, bellowing incoherent (but unmistakably violent) exhortations.

Away games are always tough. There's the early-morning rising, the travel, the almost total lack of support – all these factors work together to take the edge off even the best of teams. And we were far from the best of teams. We were our school's U16A team more by default than because of any actual talent for the game, chosen above our peers largely because we could usually manage to walk and talk simultaneously.

We'd already lost the toss, of course. The referee, sporting mielie-rows of Brylcreemed hair and an immaculately trimmed salt-and-pepper *snor*, did an average job of concealing his satisfaction when the coin turned up heads instead of tails, but that was to prove his final attempt at impartiality. He raised the whistle to his lips and a thick, anticipatory silence fell over the scene. After an exquisitely timed pause, the two-note blast shrilled and our nightmare began.

Their flyhalf chipped the ball high into the sweet morning air. Up and up it soared, and by some cruel perversity of physics its trajectory brought it down directly on top of me. Time slowed, and the thunder of oncoming boots faded. The ball became everything, spiralling slowly down from that clear blue sky, each stitch and every smear of Dubbin standing out in high relief. Thud, into my breadbasket, both arms grasping leather just as my coach had instructed. I turned, braced, waited for my team's support and the onslaught of our opponents. The support never came.

The impact was strangely painless. I lay on the grass, fighting for breath, and watched as the Paarl boys rumbled on down-field and went on to score the first of the many, many tries they would score that day.

This was the autumn of 1983. The year that PW Botha's Nationalist government was dealing with scores of bombing attacks, the worst of which killed 19 and injured 217 outside the South African Air Force headquarters in Pretoria. Schalk Burger, Bryan Habana and the United Democratic Front were born. John Vorster died. Gerrie Coetzee beat Michael Dokes in Akron, Ohio, to bring home the WBA world heavyweight title and an all-too-rare taste of what we were missing on the world's sporting stage.

This was the year that bombings, shootings and other 'terrorist' acts became an almost daily occurrence. Limpet mines destroyed railway lines, fuel depots and electricity pylons across the country. Operation Askari saw the South African Defence Force once again cross the Angolan border in force. Older brothers, uncles and friends wore uniforms, carried R1 rifles home on leave and filled our gung-ho teenage ears with grim tales of 'contacts' and 'terrs'. My middle-aged father was out in a Ford Capri from 6pm until midnight with a bunch of other terrified middle-aged men, clutching the cold and greasy steel of a totally alien shotgun as they patrolled our suburban streets against the 'black menace'. These were the through-the-looking-glass days of our youth, days of mundane mayhem and abnormal normality.

This was also the time in which the geography and history teachers in my (English-language) state school could still keep a straight face while they taught a generation of white kids that the development of South Africa was due entirely to the courage and determination of the plucky Boer settlers in the face of savage Native aggression and brutal Colonial oppression. Oh *ja*, and that the continued survival of our civilised way of life was dependent on the heroic actions of our political leaders and our Boys on the Border. These were our teachers. Such was our education.

I played hooker. I have no idea why, because I was so short that I had to bind under my props' arms rather than over their shoulders. Size notwithstanding, I usually loved it down there in the engine room, kicking and clawing with the best of them in the unseen micro-battles that decided the course of so many matches.

My opposite number on that day in Paarl looked like a junior version of Os du Randt – cuboid, crewcut and totally lacking a neck. He was bigger than his props. He smiled at me when we lined up for the first scrum, a slow smile that said all there was to say about how he saw us *Engelsmanne*. Facing up to those monsters was terrifying, but I discovered that my lack of stature had some benefits. Once the scrum was packed down, my feet were dangling in the air. I wouldn't go so far as to call this an advantage, but it did mean that I could strike at the ball just that little bit quicker than a hooker with both feet firmly planted on the earth. As the Paarl Boys scrumhalf put the ball in, I darted out a boot and won it against the head. Bad move. As I soon learned, any act of defiance was to be rewarded with an exponential increase in aggression. Next scrum, one of their locks punched me in the face just before the put-in, and the ball was lost in a smeary mist of involuntary tears.

And so it went: injury heaped upon insult. The half-time whistle sounded like Handel's Hallelujah Chorus to our sorry band of infidels. We limped from the field and stood in a loose and lonely huddle, wincing as the juice from the quartered oranges stung our bleeding lips. We stared at each other in speechless horror. Half way? Only half fucking way?

This was like being a conscript in 1916 or 1942 or some other blighted rest stop on the road to hell – so much pain already borne, so much more to come. The five-minute break (or whatever it was – it felt more like ten seconds) ended and once again we faced up to our adversaries. Only now they were pumped up on the evil adrenaline of total domination, and we were reeling in traumatic shock.

Their flyhalf picked me out again at the kickoff, and to my eternal shame I intentionally knocked it on rather than take another beating beneath their studs. Youthful courage and idealism were swiftly being usurped by their older and wiser cousins: pragmatism and cowardice.

In that second half we played like girls – like the U11D girls' net-ball team, but without their enthusiasm or commitment. We were embarrassing to a degree that must have taken years off our poor coach's life. The Paarl Boys backline could have held passing prac-tice sessions before our so-called defence reached them. Instead, they concentrated on scoring tries. They succeeded, with monoto-nous regularity.

So we lost. We lost so badly that there was no refuge to be taken in maybes or coulda-beens or ref's decisions. If there was one lesson that each and every one of us part-timers might have taken from that match, it was that these biltong-based life forms from north of the *boerewors* curtain were serious. Serious in a bone-crushing, body-on-the-line kind of way that we had never dreamed of. But there was no time for reflection that day, no lessons were learned or parallels drawn. All we could do was endure. We knew that the final whistle would eventually blow, and that no matter how deep our misery might seem there was eventually going to be an end to it all.

It took years for me to think about that match in a different way and to see the value to be found in crushing defeat. That game, I realise now, was my first real taste of what it felt like to be truly powerless. There was nothing that I, or anyone on my team, could do to change the course of events. We had no tricks up our sleeves or rabbits in our hats. We were simply not big enough, not fast enough, not strong enough, not good enough. The lesson of humility is, by definition, never easily learned.

Memory is a strange beast, though. Looking back on that day now, a generation later, it's not what I can remember about that game that's surprising, but rather that I can recall things that I didn't even notice at the time. Like the fact that every boy on that field was white, as was every member of the watching crowd. There might have been a black face about – a groundsman perhaps, or a nanny brought along to look after the young kids while the *baas* and *mêrrem* watched the game – but I didn't see any and I didn't find that strange in the slightest.

Why would I? That was the just the way it was, the way it always had been. After a lifetime under National Party rule, it would have taken a far more independent spirit than mine even to recognise, let alone protest, the inequality of the system. Then, over the years, the idea started to nag me that maybe, just maybe, in some miniscule way we got a taste in that game of what those absent black faces were dealing with every single day of their lives. When the final whistle blew, we climbed into our bus and drove back to our comfortable southern suburbs homes. After a bath, some parental sympathy and a good night's sleep we would once again be the little lords of all we surveyed.

The invisible black kids in the invisible townships would wake up to more of the same – to yet another pounding in an endless series of games they couldn't win.

The end of high school and the refusal of my body to break its 1.78m, 75kg mould signalled the end of my inglorious rugby career. I put down the oval ball, picked up a beer and a packet of smokes and said goodbye to all that without a great deal of regret.

I still loved the game, but I loved it from the safety of my couch, where I could scream at the referee and the players with impunity and enjoy my vicarious share of the agony and ecstasy in complete safety. I watched Western Province dominate for half a decade, revelling in the surrogate vengeance against all comers, then suffered through ten years of hurt as the Boere and the Durbanites hit back. When the political landscape began to change in the early 1990s, I'll confess that I regarded possible readmission into international rugby as one of the major up-sides of handing the country over to the former enemy. I was still very much a child of my time.

And then came the 1995 Rugby World Cup.

Sport, by its nature, is something that attracts hyperbole. It's war by proxy, after all, and the raw emotion, the pride, the sheer *aaarrrggghhh*-ness of it all simply can't be expressed in a sober and understated fashion. What would be the point? So when the commentators say that the 1995 World Cup brought an entire country together, for once they aren't exaggerating. Maybe it didn't break down the racial barriers of half a century in one fell swoop and maybe most of the goodwill it engendered was transient, but for a few weeks in the chilly winter of 1995 rugby played a huge role in giving our newborn nation some desperately needed common ground, a dream that everyone could buy into and one which paid dividends in spades. That the Springboks went on to actually win the bloody thing remains incredible to this day. Someone should really make a movie about it. Oh, wait . . .

Cynics (a group of which I'm normally a card-carrying member) would say that that famous victory had little or no effect on the course of our country: race relations remain a huge problem in South Africa, rugby is still largely a white man's game, *et cetera ad nauseam*. My response to them would be that either they weren't there or they've forgotten what it was like to be South African at the time. The fact that when the Bokke won the World Cup again in 2007 the feat was greeted with comparatively understated joy is just one sign of how much things have changed, both on and off the field.

In 1995, nobody truly believed that we could do it. Nobody believed the country could host the event without trouble; nobody believed the Springboks would get further than the quarterfinals. Twelve years later, we had belief. We knew they could win it, and they did. Sixteen years later, as I write this, South Africa has just hosted another of the world's major sports events, the FIFA World Cup, with aplomb, and once again our country is united in proud achievement despite the usual background whine of nay-saying and doubt. Today, we believe.

Today, that Os-like hooker from that long-forgotten rout in a very different country would sit next to me in the stands, screaming with equal passion and volume as Gio or Bryan streak for the line. Black, brown, white – who cares as long as they're wearing green and gold? Tell me again that 1995 changed nothing.

Ja, boet. Rugby, politics, despair, elation. It's a part of us, part of the warp and weft of our country and our national soul. Like South Africa itself, our rugby has had its times of shame and its times of glory, times when it deserved its punishment and times when it rose beyond any reasonable limits to achieve truly remarkable things. Because of, and sometimes despite, the people who love the game in this country, our rugby has displayed a resilience and determination that shows the very best South Africa has to offer. It's far from perfect, no doubt, but it's a long, long way from where it used to be.

The final score in that long-ago school match was, I believe, 118-0. We were silent on the bus as we waited for the driver to start the engine and begin the long journey home. Until Rob the tight-head prop spoke up through battered lips: 'Shame we lost the toss, hey *ouens*? I reckon we would have klapped them otherwise.'

It hurt like hell to laugh, but laugh we did.

When **FRASER THOMSON** isn't working on an oil rig in some godforsaken corner of the globe, he is a freelance writer whose work has appeared in numerous print and online publications. Fraser currently lives in a tiny fishing village in West Cornwall, spending far too much on imported Klippies and the monthly TV subscriptions that keep him in touch with his beloved WP, Stormers and Boks. He is desperately trying to convince his seven-year-old son that wearing an English rugby jersey is simply not an option.

JAKE WHITE

A Rugby Life

Dale College in King William's Town and Lord Milner in Settlers were both the traditional type of boarding school where you didn't go home every weekend and order a pizza from Mr Delivery. As a boarder in the 1970s, you went home a handful of times a year; and if you were lucky, you would be invited back for a couple of weekends by mates whose fathers farmed nearby. Being captain of the A rugby team definitely made you more popular because the guys who invited you home for weekends were typically teammates of yours.

At Jeppe High School in Johannesburg, where I matriculated, rugby was what determined the pecking order and the privileges. If there were four boys of the same age at the dinner table, the A team guy could serve himself first, the B team guy went next, then the C team guy. I started playing rugby as a flank, and then played hooker from Standard 6 onwards. By the time I reached matric, I had been lucky enough to play for the first team, which brought its own, new set of privileges.

The game continued to offer me unique opportunities while I was a schoolmaster.

In 1994, I took a Jeppe schoolboy side to England. We toured extensively and even visited Rugby School, where William Webb Ellis supposedly picked up the ball and ran with it towards the goal line. How much more can you do for a rugby-playing boy in South Africa than take him to Rugby School and show him where the sport began?

After leaving teaching, I worked full-time for the Transvaal Rugby Union, coaching the U21s and then being appointed fitness trainer to the senior side. Ray Mordt was coach at the time, and I remember standing with him at Eden Park in Auckland during Transvaal's Super 12 tour. Ray had scored a hat trick of tries against New Zealand in 1981, and as we stood in that same corner of the field, chatting, I thought to myself how lucky I was to be there with a man who had been the first Springbok to score a hat trick against the All Blacks.

While I was at Transvaal, I got a call from Nick Mallett, the Springbok coach. I joined the squad as technical advisor in time for the 1997 end-of-year tour. Nick himself had just got the Bok job, after coaching Boland and having coached a bit in France. I suspect we were both thinking the same thing: how fantastic it was to work with such talented players and – win or lose – become part of the rugby history of a country in which rugby is so massively important.

As it turned out, we were coaching the best team in the world.

When I was recruited by Nick, the Boks had just started their run of 17 consecutive Test victories, which would eventually equal the world record. Beating France at the last international ever played at the Parc des Princes was memorable, as was beating the All Blacks 13-3 in Wellington the next year in the Tri-Nations. That was also the last time the Springboks played at that particular stadium – Athletic Park – before it was demolished, which was significant, as South Africa had been playing there since 1921. The Boks wrapped up the Tri-Nations that year by coming back from 20-3 down to beat the All Blacks 24-23 at King's Park in Durban.

I was with Nick for more than 20 Test matches, of which we won the first 16 in a row. It really doesn't get better than that. I regarded myself as exceptionally fortunate to have been part of that journey, especially considering how quickly I had moved from Transvaal juniors to Transvaal seniors and on to the Springboks. In 1995, I had just left teaching, yet two years later I was part of a Springbok squad scoring 50 points against France in Paris.

After parting ways with Nick, I took on the Baby Bok assistant coach job in 1999. We won the 'U21 world championship', although it wasn't called that until a couple of years later. Eric Sauls and I took a team to Argentina, with John Smit as captain, and we became the first South African team to win an international U21 title. I then joined the Natal Sharks, where we endured one of the Sharks' worst seasons ever – winning just one Super 12 game in 2000.

Harry Viljoen was the next Springbok coach I worked with, when I came on board as assistant coach later in 2000. One of the strangest experiences of my rugby career occurred when the Boks played Argentina at the home ground of the River Plate football club in Buenos Aires. Percy Montgomery, playing flyhalf, didn't kick the ball for 72 minutes of the Test match. There we were, playing at the home of one of the most famous football clubs in South America, and Monty had been instructed by Harry not to put boot to ball. Bizarre!

After my second stint with the Springboks, it was back to the South African U21 side, coaching them to the U21 world championship on home soil in 2002, and I stayed on with them into 2003.

Apart from the obvious achievements of winning the Tri-Nations in 2004 and lifting the World Cup in 2007, one of the highlights of my tenure as Springbok coach was actually being appointed. Never in my wildest dreams did I think that an English-speaking guy who had never played provincial or Springbok rugby was ever going to coach at that level.

But as you can imagine, there were plenty of lows. I had a lonely time of it in 2006. We had a lot of injuries, I was trying out new combinations, and the results weren't going our way. One of the most frustrating aspects of coaching is sticking to a plan – maybe resting players, blooding young guys, testing the team's depth or trying out new ideas – and it not working out as well as you would like. You can't very well explain your thinking to the public and the fans. That would be like giving away all your insider information to the opposition so that they can beat you later, when it really counts.

Unfortunately, there is no way out of this kind of frustration for a coach. And that's one lesson I've learned since leaving the Bok job. There are some things that you cannot change. Having accepted that, I hope I would now handle those things a lot better.

Being nominated and selected as the best coach in the world by the International Rugby Board in 2004 and 2007 was a great honour, but seeing how the core of the Springbok team that was selected seven years ago has endured is also pretty satisfying. Hearing names like John Smit, Fourie du Preez, Schalk Burger, Juan Smith, Victor Matfield, Bakkies Botha, Jaque Fourie and Jean de Villiers being called out makes you realise it was worth it. Putting that original team together didn't come easy. There was always a lot of criticism: Smit was supposedly never good enough to be in the team. And Burger was never enough of an out-and-out fetcher. It's good to see that the class of 2007 wasn't a once-off.

There were two things that stood out about the Boks while I was in charge. Firstly, they were winners. Those guys have won probably every tournament they've ever been able to play in: U21 world championship, Currie Cup, Super 14, Tri-Nations and the World Cup. Secondly, more than anything else, they were desperate. The Boks had come out of the Kamp Staaldraad and World Cup debacles of 2003 and they had had enough. They would have done anything to change. They were ranked fifth in the world, their market value was a disgrace, and their image in world rugby was embarrassing.

But the players were young and coachable. That was critical.

It goes without saying that a successful team is one that best executes its game plan, and that has a good balance between attack and defence. South Africa is known as the best defensive team in the world; a team that can win a Test match without seeing much of the ball. That is nothing to feel embarrassed about. Look at England: they play a particular brand of rugby which everyone says is boring. Yet they've reached three out of six World Cup finals. That makes England the Brazil of rugby football. Australia are the thinkers of the game; Fiji are famous for running, as are Argentina for their mauling and scrumming. That's just how it is. If South Africa wanted to exploit their strong point, it would mean building a game plan around our defence.

If you can win a Test with 30% of the ball, why chase 70% of the ball? Granted, some teams need 70% of possession to win, but the Springboks aren't one of them. Don't get me wrong: if the Boks get more than 30% possession, that is fantastic. But they don't have to. They can put the opposition under more pressure when the opposition have possession.

South Africa's best game plan is based on being more organised defensively than the opposition can be offensively. South Africans have a gift for playing like that. We don't panic if we don't have possession. I think it stems from our schoolboy rugby. Just watch a primary school game: the one thing all those little kids can do is tackle each other.

South African rugby is all about being confident that we can handle whatever the opposition brings. And that is extremely important, because in rugby, as in life, you're not always going to have the ball.

——— *As told to Angus Powers*

JAKE WHITE is one of the most successful coaches in Springbok history, seeing out his full four-year contract (no mean feat in itself) and guiding the Boks to their second Tri-Nations title in 2004 and their finest hour during the 2007 Rugby World Cup. If a coach's achievements can be measured by the quality of the team he bequeaths to his successor, Jake is probably the best Bok coach of them all. He now lives in Cape Town, where he runs a coaching academy and consultancy.

ON TOUR

Toks and the Paris Panties

Most South African kids either become serious sportsmen or sportswomen or they end up becoming serious sports lovers. That's the kind of society we have. We are natural sports lovers; we are passionate and competitive. And I was no different, even though I grew up in the town of Lüderitz in Namibia.

When I played U9 rugby, I began as a wing. I thought I was extremely quick, but I clearly wasn't; the next year I switched to lock, and that's where I played for the rest of my career. My family were keen followers of the game, but in the early 1970s the closest we could get to a match was to listen to it on the radio. When the Springboks were playing in New Zealand, my dad would wake us up at 4am to follow the broadcast.

The very first big live game I saw was in Upington, when the old North Western Cape played the formidable All Blacks in 1976. Every man and his dog were at the match. I played for the North Western Cape U12 side against the Griquas U12 side in the curtain-raiser, and that's how it all started.

There were big-name New Zealand players – like Sid Going, Grant Batty, Bryan Williams and Billy Bush – lining up against a North Western Cape side captained by Herklaas Engelbrecht. Herklaas was a lock, and he played on until he was about . . . *ag*, I thought it was close to 60. But he was hard as nails, and even if he never represented the Springboks, he was a legend in South African rugby.

The All Blacks demolished the North Western Cape, but that was irrelevant because, in the final minutes, the home team got a penalty on the halfway line. Herklaas stepped forward (his team were trailing badly; they didn't have a hope in hell of winning) and he indicated to the ref that he was going to go for posts. He put the ball down on the spot where the penalty would be taken from; there was a deathly silence, as if this were a kick for the game. And it was only a penalty! The kick went over and Herklaas was carried shoulder-high from the field.

I went back home and said to my mom, 'This is a game I have to play! If that's how you get treated when you lose, then how is it going to be when you win?'

Two weeks later, we were on holiday in Cape Town when Western Province played that same All Black side. It was raining, absolutely bucketing down. Guys like Morné du Plessis, Boland Coetzee, Agie Koch, Chris Pope and Robbie Blair were playing, and there was only standing room available. My elder brother and I were both too short to see anything, so we took turns to sit on my dad's shoulders. Province scored in the dying moments in the corner of a very muddy Newlands, and Robbie Blair had to place that ball on the touchline and land the kick from an acute angle, which he did, for the win. Those were two hectic games, for different reasons, but they were my introduction to live rugby. I was hooked.

I was always destined to be a team player. Not that I've got anything against individual sports, but I am a team animal. The team environment poses a completely unique challenge; in a team sport you have to get different characters from different backgrounds with different goals to play together. Team sport teaches life lessons which you can't read in a book or learn at university: for instance, that you're dependent on other people. Or that sometimes you have to give before you can receive back. And when a team gels, generates team spirit and has a hunger to perform . . . there's nothing more powerful in life. It's like a beautiful Rolls-Royce engine just purring along. When a team clicks, they become unstoppable.

I've been fortunate to be part of two such teams: the Transvaal and

Springbok sides coached by Kitch Christie. While those were really talented teams, it was also important that we believed in each other and had a wonderful rapport. We trained like animals, but we also had certain goals, which we reached – every last one of them. In 1993, Transvaal won everything on offer: the very first Super 10 tournament, the Currie Cup, the Lion Cup and the night series. Four trophies in one season, which had never been done before. The next year we won the Currie Cup and the Lion Cup, and then the Springboks won the Rugby World Cup in 1995.

What I miss about the game are the guys I played with and against. Some of my best friends around the world are men that I played against. When you bleed and suffer together, it creates a special bond. You become a sort of family. It's similar to the special rivalry between South Africa and New Zealand. The All Blacks don't regard themselves as true All Blacks until they've played the Springboks in South Africa. It is their ultimate test. And I know the Boks feel the same. It's always been like that: a love–hate relationship, but with huge respect for each other.

I am a big fan of humour, and I have seen the funniest things on a rugby field and on rugby tour. I remember touring France with the Springboks when Toks van der Linde and I were roommates. Toks was extremely gullible, and when he asked me what he could buy for his wife to make an impression when he got back home, I said, 'You know, Tokka, there are two things that Bordeaux is famous for: good red wine and some of the most beautiful women's lingerie. I guarantee that if you buy some nice lingerie for your wife, she'll fall for you as soon as you put your cases down.'

Toks said that sounded great, but he was worried about not being able to speak the language. I said, 'That's no problem. I played in France as a student and I've lived here for eight months, so I can get by. I'll come with you and I'll translate.'

'No problem,' he said.

As we walked into the lingerie store, I explained to him that I should do the talking.

'No problem,' he said.

'*Bonjour*,' I said to the lingerie shop assistant, continuing (in my best French): 'This is my friend, he is a cross-dresser and he's looking for some lingerie.' She looked us up and down in disbelief, and then said to me, '*Bien sur, quelle couleur?*' (Of course, what colour?).

'He loves pink,' I replied.

She went into the back of the shop and rummaged around and eventually came out with a pair of massive panties. I didn't know they even made them that big. Toks said to me, 'No, no, no! My wife's not that big!'

'Don't worry, buddy,' I said, 'all she wants to know is, do you like the design?'

So Toks said to her, 'I love it!'

She went back again and returned with a massive bra which both of us could have fitted into. At that point Toks caught on and I had to explain everything, but he was properly fooled, and to this day he hasn't forgiven me!

That is another reason why I think touring is extremely important: you soon see which players can perform when they're out of their comfort zone. Not only do you grow as a player, but you also see the world. You travel in comfort and it costs you zip. Obviously, you can get up to a lot of mischief, too, and there are a lot of tales I could add here, but I don't think this book is the place.

Nonetheless, the props and hookers always somehow seem mixed up in the nonsense. Ollie le Roux, playing for the Sharks, once faced Johan le Roux at Ellis Park. Johan was our tighthead, and although he was a reserved guy he was a hard bastard. He could dish it out and he could take it on the chin. Sharks coach Ian McIntosh had obviously said to Ollie that his chance had come; he's playing against the Springbok incumbent, and if he can make a good impression then the selectors will have a look at him. Because, when he ran onto the field, Ollie was psyched out of his mind, his eyes open wide and literally foaming at the mouth.

The first three scrums collapsed. After the fourth one went down, Ollie jumped up and, looking down at Johan lying on the ground, started screaming like a man possessed: 'Welcome to hell!' Both packs of forwards stood around, watching this spectacle. Johan got up and while he was brushing the grass off his chest and face, he looked at Ollie and said, 'Meet the devil.'

That broke the ice, and all the forwards and the referee burst out laughing. Then we got on with the game. It is moments like these that make rugby extremely special. And it happens more often than you might think.

———— *As told to Angus Powers*

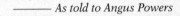

KOBUS WIESE is one of South Africa's most iconic rugby players. After debuting for Boland, and learning his trade at Western Transvaal, Kobus became a Transvaal and Springbok stalwart. His 135 games for Transvaal included five Currie Cup finals (and two trophies), two Super Rugby finals (one trophy) and three Lion Cups. As a Bok, Kobus lifted the 1995 Rugby World Cup, and his inimitable insights and commentary are now enjoyed by rugby fans all over the world.

The Rugby Brotherhood

I've always said that I fell into rugby, and for ages that's exactly how it felt. The transition from country to country and school to school, even team to team – usually so difficult – were all smoothed by my love for and participation in the game. But looking back now, it has become clear that I didn't fall into rugby at all. Rugby chose me.

That's the truth. Rugby has a beauty and power all its own, which is why it has so many disciples around the world. The game chose me, and then concerned servants of the game, the greatest givers, were all involved in nudging, cajoling and leading me along a life held together by a passion for the sport. Snatches of memory – often featuring a trip to a match, or the coach, captain or opposition player who defined the afternoon's play – litter the journey.

I was a three-year-old in the lowveld of Rhodesia and my dad had turned out for Hippo Valley, his local team. As the early-evening game ground to a sudden halt, I sprinted onto the pitch, concerned at my father's lack of movement. It turned out that he was concussed, something I felt in my bones even as I watched him go down, but surely something I could never have comprehended at that age.

As my father was carried from the field of play, the colours of his rugby jersey burned themselves into my memory. Years later, during our family holidays, he still proudly pulled that jersey on to go fishing on the rocks at Cape St Francis with the now deceased Dr Tony Mullins, the accomplished front-ranker for the University of Cape Town and Zimbabwe.

As that three-year-old, I ran on and registered the confusion of players and friends on the field – they were as concerned by my presence as they were with the plight of my father. The same faces, in different jerseys, now look out from the photograph of the varsity first XV that hangs in the hallway of our family home.

My dad got his own back in a big way, many years later. I was lying in the middle of the pitch in Twickenham stadium, my vision watery and blurred from the pain of a dislocated shoulder. I thought I was dreaming when into the circle of faces above poked that of my father . . . who wanted to know if I was OK!

I suppose we had learned from each other. At the age of three, I was whisked off by my mother, and at age 53 he was marched away by Twickenham security, ejected for illegal entry to the Test match field of play, and left to talk his way back in through the main gate half an hour later.

Years before, as a student at Stellenbosch University, I had been a fan myself and had seized the opportunity to go to the opening game of the 1995 Rugby World Cup. I had bought tickets for my dad and brought him down from Zimbabwe for the game. Displaying sterling commitment, I had queued all night outside Newlands, but being a mere student I could only afford standing-room tickets – not ideal when anyone shorter than six foot four couldn't see a thing!

In a moment of inspiration before the anthems, one of my mates grabbed a plastic dustbin from the toilets and slipped it past the guards and ushers. We lifted my dad up onto the dustbin and he leaned back against a wall and enjoyed a perfect view. In fact, it was so good he was level with the Australian team management, who were seated in the row above and behind us. Delighted, and very chatty after a morning spent at Forester's Arms, he nattered away to the non-playing squad members, and then ragged them after the Springboks pulled off a famous victory.

The 1995 World Cup was memorable for a number of reasons,

not least South Africa's eventual victory, and a carefree student life-style added great momentum to an already enjoyable time.

Watching the semifinal in Durban had its ups and downs. We wore Springbok fan hard hats, adorned with real horns, and got some tickets off Fritz van Heerden, who was playing at Stellenbosch with me at the time. The delayed start to the match, caused by the torrential rain, was extremely tense as we knew that if the game had to be called off, the French would go through. The 'Battle of Boet Erasmus' between South Africa and Canada in Port Elizabeth had badly tainted the Springbok disciplinary record, which would have been the decisive factor in the result not going our way.

The nerves were alleviated by our close proximity to a large sup-ply of South African Breweries' finest product, and the longer we waited, the louder we became. We were joined in song by two funny and enthusiastic fans who had driven down from Johannesburg. We became firm friends, and made a pact to carry on our celebrations regardless of the outcome of the match, which, after a famous vic-tory, we did, and created some long-lasting memories.

A few months later, while trekking my gear into my second year at university, a familiar face peered around the door. My assigned 'new-bie' for the year was none other than my friend from Durban. I had an extra pal, and he had the benefit of knowing his way around the system from day one.

Good things happen to good people, and with rugby relationships as the oil, the machine runs a little smoother!

Rugby's hallmark is a brotherhood who understand each other. It fell away for a while as the wheels of commercialism started to turn and the fellows forgot that friendship and rivalry amount to the same thing in the end. There is always a second half to a rivalry, and it's great to see Grant Fox now speak fondly of Naas Botha, or Justin Marshall respectfully talk up both Joost van der Westhuizen and George Gregan.

I found that this respect and fellowship became strained by the early days of professional rugby, but it was strong enough to survive, and showed itself to be healthy and thriving later on in my career.

Some of my greatest memories stem from playing Barbarians, social or amateur rugby. For instance, tours to the Dubai Sevens with former international rivals always ended in plenty of beers and laughs and apologies for a careless boot, punch or late hit, and the promise to keep up the friendship and *gees* in the future.

The Barbarians are a particularly special outfit. I toured with the side when we took on Scotland, Wales and England in 2004. For the week before the Scotland game, we stayed in St Andrews, a wonderful medieval town where the Barbarians, uniquely, enjoy a lifetime association with the Jigger Inn, a little caddies' pub on the grounds of the hotel that borders the 17th fairway of the famous Old Course.

When talk turns to the mecca of golf, it's always with much pride that I tell the story of how Brian O'Driscoll, Bruce Reihana, a few other rugby luminaries and I – after a good few pints of Guinness – were allowed to have a crack at one of the most famous holes in golf.

The old wicker golf clubs and a few vintage balls were taken down from the wall behind the bar and passed around, and the boys had their way with the course, pot bunkers and all. No one batted an eyelid. In fact, the barman virtually encouraged it, seeing as the relationship between the course and the Baa-Baas goes right back to the beginnings of sport, when friendship, touring and gentlemanly conduct were a way of life.

Micky Steele-Bodger CBE is one of the most famous names in English and Barbarians rugby, and I am lucky to count him as a friend. Micky's notoriety comes from an extraordinary history in the game. Forgive me if I leave anything out, but, as I recall, he was player, manager and selector for England; selector for the British and Irish Lions; president of the Rugby Football Union; chairman of the International Rugby Board; and player, captain and current president of the Barbarian Football Club – and a very able one at that.

The best story I've ever heard about Micky took place after he suffered a heart attack on tour. After a night or two in hospital, he turned up in the change room to spur his boys on. He still claims an Irish doctor saved his life and to this day won't tour without him. More importantly, when the duty physician at the hospital informed him that he was far too infirm to attend the match and that the stress might kill him, Micky replied that he would much rather die on the touchline at Twickenham than closeted in some godforsaken hospital. After hearing that, the physician sensibly allowed him to take his leave . . . and help inspire his team to a famous victory. It might not be so obvious nowadays, but exceptional characters and rugby still go hand in hand.

BOB SKINSTAD, born in Zimbabwe, made South Africa his home and carved out a career as one of the most charismatic Springboks of his era. Famous for flamboyant loose forward play early in his career, Bob went on to captain the Boks in twelve Tests, earning 42 caps, scoring eleven tries, and helping the Springboks win the 1998 Tri-Nations and the 2007 Rugby World Cup. He also won three Currie Cups with Western Province. Bob is now one of SuperSport's most popular rugby pundits.

JON PATRICIOS

What the Doctor Saw

The life of a rugby doctor, in three scenes.

SCENE 1

In 1997, on tour with the Lions in New Zealand, after a heavy defeat to the Auckland Blues, I was picking up the pieces in my hotel room, which doubled as a medical room. The players had a bad habit of wanting Voltaren injections before and after the game, and I was trying to move away from this as it is poor medical practice. I suggested that they should use Voltaren suppositories instead. This came as quite a shock to most of them, especially the forwards, who intimated that they couldn't possibly do this because they weren't sure how it worked. Without blinking an eye, big prop Balie Swart asked for a suppository, stood up on a coffee table, stripped naked, bent over and *slowly* inserted the suppository so that everyone knew exactly how it was done.

SCENE 2

New Zealand, being an island nation, is absolutely paranoid about any sort of contamination by alien fauna and flora. For example, players have to scrub their boots clean of any mud before disembarking, and no biltong, fruit or vegetables may be transported off an arriving aeroplane. Beagle sniffer dogs await disembarking passengers, who are asked to bin any foodstuffs thus detected before passing through an X-ray machine. This is usually a minor inconvenience and little else.

On a trip to New Zealand in 2003, we embarked in Sydney at about 9pm, sat on the plane for an hour, and were then told that due to a technical malfunction we would have to disembark. We sat in the lounge for a further two hours waiting for a new plane. In the lounge there happened to be bowls of apples. Team physiotherapist Jacques Nienaber (now the Stormers and Western Province defensive coach) is a great friend of mine, and we thought it would be an excellent prank to insert an apple into coach Tim Lane's hand luggage. In Christchurch, the beagle would sniff it out and we would all have a good laugh at his expense.

Eventually we boarded after midnight. As Tim was putting his bag in the overhead locker, he noticed the apple, realised it was us and threw it back at me. Not wanting to lose out on the entertainment, I promptly put it into the closest Cats rucksack I could find. We landed at about 3am and waited eagerly to see whose bag it was. It turned out to belong to prop Baksteen Nel. What we hadn't factored into our plan was that the beagles were now asleep. However, the X-ray machines were not. The apple was detected, the offending passenger apprehended, arrested and handcuffed. It took a further half an hour, keeping an exhausted team waiting on the bus, to negotiate a hefty fine.

Needless to say, Baksteen was fuming. So much so that we were too scared to own up at that stage for fear of being beaten to a pulp. What made it even funnier was that when we arrived at the hotel and caught the lift up to our floor, a bowl of apples greeted us. I entered into some peace and reconciliation negotiations with Baksteen the next day and paid his fine, but Jacques and I never looked at an apple the same way again!

SCENE 3

On tour, you often have to find ways to keep things interesting. So, while in Auckland in 2004, I engaged in some friendly banter with Jacques Nienaber about who was quicker across the field to an injured player.

This conversation developed over a couple of days until it was decided that we had to settle the matter over a 100m dash from poles to poles. The team became involved and were laying bets of up to R500 on their favoured 'athlete'. At training the next day, as the team finished their preparation, Jacques and I limbered up and performed a few stretches. Wanting extra traction, we each borrowed boots from some of the players. We took our marks and were set off.

At about 70m I nosed ahead, only to experience a painful twang as one of my left hamstrings tore. I was determined not to lose, even as I saw Jacques edging ahead, before he too stumbled with a torn hamstring.

In medical terms, these were significant grade 2–3 injuries that manifested in massive bruising behind our knees. We spent the next three days treating ourselves more than the players. When we hobbled onto the pitch against the Chiefs it was with strapped legs and slightly bruised egos.

(PS. Patricios beat Nienaber by 0.5m!)

DR JON PATRICIOS is a sports physician based in Johannesburg and is the president of the South African Sports Medicine Association. He has been involved in rugby at school, club, provincial and international level for 15 years. From 1996 to 2005 he was team doctor to the Cats and the Lions teams during ten Currie Cup and six Super 12 seasons. Jon currently serves on the South African Rugby Union's medical advisory committee and is a consultant to the Boksmart rugby safety programme.

SHERYLLE CALDER

The Eye Lady

The second time I met the Queen, she called me 'the eye lady'. I'd met her before, when I was touring England with the All Blacks. But by 2003 I was back at Buckingham Palace with the England team after they had won the Rugby World Cup. The Queen recognised me and asked where we'd met before. I said that I'd been to the palace with the All Blacks, and she replied, 'Oh yes, I remember – the eye lady!' She was interested in my line of work, which involves developing visual performance skills, so we chatted about what I'd been doing.

The first thing that had struck me about the All Blacks was that they were such wonderful guys. They were very down to earth, probably more so than any other rugby players I've dealt with. I was with them for two years from 2000. I was appointed by Wayne Smith but I never got to work with him, as he was soon replaced by John Mitchell and Robbie Deans. I'd fly over for their training camps, work with the team, and then fly back to South Africa. It actually killed me, travelling to and fro like that. Because there was a 'restriction of trade' clause in my contract, I couldn't tell anyone that I was working with them. I used to fly out of Johannesburg without telling a soul. It was very secretive!

That was the era of Christian Cullen, Andrew Mehrtens, Ben Blair, Aaron Mauger and Byron Kelleher. Tana Umaga was a really impressive, friendly guy. Whenever Mehrtens saw me, he would pretend to walk into something. It was a regular joke between us. I once asked Christian Cullen what skill he'd like to improve, and his answer was his vision. I thought he was one of the guys who had great vision on the field, but for him it was still a skill that he could really improve.

For my very first day with the All Blacks, I flew in at midnight, found my hotel and decided that the next day, which was Sunday, I would just relax and find my feet before meeting John and Robbie at 10am on Monday morning. I woke up, went to breakfast at 9am and then picked up a newspaper outside my door. That's when I realised that it was already Monday morning! With the time zone changes, I had completely lost track of what day it was. I had to shower quickly, gather my thoughts and get down in time for that meeting at 10am. That was my start with the All Blacks!

Throughout my time in New Zealand, I tried not to fraternise with touring South African teams or fans, as it would have presented a conflict of interest. South Africa never found out I was working with the All Blacks, but England did. Clive Woodward, who wanted to win the next Rugby World Cup, sent Andy Robinson (who is now coaching Scotland) and England kicking coach Dave Alred out to Durban to watch the 2002 Tri-Nations Test between New Zealand and South Africa (when that fan tackled the ref). And to find me.

Jake White, who was the South African U21 coach at the time, had introduced me to the Springbok management, but at that point South Africa weren't ready for my science. When Clive first approached me, I was still working for the All Blacks and I had to decline. But he phoned me about a hundred times, asking, 'Are you coming? Are you coming?' And I kept saying, 'I'll let you know. I'll let you know!'

As soon as my All Black contract was up, I got in touch and asked him whether he was still interested. He emailed back straight away, 'Yes! Can you come tomorrow?'

They flew me over: I arrived in London at 6:30am. It was winter, and just before the Six Nations. I'll never forget it. I caught a taxi to England's base at Pennyhill Park, a most beautiful place. Woodward had said that if I spent a week there I'd never want to go anywhere else, and it really was like that. It was a fantastic facility. I walked in and they said, 'Hi, we're having a team meeting in a moment. Could you do a presentation?'

I had to put something together quickly, and when I walked into the meeting room the whole England team were sitting there – coaches, management, everyone. Martin Johnson, Lawrence Dallaglio, Neil Back, Richard Hill, Austin Healy, Matt Dawson, Jonny Wilkinson – real big names. Forty or 50 people, and my presentation was about something they'd never heard of before! It was really daunting. No one said a word or blinked or smiled. I did the presentation and in the evening I did some work with the backline players. The next morning Woodward phoned and said, 'Pack your stuff, you're working for us!'

I loved working with England. Their attention to detail was way beyond anything else I've seen, and they had an unbelievable work ethic. I'd never seen a team with such a special combination of skills. It made a big impression on me, as it was exactly how I thought teams should function.

Jonny Wilkinson is probably one of the best guys I've ever worked with. I admire his professionalism, and he is so well-mannered. After England played a warm-up game – with kickoff at 9pm – in Marseille before the 2003 Rugby World Cup, we were waiting to have our team dinner (compulsory after every match) at about 1am. Wilkinson hadn't been playing, and instead of wasting his time he had started doing EyeGym training exercises on the computer that we'd set up in the team room. I can tell you now: no one else in the world would train at that hour.

His philosophy in training was that he had to kick the last ball as if he was in the World Cup final. It had to be that good. Even after dark, when all the other players had already showered and eaten, I would still be picking up balls for him. Many people said he was over the top, but I didn't think so. He was just training for that one moment, and he got it in the World Cup final. And that is what he will always be remembered for.

While we were being driven through the streets of London on the way to meet the Queen after England won the 2003 World Cup, I asked Jonny if my work had influenced the way he played. He said that EyeGym training gave him more time on the ball, which in turn allowed him to make more effective decisions. Even Martin Johnson told me recently that it was unbelievable how his vision and his awareness of space had improved. And Johnson doesn't just talk for the sake of talking. On the field he leads by example, and I don't think he got nearly enough credit for England's World Cup win. To put it simply, I don't think England would have won it without Johnson.

It was interesting how, at that World Cup, after watching the team prepare all week, I'd know on the Thursday or the Friday whether we were going to win the next match or not. It was a gut feel that's difficult to define, but by watching the players' body language, listening to their chat and their interviews, and by seeing how they trained, I just knew. It got to the point that, from the Friday onwards, I'd make myself scarce because everyone wanted to know what I thought would happen the next day. When we played Wales in the quarter-final in Brisbane, we were 10-3 down at half-time and people were asking, 'Well, what do you think?' I told them not to worry and that we'd still win the game. Everyone was quite relieved!

On the morning of the final, I noticed Jonny at breakfast and I could see something special in him. I had seen him every other morning before every other match, but he was never as confident as he was before that final. I knew that we would win that World Cup.

Funnily enough, the South Africans didn't know I was at the 2003 World Cup until the opening function, when I got off the bus with England. The South African team were standing around, and Breyton Paulse noticed me and asked, 'What are you doing here?'

I had offered South Africa my services, but they had turned me down. For the duration of that World Cup, I tried not to talk in public. If English fans heard me talking to the England players, they'd say, 'Don't trust her! Don't trust her! She's a traitor and she's gonna give away our secrets!' And if South Africans were close by, they would shout at me: 'Who do you think you are, you traitor? You're cheating your country!'

But in 2007, when I was working with the Springboks and we played England in the Rugby World Cup final in Paris, two guys walked straight up to me after the final whistle. One was Dallaglio and the other was Ben Kay (who was instrumental in England beating South Africa in their pool game at the 2003 tournament). They congratulated me on the Boks' win and said they'd never have been able to win the World Cup four years previously without me. I actually went into the England change room afterwards to chat to the players and team management, and they received me very warmly.

In 2004, Jake White asked me to come back to South Africa to meet the Boks. I was really happy to be back home and to be able help the Boks prepare for the World Cup. It turned out to be a very different experience and a bit of a shock to the system! Here I was, coming from England's incredibly structured environment to one that was much less so, with less attention to detail. Instead we relied on Jake's exceptional coaching and pure player talent. I realised immediately that South Africa has so much talent, more than any nation I've ever worked with.

The players were great. Everyone accepted me, and, as one example of my work, their handling got so much better. CJ van der Linde used to go onto the field saying, 'Don't give me the ball!' because the traditional role of a front-row forward was simply to scrum. But by the time we got to the World Cup, it was, 'Just give me the ball!' After the first game Gurthrö Steenkamp played once he'd trained in the EyeGym, he came off the pitch saying, 'I saw more on the field today than I've seen in my whole rugby career!'

It meant so much to start getting that kind of feedback from the front-row guys.

Then Bryan Habana and Jean de Villiers started scoring those intercept tries. It was all about the quickness of the eye, getting your hands to where they needed to be, reading the play and seeing things before they happened. Jean, without fail, would come out of the tunnel, look around to find me and come straight over to do some visual warm-ups – two minutes' worth, even one minute – and then he'd be ready to play.

The players embraced my techniques, and they could see the difference it made. Even a guy like Juan Smith, once we had improved his peripheral awareness, was suddenly seeing players all around him and finding them with offloads. At a certain point in the 2007 World Cup, Os du Randt was ranking first on our EyeGym programme. We helped make his running lines more economical and we improved the timing of his tackling. Os put in some amazing tackles at that World Cup.

When the Springboks won the 2007 World Cup, the first thing that went through my mind was that I probably won't have to explain what I do any more, because it's obvious that it plays a role. And my second thought was: I'm not going to do this again! (But that was just a fleeting thought.) My science had been in the spotlight throughout the tournament because I'd won a World Cup previously and I would become the first person to receive back-to-back World Cup winner's medals. The pressure had become quite intense.

After winning the World Cup with the Boks, I worked for the British Olympic Association with, among others, boxers, synchronised swimmers and badminton players. Since then, I've also worked with cricket, baseball, netball, hockey, tennis, volleyball, sailing, golf, polocrosse, Aussie Rules football, ice hockey, skiing, canoeing, surfing and motor racing. I helped get Wolverhampton Wanderers promoted from the Championship into the English Premier League in

2009. In rugby, I've worked with Grey College, the University of Cape Town's Varsity Cup team and the Lions Super Rugby team.

The one downside of my work is that, once or twice, trial software has been stolen off my laptop while working with teams. It might once have helped a provincial team win the Currie Cup, but the science moves on so quickly that without a complete understanding of current techniques, any stolen software is useless.

Before we left for the 2007 World Cup, I was the only person in South Africa who had a winner's medal from 2003. It's a beautiful gold medal, with a picture of the William Webb Ellis trophy etched onto it. In the team room before we left for the airport, John Smit addressed the team: 'Guys, Sherylle's got something to show you. And listen up, because we're not coming back unless each of us has one!'

So the medal got passed around: some players looked at it, others felt it. Everyone had a different reaction. It was very interesting to watch them. I think that moment was instrumental in motivating the guys.

But when we got up on the podium to receive our medals after

My Rugby World Cup winner's medals
from 2007 and 2003.

winning the final against England, they didn't turn out to be as well made as the one I had shown them. The country that hosts the tournament designs the medals, and some of the Boks were saying, 'Gee, Sherylle, what's going on here? They've given us the wrong medals.' As runners-up, the England team had also received medals, but because ours looked fake compared to the one I had from 2003, our guys were convinced the organisers had given England their winners' medals by mistake!

——— *As told to Angus Powers*

SHERYLLE CALDER is regarded as the leading specialist in visual performance skills and training in world sport. Born in Bloemfontein, it was during her hockey career (which included 50 South African caps) that she realised the critical importance of using your eyes and visual awareness skills. Armed with proprietary visual performance training programmes and techniques (such as EyeGym), Sherylle is the only person in world rugby to have won back-to-back Rugby World Cups – with England in 2003 and with the Springboks in 2007.

LEON SCHUSTER

The End of my Rugby Career

When I was still young and handsome, I was selected for the first team of the University of the Orange Free State. The Shimlas, as the team are known, toured Europe in 1974. (That is so bloody long ago, the Dead Sea wasn't even sick at the time.) We were a squad of about 40 guys. I was the reserve hooker, and it was without doubt the most fantastic tour of my life.

We toured France, Italy, Germany and England by bus, and if I wasn't grabbing the mike – singing songs and making up the words as I went along – I'd be playing pranks on my teammates. I used to put mixed veggies in my mouth and pretend to vomit them up after loads of German beer, which tasted like double-diluted Castle Light. My pranks annoyed the guys, especially when I found a 'lady of the night' in Paris, gave her some money, and got her knocking on their doors at three in the morning, saying that she was a 'freebie', paid for by one of their teammates.

This *really* upset the guys. During those days, young Free State *boere-boykies* were extremely moral, and I think there was only one non-virgin in the squad – our fullback, Piet Strydom, who was married. The next morning I revealed myself as the prankster, and I went through the 'oven' more times than I can remember. (The 'oven' was 39 teammates lined up one behind the other, feet planted shoulder-width apart . . . with the victim crawling on all fours through their legs while they slapped his butt with a vengeance. Coming out of there, your bum burnt like hell, hence the name!)

When we were in Montmartre, in Paris, the guys bought expensive paintings to keep the girlfriends back home happy, and had them wrapped in brown paper and string. I bought a cheapie, had it similarly wrapped, then secretly swapped it for one of my team-mates' paintings. That night in his room, I picked up the painting, punched a hole through it with my fist, and pronounced, 'Definitely not quality canvas.'

The guys were continually plotting how to get me back . . . and eventually they did. We used to drink loads of orange juice from huge glass bottles in Germany. I loved the taste of that very special, very pure orange juice. A few hours before a game, I'd stuff myself with the juice. I used it like they use energy drinks today. It was obvious how much I loved that juice.

In the Reeperbahn, in Hamburg's red-light district, we had come upon a guy selling what we called *bul pille* (bull's pills). The seller promised that these were the best aphrodisiacs this side of sexy town. Some of the guys bought the pills and reported innocently the next morning that the pills really worked, because 'we tested them on ourselves, and the results were hair-raising, also raising something else.' One oke even went so far as to crush the tablet, as it then worked faster. He labelled it 'self-raising flour'. A touring rugby squad is a naughty bunch, believe me.

We played a game against Hamburg Police, and our scrumhalf (who was promoted from eighthman to No. 9 by our coach, Nelie Smith, and played a Test against the 1974 British and Irish Lions) was about to put the ball into the scrum for me, his hooker, when he said, 'Schus (my nickname with my teammates), we put a crap-load full of self-raising flour in your orange juice during lunch!'

Having a very vivid imagination, this sent shockwaves down my spine. I was continuously monitoring myself, waiting for the self-raising effect to take place. I lost sight of the game completely, and conceded at least seven heels against the head. I still don't know whether they really put the stuff in my juice, but my imagination took over and soon something was happening down under, and I'm not talking about Oz. It was extremely embarrassing. Imagine tackling an opponent and landing on him in this state! They'd think I was straight from the Reeperbahn's *moffie* division!

I was useless. My scrumhalf and the rest of the team revelled in my dilemma. I was extremely nervous, upset and traumatised. Just before half-time, during a scrum, I popped my head out, shouting, 'Einaaaaa!', and went down faking injury. I lay there, crumpled in a heap, holding my hands in front of my crotch, and complaining that someone had kicked me right where cricket players normally wear protection. I didn't ask my captain for permission to walk off – I just left the field, hands covering my embarrassment.

The guys pissed themselves laughing, and the Germans were dumbstruck, not knowing what it was all about. The referee approached me and I said in my best German: '*Sie haben mich in dem balls geskoppen.*' ('They kicked me in the nuts.') That's when my teammates *really* packed up. Luckily Hamburg Police were a rubbish team, and the Shimlas won comfortably.

I was mocked, ridiculed and became the butt of every joke after that . . . until the day we were travelling by bus to the town of L'Aquila, in Italy, where we were to play a local side the next day. On this particular day I was baggage master; this was quite a job, and involved organising lunches, vitamins, drinks and so forth. The bus was loaded with Italian beer, which was weaker than a triple-diluted Castle Light, so the guys drank loads of it. Our scrumhalf trickster was in high spirits, and shouted, '*Schus, pass nog 'n bier daar!*' ('Schus, give us another beer!') And so I got my revenge. Unbeknown to him or anyone else on that bus, I had prepared a special beer for him – one containing liquid that had passed through my kidneys.

He proceeded to down the beer, then froze, his eyes growing saucer-wide, cheeks bulging . . . but, alas, too late. He had already taken a few swallows. I smiled, looked at him and said, 'Kidney juice, *ou boetie*. Home-brewed and poured from my self-raising tap.' The poor oke showered half the team with my kidney juice before leaning out of the window and barfing into the wind.

The guys were in stitches. And I don't think that *boykie* has forgiven me to this day.

I pointed my middle finger at him, and said in a German accent, 'Don't mess mit der Zschuster.'

Years later, Adam Sandler made a movie called *You Don't Mess with the Zohan*. Little bugger. I think someone told him my story.

A sports reporter from *Die Volksblad* accompanied us on that tour. He filed an article, recommending that this Schuster character join the SABC and make comedy programmes. I took this to heart, but first I had to deal with my rugby career back home in the Free State for the rest of that year.

I had been on the bench for my provincial side for more games than I can remember, but unfortunately the first-choice hooker in the Free State squad was a tough oke and never got *blerrie* injured. I finally got my chance to pull the white jersey of the Free State over my head during the Springbok trials of 1974, in preparation for the British and Irish Lions tour later that year.

We played a Junior Springbok side in Bloemfontein, and my front row opponents were Rampie Stander, Piston van Wyk and Hannes Marais (who went on to become Springbok captain). Believe it or not, I hooked four heels against the head against *ou* Piston! I was in seventh heaven, out on the town with my girlfriend that night, scheming that I might become a Bok!

Of course, that never happened, but my prankster ways continued and I finally joined the SABC in 1976 as a junior broadcaster. I went on to make an Afrikaans hit series called *Die Vrypostige Mikrofoon* (The Cheeky Microphone), which was all about playing telephone pranks. Owing to its popularity I resigned from the SABC, recorded an album of rugby songs and made my first candid-camera movie, *You Must Be Joking*. I have since made eleven movies and about 30 CDs.

I've recorded on my albums many of the songs we used to sing on tour, and had an enormous hit with *'Hie' kommie Bokke'* during the 1995 Rugby World Cup. That irritating All Black captain, Sean Fitzpatrick, even complained that the Boks had an unfair advantage with the continuous blaring of *'Hie' kommie Bokke'* over the Ellis Park PA system!

There's no doubt about it – that Shimlas tour kick-started my movie career. If that reporter hadn't alerted me to my full singing and pranking potential, I would probably still be doing today what I started out with after varsity – teaching English at my old high school in Bloem!

Viva la Shimlas!

———————————————

LEON SCHUSTER is a bald old *toppie*, nearly 60 but still going strong and making movies. He grew up in Bloemfontein, played for the Shimlas and one game for Orange Free State, but is better known for his pranks and funny songs. He lives in Roodepoort and, with time on his hands as a bachelor, writes screenplays for movies like *Mr Bones*, *Mama Jack* and *Schuks Tshabalala's Survival Guide to South Africa*. He has been klapped more times in his movies than Jacques Kallis has klapped sixes.

HUGH BLADEN

Rugby Diplomacy

The year was 1970. The mighty All Blacks, led by Brian Lochore, were in the country to play a host of provincial games and a four-match Test series. The New Zealanders arrived with a world-record 17 Test wins under their belts and quickly showed why they would be firm favourites to win the series. They had a string of provincial fixtures to fulfil before the first Test at Loftus Versfeld in Pretoria, and they swept all before them.

I was picked to play for Transvaal against the All Blacks. The tourists had not yet even conceded a try, a matter our captain Dawie de Villiers put right when he scuttled over after taking a quick tap penalty. Dawie had moved to Johannesburg to lecture at the Rand Afrikaans University (now the University of Johannesburg), and as the incumbent Springbok captain was a great acquisition for Transvaal. For myself, it was a great privilege to play at flyhalf outside this outstanding half-back. But Dawie also revealed a talent for diplomacy, which would serve him well in later life.

At Ellis Park, the All Blacks came at us with great skill, power and speed. It was my third game against international opposition, and I remember thinking very early in the game that I had not experienced this calibre of play before. Not long after the start of the game, things got particularly rough, beginning in the scrums. Transvaal had a powerful tight five, all of whom, with the exception of Piet Bosman, were or would become Springboks. Our tighthead prop, Martiens Louw from Vereeniging, was giving their loosehead, one Alister Hopkinson, a torrid time. In those days the front-rankers did not have to scrum with their shoulders above their hips, so if the tighthead was strong enough, he could take his opposite number down and hold him about 40cm off the ground, and as a result the opposition hooker would be unable to lift his feet to hook the ball.

Transvaal's front row of Piet Bosman, Robbie Barnard and Martiens Louw were getting the better of the All Blacks Test front row of Hopkinson, Bruce McLeod and Jazz Muller, and the Kiwis were not enjoying this one little bit. A scrum was formed and then broke up, with the front rows having a fearful fight, ably assisted by the locks – in Transvaal's case, Piet Botha and Sakkie de Klerk. It took the referee a while to quieten things down, but the niggle continued.

After a particularly robust ruck, an All Blacks lock was left lying on the ground. Alan Smith by name, he had come into the side because that world-class lock Colin Meads had broken his arm against Eastern Transvaal the week before. Smith lay on the ground, complaining that somebody had kicked him. Brian Lochore approached Dawie de Villiers in a threatening manner. (Remember that these two would soon lock horns as captains of their countries in the Test series.)

'Listen, you. We can have a fight or we can have a rugby match,' Lochore said, and folded his arms across his considerable chest.

Lochore was the No. 8 and stood about 1.94m tall. Dawie, all of 1.78m, did not back down. 'Hold on a second, Brian,' Dawie said, and turned to approach his pack of forwards, who had gathered to one side.

'*Wie het hom geskop?*' (Who kicked him?), he asked. All looked at Dawie rather quizzically, and no one said a word.

Dawie walked back to Lochore, who was waiting for an explanation. Dawie looked up at the expectant All Blacks captain and said, 'I'm terribly sorry, Brian, but all of my players failed to kick your guy.'

As young as I was, I thought, 'Now there's a man who could go far in politics.'

The All Blacks beat Transvaal that day, but the 'Vaal had the distinction of outscoring the visitors in the second half. Dawie de Villiers went on to lead South Africa to a thrilling 3-1 Test series victory that year.

That would prove to be Dawie's last act in a Springbok jersey. As soon as the Lions tour was over, he retired from rugby and began a career in politics, and was named South Africa's ambassador in London nine years later. After returning home, he became a cabinet minister and a National Party delegate both at the Groote Schuur talks with the ANC and at the Convention for a Democratic South Africa (CODESA), which laid the foundation for South Africa's new constitution.

HUGH BLADEN started his rugby commentary career in 1976, and has since commentated on 160 Springbok Test matches, close to 250 Super Rugby matches, and three Rugby World Cups (1999, 2003, 2007). Hugh captained the KES first XV, played flyhalf and centre for Transvaal from 1965 to 1971, and represented the Junior Boks against Argentina in 1965. He served as a Transvaal selector from 1984 to 1992, and still sits on the Golden Lions Old Boys Trust.

ROB WALTER

Partying with the Boks

I was born into a family of Natal supporters, which in the late 1980s didn't hold as much prestige as it does these days. On countless occasions in the common room of the boarding school I attended in Pretoria – after yet another disappointing performance by the men in black and white – I faced the scorn of my schoolmates, who were mostly Northern Transvaal fans.

At that stage there wasn't much international action for the Springboks, so we had to be content with supporting our local sides in the Currie Cup or watching the Five Nations with great interest. In high school, things took a turn for the better as Natal continued to show signs of promise and the Springboks re-entered the world of international rugby . . . albeit not very successfully at first, but within a couple of years they had brought the nation together with their Rugby World Cup win in 1995.

At school, we were spoilt for choice of sports to play, and while cricket was my passion, the thrill of running onto the rugby field couldn't be rivalled in terms of adrenaline and excitement. In the afterglow of the World Cup glory, I don't think I was alone in shifting my allegiance from cricket to rugby, and our break-time games shifted from the trivial in nature, such as Stingers or Toilet (which had a very undesirable ending if you were the loser) to rugby-oriented games like touch rugby, gaining grounds and carpet rugby.

Turning out for the school's first team really laid the foundation for my love for the game, even though I knew that it would not extend much further than school level and the odd social game at varsity. Like the majority of rugby-loving South Africans, my involvement in the game then became purely that of a spectator and avid Bok supporter. But, unlike most rugby fans, on the night of my thirtieth birthday I happened to meet a couple of Springboks face to face, which produced a story that has been told and retold ever since.

My thirtieth birthday party was held in Pretoria, and since I was the trainer of the Titans cricket franchise at the time, the majority of my close friends were present, many of whom played for the Proteas. It was great to have them in the country and free from international duty. Coincidentally, on the same day there was a Currie Cup game at Loftus Versfeld involving many of the Springboks.

The party ran a similar course to that of most other thirtieth-birthday bashes, with large quantities of alcohol being consumed. As the night gathered momentum, so too did silly drinking games, poor dance moves and the usual skullduggery associated with young sportsmen under the influence. In particular, the guys were going through a childish stage in which they thought it funny to give a mate a clip on the ear or cheek when he least expected it. Revenge was the sweetest part of this foolish game, and there was no surprise when the strength of the clip increased as intoxicated, athletic men lost touch with their coordination.

When we were asked, for the umpteenth time, to leave the venue, the lads were in fine form and there were no thoughts of the party concluding so soon. I had already come close to paralysing myself in a 50m sprint against my girlfriend on the hockey astroturf; a golf ball I'd brought back from St Andrews in Scotland had made its way through almost everyone's drinks (with the consequence that you had to finish whatever you had left in your glass); and the game 'fives alive' had seen plenty of shooters being consumed.

Unfortunately, we weren't left with many options nearby, so the logical next step was to move the party to an institution in Hatfield Square called Drop Zone. It was a favourite with students, but the younger cricketers had some contacts at the front door, so it was easy getting all of us in.

Not long after we got there, a few of the Springbok rugby players arrived. They were also fairly jovial, as the Bulls had beaten their big rivals, the Sharks, that evening at Loftus. Owing to the mutual respect between the two sporting codes, and the fact that some of the boys had been at high school together, the scope of the party expanded. My association with the cricketers meant I was part of the fun, but it was this affiliation that probably saved me from serious injury later that evening.

With my judgment by now severely impaired by alcohol, I decided that it would be a great idea to keep the rugby players on their toes by including them in our idiotic game of delivering a surprise slap to the cheek or ear. While the names of the rugby players need not be mentioned, I can confirm that they were all Springboks: a scrum-half, a lock and a utility forward. Despite my towering height of 1.75m, I chose the largest of the three as the first candidate for a surprise tap on the ear.

I approached him from behind, but only when I reached up did I realise that I could barely get to his ear, even with my arm outstretched. But I had come this far, and there was no backing down now. In the meantime, my friends had caught on to what was about to happen, and, like good friends do, they opted to let me continue with this stupidity rather than step in to prevent a disaster.

A split second after I clipped him on his ear, the 2m-tall, bearded hulk swung around with a look of enraged surprise. People in close proximity were stunned into silence, and my mates held their breath. I wasn't sure what might become of me, but I remembered something I had told a close friend one evening, namely, that you can get away with anything as long as you do it with a smile on your face. So I put on my finest grin and went in for a big hug as a sign of friendship. This was also to deny him room to throw a massive sidewinder punch, which would have almost certainly put me in hospital. (Incidentally, my nose came to rest quite snugly between his pecs.)

When I felt both his hands on my shoulders, I was sure the end was nigh. There was a concerned note to my friends' chuckling, and the uneasy murmuring from the rest of the onlookers had become a deathly silence. The man-mountain tore me away from his chest and looked me in the eye. In desperation, I forced my sickly smile wider and congratulated him on a 'great game tonight'.

Slowly the anger seemed to leave his eyes, and it looked as if I might escape unscathed. But before clasping me in another crushing bear hug, the Springbok politely said, *'Doen dit weer, dan poes ek vir jou'* (Do that again and I'll fuck you up).

The silence dissipated, and relieved laughter seemed to celebrate my survival. As a sign of goodwill, the next round of drinks was on me. As I (still shaking slightly) passed the big guy a beer, I couldn't help but notice that the other lads had grown in confidence in the meantime. My closest friend was giving the Springbok lock some tips on body position when clearing out the fringes of a ruck, and another of the cricketers had traded a brand new Pringle golf shirt and short-sleeve jersey, which he had bought that day at great expense, for the scrumhalf's Bulls jersey. There was a marked size difference between the two, so the Bulls jersey was a very tight fit, just for the record.

The festivities continued for a couple of hours, with much reminiscing of school rugby days, cricketers' rugby aspirations, rugby players' cricket aspirations and, of course, the reliving of my prior madness. The saying 'All's well that ends well' rings true for this story, which is regularly dusted off at braais or social occasions whenever those who were there meet up again. It was a birthday to remember.

ROB WALTER is the strength and conditioning coach of the Proteas cricket team, and served the Titans cricket franchise in a similar capacity from 1999 to 2006. He played first-team rugby at school (as a scrumhalf, outside centre and under-achieving goal-kicker), as well as senior provincial cricket and hockey. Rob is one of the dedicated rugby fans in the Proteas squad, who go to great lengths when on tour to ensure that they can watch Springbok matches live.

MARK ANDREWS

The All Blacks Connection

Growing up as young white boy in the 1980s, there was no real way of knowing that South Africa was the pariah of the world. Life was simply to be enjoyed, isolated as we were from the chaos elsewhere in the country. To a sports-mad boy, one indication that something was not quite right was that, thanks to the sports boycott, South Africa was unable to compete with the rest of the world, most significantly in rugby, the sport that I enjoyed above all.

I spent many winter days running around with my old leather Super Springbok rugby ball, dreaming that I was a Springbok beating all defences and scoring every try I attempted (mostly thanks to having no defence in front of me). The Springboks were an almost mythical team to me. I was eight years old when the Boks toured New Zealand in 1981. I had to wake up early to watch the matches, and usually fell asleep again before they began. This was in the days before VCRs. It's difficult to explain those days to my sons, who only have to push the pause button on the PVR if their dad is going to be late for a game on TV.

On the morning of the final Test of the tour, I woke up excited at the prospect of watching the Springboks beat the All Blacks and take the series. During the match, silence descended on the room as my father explained to me why the New Zealand supporters were dropping flour bombs from a light aircraft onto the players on the field, and why other supporters were charging onto the field and getting beaten by policemen. I had assumed this was the way the New Zealanders supported the All Blacks and how they went about intimidating the Springboks. Until my father's explanation, I was oblivious to the real reasons behind the protests and merely thought that New Zealanders were a bit daft, even rough, and were without a shred of sportsmanship.

Ironically, 13 years later I was part of the Springbok team that arrived in a cold and wet New Zealand in June 1994. That Bok tour made a small but significant contribution to erasing the pain and conflict that the Springboks had caused New Zealand more than a decade earlier. It was only on that tour that we South Africans fully realised what had happened to New Zealand society back then, with families split apart by those who wanted to watch the two greatest rugby nations play each other and those who felt that no game should take place until apartheid was abolished.

I learned on that tour that the Kiwis are generally great people who have a genuine passion for the game, and although they didn't charge the field or throw flour bombs again, certain of their players still liked to throw haymakers and right hooks, both on and off the field. During the two months spent travelling all over the country, we saw the sun come out only once, in Christchurch. Even I became grumpy after eight weeks of clouds and rain. But when we left, we had made many good friends and gained a new appreciation of why our hosts could be roused to such anger.

I have been fortunate to be part of many successful rugby teams, none more so than the Springbok team who won the 1995 Rugby World Cup in South Africa. As with all successful teams, a few stars and planets had to come into perfect alignment for the team to be truly special. The one other requirement for competing with the world's best was a high level of fitness.

I had been put through some serious fitness sessions by a host of coaches, but few matched the levels of intensity and pain that coach Kitch Christie visited on us before and during that World Cup. At the time, I thought he was a mean bastard who took pleasure in our enduring such painful sessions (which often seemed more than was required), but thankfully he was proved right in those last 20 minutes of the World Cup final.

Once during a forwards scrum session behind the poles at the Wanderers training ground, we were halfway through scrumming a few tons of unforgiving steel a full 120m. I had scrummed the skin off my left shoulder, and the blood was starting to seep through my jersey. My neck was also starting to spasm. Seeing my obvious discomfort, Kitch asked me, 'Mark, do you think Ian Jones is training this hard? Do you think he is bleeding like you are and working as hard as you are now?'

As much I wanted to believe that the All Blacks lock was not, I also did not want Kitch to think he could up the fierceness of the session. 'No way, coach,' I said, and tried to focus on the next scrum.

Kitch's question to me that day was answered twelve years later when Ian Jones interviewed me in my home for a New Zealand rugby TV show. While we were chatting about the classic Bok–All Blacks clashes of the last decade, we started talking about the 1995 World Cup. Ian spoke about his team's preparation for the tournament and how hard they had trained. He also mentioned that, during a particularly fearsome fitness session, his coach had asked him if he thought Mark Andrews was training as hard as he was. Ian had also replied in the negative, and never gave it a second thought until that day of our conversation.

When I related my almost identical experience, Ian smiled and said that since neither side was fitter, the difference could only have been our 16th player. Puzzled, I asked him who that was.

'Nelson Mandela,' he replied.

Sport invariably gives you a winner and loser, and as a sportsman the hardest thing to do is to accept a loss when you've had the better of the opposition. During an especially hard Super 12 series in the late 1990s, the Sharks had suffered another narrow defeat. As a team is inclined to do after such a loss, the players were sitting around on the benches in the change room, in various states of undress, feeling sorry for themselves and talking about the bad reffing or whatever other excuses they had for not having had their best game.

I was sitting next to Gary Teichmann, André Joubert and Henry Honiball, when Henry announced that he had worked out why a team sometimes loses games when there is no properly superior side on the day. We all looked at him expectantly because 'Lem', as the guys called him, was known for simplifying things to the extreme and appeared to see life only in black and white. Lem went on to explain that there is this 'something' which comes down the tunnel before a game; it looks left, looks right, and then decides which team is going to get the 'something' that will make the ball bounce their way and help the ref's decisions favour them.

We all looked at him as though he had taken a knock on the head, until we realised that Henry always gave 100%, even on a bad day. For him, it was never an option to give anything less than his best. Henry must have assumed that other players would also never give less than 100%. Therefore the only difference in a close game could be that 'something' which would gave one team the edge over the other.

It's hard to accept losing when you've given everything and felt like you had the game in the bag. Afterwards, your head is always filled with the 'What if?' and 'If only . . .' kind of questions. Even after a post-match video analysis, it can sometimes be unclear why you lost.

At moments like those I always remembered Lem's explanation that 'something' must have gone under our opponents' change-room door . . . and not under ours.

MARK ANDREWS was a towering presence in the Springbok jersey for eight years and 77 Tests. Although feared and respected for his uncompromising athleticism at lock, Mark played the 1995 Rugby World Cup final at eighthman, giving the Boks a huge pack and an extra, vital line-out option. Mark's Bok career included a Tri-Nations trophy, 13 mid-week games and twelve Test tries. He also won two Currie Cups with the Sharks, and now enjoys life as a successful businessman in Durban.

ON SECOND THOUGHTS

SIMNIKIWE XABANISA

Travels of a Rugby Writer

At the risk of invalidating everything I've ever written on rugby, I must confess that my introduction to the game never once suggested I might end up being considered an 'expert' at it.

In 1991, I was a Standard 7 new boy at Dale College in King William's Town, and part of my duties was to be a sand boy for the goal-kickers at the rugby tournament held to celebrate the school's 130th anniversary that year. The job was simple enough, but the problem was that my only understanding of rugby at the time was that it was a rough game and I should steer well clear of it. When I asked the teacher who shoved a bucketful of sand under my nose how I would know when to deliver its contents onto the field, he said that the referee sticking his arm out (in the penalty signal) should be my cue.

The first few penalties went well, until the ref gave one of the two sides a penalty on their own 22m line. I charged onto the pitch and made a beeline for the kicker, who pointed me back in the direction of the laughing crowd on the touchline! I wish I could say things got better from there onwards, but the short playing career I enjoyed at school was steeped in ineptitude too.

Having come from a cricket school, I was at Dale to become a fast bowler like Richard Snell, and hopefully get an education while I was at it. But Dale College at the time – and I'd be surprised if anything's changed – was the kind of place where the prospect of an unbeaten first XV was more appealing than a 100% matric pass rate. Rugby was something you couldn't avoid, especially when one of your first tasks as a new arrival was to learn everything about Dale's most famous Springbok, HO de Villiers, who'd left the school a good 30 years previously.

The need to memorise all matters rugby extended to the first team and all the rugby songs. You had to know the names, heights, weights and favourite, illicit after-match drinks of all the first-team players . . . and sometimes the colours of their girlfriends' teddies too. The fact that the Dale first team was a great one at that point made up for the apparent stupidity of these traditions.

In the first three years I was at the school, we lost just three games. One was to Selborne College in 1991, and the other two were to Queen's College and Grey College a year later.

The loss to Queen's, on our old boys' reunion weekend, was a memorable affair simply because it was the most frustrating 70 minutes of my life. The cheeky bastards – who had a ginger-haired prop named Robbie Kempson playing for them – got a penalty in the first minute of the game. They nailed it, and proceeded to put in the kind of heroic defensive effort that meant the final score ended up 3-0. We shouted ourselves hoarse in the stands, but the Queens weren't averse to getting those white uniforms dirty that day, and kept us out. Apparently Robbie K still rates it as one of his favourite matches.

The following year, Dale's last unbeaten year, more than made up for that freakish event. Playing with a bunch of midgets – the tallest player in the backline was our six-foot scrumhalf – we beat all comers in a faultless season. An unbeaten schoolboy season is nothing without a win over Grey College. I'm happy to say that they too – with one Stephen Brink on the wing – came in for their 35-11 punishment in King William's Town.

The star of that show was flyhalf Sean Sharp, who in my opinion was the best rugby player Dale ever produced. Sharp was an all-purpose flyhalf who was strong, quick, had great hands, superb distribution and rarely missed a kick at poles despite not being a natural kicker.

A bloke who can't have said more than five words in the three years he was at the school, Sharp was a rugby tragic in that everything he did was aimed at making him a better rugby player. He was the kind of guy who would stay in his room after starring in one of the school's victories to work on his handling because he had dropped one pass that afternoon. One Saturday I saw him bounce a rugby ball against the wall all night until his T-shirt was soaked in sweat. Despite making two Border Craven Week sides and being the school's all-time top points scorer, the ultimate reward of playing professional rugby was denied him after he wrote off his knee in his second Currie Cup game for Eastern Province.

With all that inspiration around, eventually I couldn't take any more touch rugby so I signed up for the real thing in 1994, my last year at the school. I found a happy home in the eighth XV, where we played ten games and won one that season. We may have lost a lot, but I certainly enjoyed being the team's 60kg enforcer at flank and lock. We never saw much of the ball, so my job was to tackle anything that moved, something I did with rabid zeal. I even had a motto – borrowed from a Dr Dre song off his debut album, *The Chronic* – for my handiwork: 'I never hesitate to put a nigger on his back.'

While it may have been considered a relaxed form of the art, playing for the eighths had its challenges: the Tuesday practice matches against the U15A team. Loaded with the likes of Gcobani Bobo and Oginga Siwundla – future pros – they were basically big kids getting their own back on the matrics. To this day, I try to remind Bobo that I was but a mere speed bump en route to his becoming a Springbok!

When it finally came, our win was quite an achievement, because it was against those ponces from Selborne (who had beaten us 44-0 earlier in the season), in full view of the grandstand on the main field *nogal*.

Funnily enough, with all that winning and losing, my greatest schoolboy rugby memory came from a match that never really happened. The sevenths were playing the team from Daniel Pienaar Technical – Mornantau Hayward, Dewald Senekal and Dewald Potgieter's old school. At the first scrum, one of the boys from Uitenhage used the k-word. He was warned against using it by one of Dale's white players, but he thought he'd repeat it at the next scrum. The mother of all free-for-alls ensued, with every team member – including the wingers – getting stuck in. The referee had no choice but to send everybody off before the game had reached the tenth minute.

Up until then, my explanation for why I liked rugby was that it suited my fiery, quick-to-anger temperament. But that day I learned about the ethos and spirit of rugby union: it's an all-for-one and one-for-all sport. As deep-seated as my individualism is, there's nothing like playing your part in an effort that needs the cooperation of 15 men to work – even if it means throwing one measly punch.

The Monday after that episode sealed the existential element of the game for me: the headmaster called the whole sevenths side into his office and caned the lot. So there you had it: 15 multiracial kids who took a stand against racism being rewarded with a caning for not representing the school particularly well. Shades of grey indeed.

Of course, playing for the eighths would come back to haunt me in my guise as a rugby writer. One such moment was when I first met former Bok coach Jake White. At the time, he was still known as a technical analyst, but he appeared to have read a few articles I'd written and he was curious about my background. He consulted Bobo, who must have embellished things in telling him I played at Dale College because White was of the impression that I was a former first-team man. I'm convinced that he lost whatever regard he may have had for my opinions when I set him straight.

Another instance occurred during a press conference during the 2007 Rugby World Cup, when I asked White a question he had been dreading. He came up to me afterwards and almost congratulated me, a rugby writer, for asking a question in a press conference. I got the impression he had to restrain himself from asking if I'd come up with said query on my own.

In all fairness to White, if he had known how my first foray into rugby writing for the *Sunday Times* went, he probably would have felt justified in questioning why I had the right to ask him anything about the sport, let alone criticise what he'd had to say the next day. After two and a half years of hating my existence as a news intern at the paper's Durban bureau (I had studied journalism in Durban), I was given a Sharks vs Reds Super 12 match to cover, even though I had no previous Craven Week, club or provincial rugby experience. After finishing my masterpiece, I phoned the office to breathlessly ask how it went, and the voice on the other end said, 'I don't know, Sim, you spelt your own name wrong . . .'

Despite that clanger, I was offered a job as a general sports writer and moved up to Johannesburg. A few months later, after the great Dan Retief resigned, I bumped into the sports editor, the late Rodney Hartman, and asked him who Dan's replacement would be. 'You!' he said. I nearly wet myself with fear.

My introduction to the various press boxes around the country as a brand-new rugby writer was a challenge on its own. People would openly laugh at the skinny kid with dreadlocks and spectacles sleepwalking his way through the press box. Truth be told, I did look like an extra from the movie *Cool Runnings*, and, upon closer reflection, some of my earlier musings on the game appeared to have been written by an extra from *Cool Runnings* too. And, in all fairness again, the local reporters weren't the only ones to do a double take when they saw me. During the 2001 Springbok end-of-year tour, I walked into a press conference and one of the Brits said, 'Look, it's the Snoop Dogg of rugby writing!'

For all the initial leg-pulling, my colleagues turned out to be a fiercely protective lot. On that same trip to Europe, my first with the Boks, my hotel bookings were so shoddy that I ran out of money with a full week left on tour. I owed the hotel we'd stayed in that week £489 and had only £10 in my pocket, and the receptionist was not buying the story that if she got in touch with our office the next day (Monday), they'd sort it out. It took me forever to convince her, but *Rapport*'s Rudolph Lake waited patiently for the outcome despite having a plane to catch to Houston. When I was done, we caught a cab to Gatwick Airport and he paid my part of the fare, insisting that I use my £10 to buy myself breakfast.

There have also been a few occasions when my colleagues were ready to get into fisticuffs on my behalf if they felt somebody was trying to bully or racially abuse me. The only explanation I can offer for that kind of support is that rugby writing is a surprisingly tough job and all the boys stick together. The players, coaches and administrators think you don't know what you're talking about, and the pundits mostly read your stuff to confirm to themselves that they know better than you. I've even been in situations where I've been on leave and watched a game with my friends, only to find that they're in some kind of competition to show that their opinions are better than mine.

I've always said that it's not about how great the opinions are but about how well and how quickly they can be written, as deadline is the only thing that matters in our line of work. When people argue about a point in a match report, you can tell that they think you had the benefit of replaying the tape of the game before writing. The truth is, most of the time you need to press 'send' as soon as the referee blows the whistle to end the game. You really earn your post-match beer in those matches, especially when the lead changes in the last minute!

With opinions on a rugby match differing so widely, I reckon a good match report is one where you put into words what the reader thought while he was watching the match. A great one is where he disagrees but has had his point of view challenged by a lucid argument. A bad one is none of the above . . .

People often wonder what it's like being a so-called black rugby writer. Well, I've had coaches call me after a lengthy chat about the game to tell me how good the conversation was, as if they honestly didn't expect me to be what I claimed when I turned up on their doorstep. Before we all yell 'racism', I must say that some of the bigoted stuff that happens in rugby is not carefully planned. Rather, too many people in rugby are unaware they're doing it. I once had the Cheetahs' Harold Verster tell me in an interview that Kennedy Tsimba, who was the best flyhalf in South Africa at the time, was in their team on merit, 'like a white guy'.

To put the experience in simple terms: when you criticise a white person in rugby, people think it's because you have a chip on your shoulder. And when you criticise a black person, it's because you've sold out. So you might as well write what you really think.

The best advice I ever got was after I wrote 800 words for a magazine on what it was like to be a black rugby writer. My then boss, Clinton van der Berg, pulled me aside and said, 'You need to make up your mind if you're a black rugby writer or a rugby writer.'

Not that changing my tune to that of just plain rugby writer curried any favour with the Bok coaches. In over a decade of writing about the game, I have yet to have a Bok coach like me. The hostilities began with Harry Viljoen, who was so irritated with something I wrote on the 2001 tour that he told me, when we were in a lift together, to go and improve my rugby knowledge. When I gave Van der Berg a distraught call, he said, 'Tell Harry that this time next year, you'll be here and he won't.' Viljoen quit a month later.

It wasn't just the head coaches I tended to piss off. I also got White's assistants, Allister Coetzee and Gert Smal, hot and bothered by once calling them 'yes-men' in a column. Coetzee didn't talk to me much after that and later dismissed the incident, but Smal turned up in a hotel lobby in Brisbane and barked, 'You, come over here!' I sat about a metre from him as he shook with rage and told me off, but all I was thinking about was which way to run if he made a move towards me. (I'd seen the YouTube clip of him punching Gary Knight's lights out, and I figured that if he punched me, he'd probably kill me.)

Peter de Villiers and I also had a moment after I said the Dunedin win in 2008 was achieved playing Jake White-style rugby. He said that if I wanted to be white, then I must just go ahead and be white. De Villiers also told a radio boss of mine, '*As daai mannetjie jou spesialis is, dan weet julle niks!*' (If that little man is your specialist, then you know nothing!) After 2010, I suppose a lot of punters would say we make a fine pair, so I'm calling it a draw . . .

Intermittent tension aside, covering the Boks is an absolute pleasure. I've visited hallowed rugby grounds like Twickenham, the 'House of Pain' (in Carisbrook), Lansdowne Road, Parc des Princes, Newlands, Loftus Versfeld, Ellis Park and King's Park. And I've seen my share of highs and lows, from Kamp Staaldraad and the 53-3 loss to England to the glorious World Cup win in 2007.

Not bad for a kid who once didn't know what a penalty was in rugby.

SIMNIKIWE XABANISA worked for the *Sunday Times* from 2000 – 2011 covering two Rugby World Cups, five Tri-Nations tours and three end-of-year tours. In 2008, he was voted Vodacom sports journalist of the year and Sasol Springbok rugby writer of the year (after using the fact that the latter was being awarded on his birthday to unfairly influence the judges). Simnikiwe believes God possesses a tight-fitting, green and gold rugby jersey – how else to account for the Boks winning in spite of their administrators?

JACQUES KALLIS

The Ultimate Sport

Rugby is probably the best game in the world. If the opposition overstep the mark on the cricket field, there's not much you can do about it. You can't exactly throw a punch in a loose ruck and get away with it. Cricket doesn't have much scope for aggression, whereas rugby's a game in which everyone can find a place.

I played rugby from U9 until I finished school, and I enjoyed every minute of it. My dad, who played for False Bay Rugby Club as well as for Western Province U19 and U21, introduced me to the game and I fell in love with it immediately. Rugby was my winter sport and cricket was my summer one.

I started playing competitive rugby early on, and for four years – from U9 to U12 – our Wynberg Boys' Junior School side went unbeaten. We had a well-balanced team: the future Springbok Robbie Fleck was at centre, and Jake Boer (who went on to play for Gloucester) played flank. We were successful in high school, too, up until U16 when teams like Paarl Gym and Paarl Boys suddenly overtook us. We struggled a bit at first team level, but we held our own as a southern suburbs side against the northern suburbs schools.

I played flyhalf throughout my rugby career, all the way to first team in matric. I remember how, against Paarl Boys, during scrum time, the ball popped out and looped towards me, and Corné Krige (who was playing flank for Paarl Boys) got stuck into my ribs while my hands were above my head trying to catch the ball. I think I caught the ball on their 22m line and he put me down on my own 22! I couldn't breathe for a couple of minutes after that.

I also had some good games against Louis Koen at Paarl Gym, and against Percy Montgomery at SACS. Wynberg won most of the time against SACS. In fact, I can't remember ever losing to them.

Inevitably, there came a point when a decision had to be made, and it meant choosing between Craven Week trials or going on a cricket tour with the South African U17 side to the United Kingdom. I was a much better cricketer than I was a rugby player. To be honest, I was actually a pretty average rugby player, but I still loved the game. So I made my choice and kicked on with cricket from there. Apart from the odd Wynberg Old Boys' festival game against the Wynberg first team, or against SACS Old Boys, I never played rugby again.

Rugby provides a true test of character. You often get into situations where there's nowhere to hide. For instance, if you're the last line of defence and you've got some big guy running at you, you've got to decide whether you're going to let him score or whether you're going to stop him in his tracks.

I learned another important lesson when I was in the U13A team. Our coach had to leave practice early and left me in charge. It was my responsibility to ensure that the team finished their fitness session: doing shuttle runs from the try line to the 22, then back to the try line, then to the 10m line and back, to the halfway line and back, and so on. 'No problem, sir,' I said. 'I'll make sure that the guys do it.' The coach watched us do the first set, and then drove off.

I called the boys together and said, 'Look guys, I don't think we need to do this. Let's play touch rugby instead.' So we played touch until practice was over.

When my dad came to pick me up, I told him that at rugby practice I'd been left in charge but that we had ended up playing some touch rugby. The next day at school, a request came over the intercom for the U13A rugby team to meet on the rugby field at break time. When we were all there, our coach said, 'Right, now you're going to do double the number of shuttles that you were supposed to do yesterday afternoon.'

It turned out that my dad had told the coach what we had gotten up to. There was a very clear lesson for me that day: if you get away with something, don't tell anyone or it'll come back and bite you!

The Proteas go out of their way to watch rugby, especially on the subcontinent. It can be tough at times there, because there's not much to do off the field. Knowing there's some rugby on the weekend is what keeps us going from week to week. Touring countries like Australia, New Zealand and England is a lot easier because the game is guaranteed to be on TV, so we don't have to pester our team manager, Goolam Rajah, to organise a satellite feed or internet link. When we're in South Africa, it's pretty much cast in stone that we braai and watch rugby every Saturday. That's something that we really miss on tour.

I am still good mates with Percy and with a couple of the Stormers guys, like Schalk Burger and Jean de Villiers. I think we are pretty similar types of people. It also helps that our girlfriends get on well with their girlfriends. It's great to catch up with the rugby guys over a braai and chat about what works for them and what works for us. I still believe there can be a lot more interaction between the rugby and the cricket guys. Unfortunately, there's never enough time.

The Proteas are split by competing Super Rugby loyalties. There's always a lot of talk in the week leading up to a Stormers vs Bulls game, for instance. We've managed to convert Mark Boucher from being a Sharks supporter, although Schalk played a major role there. But it's nice to have him converted! The rivalries extend to the girlfriends, too. My girlfriend is from Pretoria and knows most of the Bulls players, so she's a diehard Bulls fan. I've been trying to convert her for ages, but I'm getting nowhere. Sometimes we have a bet: whoever's team loses a big derby game has to wear the opposition's jersey on the Sunday. On a few occasions I've had to wear a Bulls jersey for a whole Sunday. It can get irritating.

In World Cups, anything can happen. If the bounce of the ball goes against you on the day, you can suddenly find yourself out of the World Cup. We've seen that from a cricket point of view. However, the Springboks have been amazing in how they've managed to control their emotions and find that balance between passion and focus. Sometimes I ask myself how the hell they get up the next day. It's unbelievable how tough and professional rugby has become and how physically demanding it is out there on the pitch. I really don't know how they do it.

I've always said that I would give up many of my cricket matches and my runs to be able to run out, just once, for the Springboks at Newlands and face the haka. I don't think I'd be getting much sleep before that. That would be the ultimate experience.

——— *As told to Angus Powers*

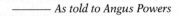

JACQUES KALLIS's reputation precedes him. He is acknowledged as one of finest cricketers the sport has ever seen, and is undoubtedly the most complete player to have come out of South Africa. His Test batting statistics alone make humbling reading: almost 12 000 runs in close to 150 matches, at an average of more than 55, including 40 centuries. Add his more that 500 wickets and almost 300 catches in Tests and ODIs, and it becomes clear that rugby's loss was most certainly cricket's gain.

ASHWIN DESAI

Hunting with Lions, Running with Springboks

When the British and Irish Lions toured South Africa in 1974, they cut an imperious swathe through the country on their way to play Natal. I read about their trip with all the studiousness of an adolescent fan. The newspapers reported that the Springbok scrum was on the retreat. My father, who followed the game with passion, had spoken to me in hushed tones about the awesome power of Fran Cotton, Ian McLauchlan and Bobby Windsor, the Lions' front row.

To me, this was difficult to take in. The Afrikaners had a stranglehold on power, and they seemed mythical, invincible people. This was put on display when Northern Transvaal or the Orange Free State played the *Engelsmanne* of our home province, Natal. They would grind our pack down and somehow make the English in our province, for all their backline finesse, seem lacking in manhood. The judgment delivered on the rugby field by the 'Dutchmen' to our *souties* extended into the business and political world as well.

But white South Africa was in a state of fear and dread. Rugby was central to Afrikaner nationalism. As renowned newspaper editor Donald Woods observed, it was 'a means of national expression of the *volk* . . . Many seemed to see international rugby as the means of impressing upon the world the existence and toughness of the Afrikaner people, and this approach was undoubtedly the result of seeing themselves as a beleaguered group, special to their circumstances but also special in their mission.' No wonder there were panic selections, like when the Springboks brought in as scrumhalf a retreaded flank forward, Gerrie Sonnekus, for the third Test in Port Elizabeth. Compared to the twinkle-toed Gareth Edwards,

Sonnekus seemed to have boots of lead. Once again, the Springboks were thrashed.

Until the tour reached Natal, my father and I were on the side of the all-conquering Lions. Forced to choose between the Boers or the Empire, like Gandhi during the Anglo–Boer War, we chose Empire.

But this was *our* province. I was torn apart by the contradictory feelings. After all, we were regulars at King's Park rugby stadium. Oddities, my father and I, high up in the stands. My favourite player was fullback Malcolm Swanby; my father's, Tommy Bedford, the provincial captain and eighthman.

King's Park was packed. But in our stand, which could seat approximately 250 people, we were just ten. This was the 'non-white' stand. A whole stand to ourselves. At half-time, since we were not allowed to buy refreshments at the kiosk, my father took out his flask and laid out a picnic. While the whites were cramped together, we lay back over a couple of seats and enjoyed the break.

At the toilets, I saw the whites in long queues snaking round the corner. I was the only one in the non-white toilet. Apartheid had its benefits.

For me, Natal had to win. I made up my mind when Tommy Bedford was attacked by the Lions fullback, JPR Williams. The 'civilised' locals went wild. They threw oranges onto the field and some even tried to run on and beat up the Lions players. I was shocked. I had never seen white people behave like this.

When my father poured the tea and spread out the cheese and tomato sandwiches at half-time, it was 9-6 to the Lions. Game on. Deep into the second half, the three-point gap remained. I was on the edge of the whites' area I was so excited. My father pulled me back and delicately took the orange from my hand. The Lions machine changed gear. Gareth Edwards reigned supreme. The Lions crossed the try line and soon it was all over. We left the ground as dolefully as any of our lighter-skinned countrymen.

Non-whites did play rugby. But it was a different world to what we witnessed at King's Park. As the veteran Eastern Cape journalist Mono Badela wrote, in this non-white world 'the images are of dilapidated stadiums which look more like cross-country courses than playing fields. Scenes of African and coloured working class people, scrumming down on a dusty stony surface, car headlights illuminating a cold winter's night.'

According to the doyen of rugby writers, Bryn Thomas, who covered the 1974 Lions tour, 'progress is being made' in South Africa, 'but it will have to be slow as the coloured and native populations are passing through stages in their evolution that are quite different from those of the European.' That was one of the reasons that the Lions played separate matches against the Africans (the Leopards) and the coloureds (the Proteas). The idea of the non-white as a yet-undeveloped child had a long lineage in South Africa. Over four decades earlier, Jan Smuts had told an audience at Oxford that the African 'remained a child type, with a child psychology and outlook'. One had to assume that the Lions played the 'children' with the honourable intention of helping them climb the evolutionary ladder to adulthood. Many of the children were long in the tooth, and it was no surprise that both the Proteas and Leopards were soundly beaten.

On Saturdays it was rugby, and on Sundays it was soccer. Across the road from King's Park was Kingsmead soccer stadium. Two teams dominated the local professional scene in those days: Durban United and Durban City. My father had a ritual before derby day. He would wake me up earlier than usual and we would make our way on foot to the edge of the Indian quarter in Durban city centre. As the first rays of sunlight lit up the shrine of the Muslim saint Badsha Peer in the Brook Street cemetery, my father – a Hindu – would offer food to ensure a win for Durban United. He was not alone. I often wondered what the saint, whose *karâmât* (miracles) are legendary, thought about grown men asking for support for a soccer game involving 22 white players. But this was a time when life twisted into a combination of normality and abnormality. When I tried to tease my father in later life, he adopted an Mbeki-like denialism while attacking my political credentials.

The epitome of white life in South Africa was contained in the advertising slogan, 'braaivleis, rugby, sunny skies and Chevrolet'. My family was getting there. We were watching rugby; my father had a Chev; nobody, not even apartheid, could deny us sunny skies; my father was dressing in safari suits and, at a late age, learning Afrikaans. He was a schoolteacher, and Afrikaans was a prerequisite for promotion. Braaivleis, though, was one step too far. My father's family came from a long line of vegetarians, where even eggs were off the menu. Soya sausages had not yet made their appearance.

But this was a world coming to an end. The South African Council on Sport (SACOS) was beginning to have an impact. Cricket administrator Hassan Howa coined the phrase, 'no normal sport in an abnormal society'. Those who played under the SACOS banner were not to attend white sport. To do so was to practise what was referred to in SACOS language as 'double standards'. There was no real clarity on what defined double standards. One could, for example, apply for a permit to study at a white university, but to play for the university team was to practise double standards. Still, the power of double standards was that it clearly demarcated 'non-racial sport' from 'apartheid sport', and this gave much impetus to the global anti-apartheid sports movement.

My father played for Crimson Cricket Club. In the team was Krish Mackerdhuj, one of the leading proponents of the double-standards rule. There was no way to escape the all-seeing gaze of Krish. As sport and politics intertwined, my father stopped going to King's Park and Kingsmead soccer stadium. Most heartbreakingly, he also insisted we did not go to Kingsmead cricket stadium. I had watched

Barry Richards make a century there against the 1970 Australians when he was at the peak of his powers. I was never to see South Africa's greatest opening batsman pierce the covers again.

At Rhodes University in the early 1980s, two of us non-whites tried to practise double standards. It was a fortnight or so before the inter-varsity football match between Rhodes and the University of Port Elizabeth (UPE). Both of us made the second team – not a difficult accomplishment given the standard of sport at Rhodes. But then the administrators at UPE announced that black students could play on their fields but not attend the dance. We withdrew from the team, expecting solidarity from our fellow white Rhodians. Wishful thinking. The episode became a powerful weapon to argue against playing for campus teams. For a while this incident was written up in black student history as a deliberate ploy to expose the hypocrisy of administrators and students at Rhodes. The truth is that we so much wanted to kick a football on a level playing field.

Much has happened since those days. Cut to 2009, when the British and Irish Lions toured South Africa again. My friend Heinrich was keen that we go to the King's Park Test. His old school friend Terry was making his way down from Pretoria. My neighbour, Glen, a former Durban Collegians fifth-team hooker, was also roped in.

When we arrived, the stands were empty. Rows of Portaloos marked the outfield areas. Hundreds of Lions supporters lined up outside them, still sipping from plastic pint containers as they waited to open the taps at the other end. Some were dressed in replica redcoat uniforms that recalled the British Empire. For some reason I wanted the Lions to win, even here in liberated South Africa. Was it nostalgia for 1974?

I did not let on to the other three. I suspected, though, that Heinrich was with me. But, as the 1989 all-Indwe poker champion, he could keep a straight face. Terry, a South African of Greek origin, had spent too long fitting into Afrikaner schools to contemplate not supporting the Boks. Glen's bubble burst when he realised that he could not afford more than two beers. As the Lions supporters passed their beer order along the row of seats, he tried on an Irish accent. As he reached for a Castle, a mighty Lions supporter slapped him on the wrist and spat out 'Springbok'. Glen was quiet for the rest of the match.

After a while, the sight of the redcoats began to make me wonder. I thought about the redcoats of 1879 lining up to be speared by the Zulus at Isandlwana. I thought about the havoc later wreaked by the British army in Zululand, their dragoons and lancers and mounted rifles moving up in formation like a well-drilled backline after the up-and-unders of artillery had softened up the opposition. The British army's task was to kill, maim and intimidate and so allow the brutal exploitation of South Africa's people and resources. The British had rifles, sidearms, horses and artillery pieces. The Zulus had spears, small wooden clubs known as knobkerries and outdated firearms with little ammunition.

If this technological advantage was not enough, the British resorted to cowardly and deceitful tactics, exemplified by the campaign against the Hlubi clan in northern KwaZulu-Natal. Women and children were blasted out with dynamite from their places of refuge, and, as the survivors staggered out, some 200 were shot down. All their land and cattle were then confiscated. The battle was followed by the murderous invasion of Zululand by the British, with hundreds of Zulus mowed down by Gatling guns in July 1879.

The consequences of this pillage and dispossession are still with us. With a land redistribution programme that has barely made an impact, the descendants of Zulu warriors are reduced to dancing for tourists at a make-believe village called Shakaland. Centuries of tradition are packaged into ten minutes of cavorting for tips. It made one rethink the role of the redcoats in this neck of the woods.

All of a sudden, the stands were full. We were squeezed into the smallest of spaces. How I wished for the non-white stand.

The opening ceremony was a spectacular take on *The Lion King*. It gave me goose bumps as Mufasa turned to Simba, his son and heir apparent, and said 'Everything the light touches is our kingdom. Everything the light touches will be yours.' We were the Rainbow Nation of God. The signs saying 'non-whites' were a distant and defeated part of history.

It came at a price though, this equality: R1 000 a seat. Still, change always required a price to be paid, did it not?

By now smarting at the sight of the redcoats, as the game got under way I noticed a *boereseun*, no more than seven years old. Bedecked in a Springbok scarf, he was hanging onto his father. I thought about the Anglo–Boer War and the concentration camps. The protective cover of apartheid was no more. The Afrikaans language was under threat. The last possession of the Afrikaner was his rugby. That too was under pressure from a cynical, elitist, racial quota system. I wanted the *boereseun* to be happy. He was me all those years ago in the non-white stand.

As the game stretched into the afternoon, the shell of the new Moses Mabhida soccer stadium across the road cast a shadow over King's Park. Sports historian John Nauright claims that 'the rugby ground became a symbol of white power, identity and collective consciousness.' What do the new World Cup soccer stadiums mean to the new ruling class? Peter Alegi, a historian specialising in world soccer, has said that image was crucial in the decision to build stadiums: 'The nation-state is relying on new playing facilities to market "Brand South Africa". Stadiums are seen as architectural expressions of a modern, technologically sophisticated, self-confident, proud African nation eager to score an Eiffel Tower-like branding effect on the world stage.'

Rather than the Springboks winning, the Lions lost. The game was one of rolling mauls and sniping channel-one runs. Beyond flyhalf, the backlines never really contributed. The Lions supporters knew how to drown their sorrows. They drank out Florida Road. We headed to the shacklands and crumbling middle-class homes of Clare Estate. The owner-cum-barman was Buds. Whites do not venture to this part of the city. Buds greeted the white newcomers with these words, 'Listen here. I hate everybody, except myself.'

Terry remarked, *sotto voce*, 'At least he's not a racist.'

We tucked into tripe, beans and roti. Talk turned to the local rugby team, the Jaguars, the only black rugby team in the KwaZulu-Natal premier league. They are under the cosh; white clubs are raiding their best players as they seek to ensure that their own teams are not lily-white. The local schools no longer play rugby, thus new talent is in short supply. Sponsorship is drying up. There is only one field, so having junior clubs is burdensome. The Jaguars' home ground is known as 'the House of Pain'. This attests to their fighting spirit at a time when the odds were stacked against them. One can only hope that this spirit sees them survive their current difficulties; otherwise the name of their home ground could come to have a completely different meaning.

The promise of change in South Africa was contained in the Reconstruction and Development Programme (RDP). The programme secured black buy-in to an orderly transition to democracy rather than a violent revolution. It regarded sport as representing one of 'the cruellest legacies of apartheid' and it promised redress and transformation. But, like the Springbok pack of 1974, these promises have been ground down and pushed back.

The fate of the Jaguars opens a window into a world in which resources are siphoned upwards rather than downwards into historically neglected areas. The same process applies to the building of big stadiums and the obsession with 'black African' representation in the Springboks, but with little commitment and money to foster the game lower down. Geographer Peirce Lewis wrote about how sporting landscapes reflect a people's 'unwitting biography, reflecting our values, our aspirations and even our fears in tangible visible form'. So true.

King's Park was the site of racial apartheid. Moses Mabhida is the site of class apartheid. The new stadium is already a drain on the taxpayers, under-used and a symbol of the bling consumerism that has come to define change in this country. The old and new elite stare at each other. Spitting images.

Sources

Alegi, P. 'A Nation To Be Reckoned With: The Politics of World Cup Stadium Construction in Cape Town and Durban, South Africa', *African Studies* 67, 3 (2008), pp 397–422.

African National Congress. *Reconstruction and Development Programme.* Johannesburg: Umanyano Publications, 1994, pp 72–73.

Grundlingh, A. 'Playing for Power? Rugby, Afrikaner Nationalism and Masculinity in South Africa, c.1900 – c.1970', in Nauright, J & Chandler, T (eds), *Making Men: Rugby and Masculine Identity*. London: Frank Cass, 1996, pp 188 & 195.

Guy, J. *The Destruction of the Zulu Kingdom*. Pietermaritzburg: University of Natal Press, 1994.

Morrell, R, Wright, J & Meintjes, S. 'Colonialism and the Establishment of White Domination, 1840–1890', in R Morrell (ed), *Political Economy and Identities In KwaZulu-Natal*. Durban: Indicator Press, 1996.

Nauright, J. *Sport, Cultures and Identities in South Africa*. Cape Town: David Philip, 1997, p 86.

Smuts, J. *Africa and Some World Problems*. Oxford: Clarendon Press, 1930, p 76.

Thomas, JBG. *The Greatest Lions*. London: Pelham Books, 1974, p 74.

ASHWIN DESAI is author of *We are the Poors: Community Struggles in Post-Apartheid South Africa*; editor of *The Race to Transform: Sport In Post-Apartheid South Africa*, and co-author of *Blacks in Whites: A Century of Cricket Struggles in KwaZulu-Natal*. While studying in Grahamstown, he helped found Phoenix Football Club, and at 21 was signed by United Teenagers. Nicknamed *'Die Boom'* (The Tree) for the sturdiness of his defence, and because he turned more slowly than Gerrie Sonnekus, Ashwin now lives and practises double standards in Durban.

PAUL DOBSON

In Memory of Craven, Louw and Pickard

DANIE CRAVEN

When the International Rugby Board (IRB) established its Hall of Fame, the first inductee was William Webb Ellis, closely followed by Rugby School and Danie Craven. It would be a tough task to find someone whose achievements and influence in the game rival those of Craven.

As well as captaining South Africa, Danie Craven played for the Springboks in Tests at scrumhalf, flyhalf, centre and eighthman, and at fullback in a tour match. After a stint in the army during the Second World War, Craven coached South Africa and was a national selector. He was manager of the South African team and president of the South African Rugby Football Board from 1956 to unification in 1992, when he became the first executive president of the South African Rugby Football Union (SARFU). He was also a member of the International Rugby Board.

Craven experimented with the laws of rugby and was influential in lawmaking. He coached Stellenbosch University until he was 80, and wrote many books on the game, including coaching manuals, biographies and histories.

Craven did not invent the dive pass. It seems that Lammie Luyt did that. It was more of a fall in those days as the scrumhalf tried to get out of the way of marauding loose forwards. Craven took it a step further and it became a dive, and it added to his fame.

After the 1931–32 Springbok tour, Craven, then 21, was asked to write an article explaining how the team had countered the threat of the loose forwards during their tour to the United Kingdom and Ireland. For the article, he set about analysing his dive pass. At night, he would practise the dive pass by himself by lamplight on a lawn outside the Wilgenhof residence at Stellenbosch University, using an old boot as a ball and a ring on a lamppost as his target. He said that analysing what he did instinctively had a bad effect on his play as it made him self-conscious. But in the long term it equipped him better as a coach and teacher.

Craven never spoke a great deal about the triumphant 1937 Springbok tour to Australia and New Zealand. One got the feeling that it was a disappointment to him, possibly because his mentor, Oubaas Markötter, may well have told him that he would captain the side. Instead Philip Nel was made captain, with Craven vice-captain. The players ran the tour after the manager left early.

For the first Test in New Zealand, they dropped Nel and made Craven captain and flyhalf. It was the only Test in five that the Springboks lost. Craven got another chance to captain the Springboks in 1938, and it was always a matter of great sorrow to him that they lost the last Test he ever played.

Oubaas Markötter believed that you should not praise a man because this destroys him, as now he believes he is good enough. Craven certainly followed that example in his dealings with his players. Jannie Engelbrecht tells a story to illustrate it.

Jannie was in his first year in the first XV at Stellenbosch, and had scored five tries at Newlands. He went back to Stellenbosch and on the Sunday strutted about, waiting for accolades. On Monday he went to practice and Craven sat his team down for their usual review of Saturday's match. Jannie waited for praise from the great man.

Craven went through each player, starting at fullback, but he skipped the right wing. Jannie presumed that Doc was saving the best for last, but when he got to the end, Jannie was still not mentioned and the practice went on. It was only on the Thursday that Craven took any notice of Jannie. He said, 'You'll never score a try between the posts again.'

Jannie, a much humbler man by this time, asked, 'Why not, Doc?'

'Because your head's too big to fit between the posts.'

The late Frederik van Zyl Slabbert, former leader of the Progressive Federal Party, once said, 'Craven had a very simple view of the world. If Wilgenhof was all right, Stellenbosch was all right, and if Stellenbosch was all right, South Africa was all right.'

Craven himself often quoted Markötter: 'South Africa first, Stellenbosch second and Western Province a poor third.' Not surprisingly, Craven's relations with Western Province were often unhappy. At one stage it was mooted that Stellenbosch secede from Western Province. But in 1981 Jan Pickard, an ex-Matie and a larger-than-life personality, became president of the Western Province Rugby Union, and in 1982 Stellenbosch agreed to stay in WP.

On one occasion we were at a curtain-raiser between SA Schools and SA Defence Force. Craven went down to wish the sides well. He opened the door to the Schools side and found them praying. So he closed the door and went to find the army boys. He opened the door and they were praying. Craven closed the door and came back to us on the stands. He said, 'We put God in a helluva position.'

Craven always had firm views on the game. 'In rugby we play against opponents, not the enemy. In war you are allowed to kill your enemy. But rugby is not war and we do not play against the enemy. It is possible to kill a man on the rugby field but we do not do it. Our opponents have the same rights that we have – to the protection of the laws, to enjoy the game, and even to win the game.'

In Craven's day, the South Stand at Newlands was known as the Malay Stand. In those times of segregation it was where 'non-whites' were allowed. The coming of the Group Areas Act and the destruction of communities such as District Six, Claremont, Harfield Village and Newlands changed a lot of that. Members of the Muslim community in particular sat in the South Stand – on big days wearing their grey suits and red fezzes – and they were always regarded as knowledgeable. Gesant Ederoos Behardien (known as Gamat), a tailor from Somerset West, was an important figure; he was the baggage man, who looked after the togs for Western Province and the Springboks for over 40 years.

Craven played for South Africa before he played for Western Province. But when he played for Province, it was in great sides that included Bennie Osler, Boy Louw, DO Williams, and so on. To go to Newlands to play for Province or the Maties, Craven would take the train from Stellenbosch to Salt River, and then the train from Salt River to Newlands, where there would inevitably be a couple of 'pikkies' (children) to carry his tog bag. Together they would stride towards Newlands.

After the match, a child would again materialise to carry the togs back to the station. Craven did not lose easily, and so on one occasion when Maties lost Craven was in a foul mood as he left for the station. As always, there was a child waiting.

'*Baas Danie, Baas Danie se togsak dra?*' (Master Danie, Master Danie, can I carry your tog bag?) the child asked.

Craven said nothing.

'*Baas Danie, Baas Danie se togsak dra?*' came the humble voice again.

Craven said, '*Gwaan, voetsek, man.*'

The little voice was not as humble when the child replied, '*Baas Danie, Baas Danie darem op Baas Danie se moer gekry vandag, nè?*' (Master Danie, you really fell on your face today, hey?).

That at least was how Craven told the story.

In the 1970s and 1980s, Craven often met with rugby men from the Muslim community, and they would come to the Rugby Board's suite at Newlands. When the South Stand was renamed the Danie Craven Stand, there was a ceremony before a Province match at Newlands. Craven and Jan Pickard were there in their smart Province blazers, each with a disa in his lapel. But Craven also had a plastic supermarket bag in his hand, which was an incongruous sight.

When it was Craven's turn to speak, he took from the bag a red fez, put it on his head and said, 'I would rather that it was called the Malay Stand and that the Malays came back to Newlands.' That was in 1987.

Danie Craven invited the Malay community to make the Danie Craven stand at Newlands their own.

BOY LOUW

*Nobody played for South Africa and Western Province with greater
devotion than Boy Louw, as Matthys Michael Louw – the Master – was
known. He played for South Africa in every position in the scrum,
playing in 18 Tests (then a record) between 1928 and 1938. He became a national selector and the coach of the Springboks, as well as a
selector and manager of Western Province and a life member of the
Western Province Rugby Union.*

*He was also a provincial referee, and the first to referee a Currie Cup
final. That was in 1939 at Newlands, when Western Province played
Transvaal, with his brother Fanie as the captain of Transvaal (Transvaal won 17-6).*

Louw, a bank manager in Paarl, had a great sense of humour, much
of it dependent on his ability to mangle English, especially verb con-
cordance, which he typically solved by putting an 's' onto the end of
each verb. A lot of it was deliberate.

One famous Boy Louw story is set in a shop in England in 1931,
when Louw went in to ask the young shop assistant for a cake of soap.

'Would you like it scented?' she replied.

'No, I'll *maar* take it with me,' he said.

Or, when a referee denied Louw a try and said, 'You didn't ground
the ball,' Boy exploded with, 'Grounded it! Must I buries the bloody
thing?'

Or, when he was a referee and, while awarding a try, was ques-
tioned by a defender who said, 'That wasn't a try,' Louw answered,
'*Ag so*? Reads about it in *The Argus*.'

Or, when told that his team had been lucky to win, Louw gave
perhaps his most famous retort, '*Ag so*? Looks at the scoreboard.'

One of Louw's other speech oddities was to pronounce a 'j' in English as a 'y', which was of course the Afrikaans way of pronouncing
a 'j'.

During the Second World War, he became Bombardier Boy Louw, a recruiting instrument for South Africa's volunteer army. He was up north, in the desert near the Mediterranean, when a soldier came up and informed his party that a U-boat had been sunk. Louw said, '*Ag nee*. How many Yews was drowned?'

There used to be a B Field at Newlands, where the Sports Science Institute now stands. Western Province would practise there. It was raining one evening and Louw and others took shelter under the scaffolding that housed a television camera. The construction was not waterproof.

Somebody said, '*Oom Boy, die dak lek*' (Uncle Boy, the roof is leaking).

Boy replied, '*Ja, dis lekker weer vir ducks*'.

But that pun gets lost in translation!

JAN PICKARD

The great Newlands personality after the Second World War was Jan Pickard. As a charismatic player, a charismatic captain and a charismatic president, Pickard knew how to make a success of everything he did, usually by ensuring that he got the best for those close to him.

As is the case with all good captains, Pickard's team came first. Once Province were playing Natal in Durban. The Springbok fullback Lionel Wilson warned that in Natal the field was hard and so were the balls. Pickard asked to see the balls. Once they were brought to him, he asked Wilson to have a look. Wilson pronounced the balls fine, but Pickard called in the Natal officials and told them that the balls were no good. Too hard. They had to let some air out or Province would not play.

It was all nonsense, of course. The Natal people couldn't find a valve (in those days valves were used to control the air pressure in the balls). But they got Roy McLean, a great Springbok cricketer and a former Natal flyhalf, who worked at King's Sports down the road, to go to his car in the car park and fetch a valve to let the air out.

In his tribute to Pickard at his memorial service, the famous Springbok centre John Gainsford said, 'The image Jan created was of somebody totally in control all the time. His players believed that he could get anything right, even rewrite the laws of the game if he wanted to – and that he'd get the refs to abide by them.'

Pickard believed in putting pressure on the referee. There was an occasion when the University of Cape Town held a course for coaches, and invited speakers to present their views. Professor Tinkie Heyns, a well-known academic, educationalist and rugby referee, spoke on refereeing. Among many other things, he spoke of the importance of setting standards early in the match. He said that early in the match the referee should, for example, pick up the backs for offside. Do it early and you'd have no more troubles.

Pickard gave the next talk. 'It's important to know your referee,' he said. 'Tinkie Heyns is always on about backs offside. I used to tell my backs, "Go offside early in the match. He'll blow you and then he will think he's got that sorted out, and you can go offside all afternoon." Ralph Burmeister was always on about barging in the line-out. I used to barge at the first line-out and he'd penalise me. Once he'd got that out of his system, I could barge all afternoon.' At the time Ralph Burmeister was the top referee in South Africa, refereeing Tests from 1949 to 1961.

PAUL DOBSON completed his 40-year career as a schoolteacher in 1994, after spending 29 years at Diocesan College (Bishops). In 1968 he joined the Western Province Referees' Society and refereed to Currie Cup level. He is now the honorary life president of the society. He also served on the South African rugby laws committee and is a life member of South African Referees' Society. Paul has written widely on rugby and now contributes to rugby365.com and edits a schools rugby website and a site for South African referees.

What Endures

Tony O'Reilly, the wing who played for the British and Irish Lions and who went on to found the Independent media empire, once told me that he remembers far more about characters and off-field incidents from his rugby career than about the games themselves. This always seemed odd to me, because as a player you are always obsessed with performance and results. The rest is neither here nor there.

Now, at 55, I realise that the great man was telling the truth and that the human dimension of sport is actually the most important. I have many memories from my career with universities, clubs, countries and the British and Irish Lions. Very few vivid ones concern what happened on the pitch unless, believe it or not, it was humorous. Like flyhalf Tony Ward arriving at the deciding Test of the 1980 Lions series against the Boks and discovering that he had forgotten his boots at the hotel.

Tony has tiny feet, and the rain was bucketing down outside and the roads were jammed, so we decided not to say anything to anyone. But, as a reserve, he almost got called onto the field in his stockinged feet! I swear that is true. Ask Brent Russell's dad, Robbie, if you don't believe me. He played in a curtain-raiser that day and saw the confusion in the grandstand as we unsuccessfully tried to find another pair of small boots for Tony. With the professionalism of modern-day rugby, I can't see something like that happening again.

Another favourite took place at my club, Greystones, in Ireland, where we had a fabulous backline but a tiny pack. We compensated for this by developing a vigorous and effective rucking pattern in the loose that depended on the forwards linking arms with each other before they hit the ruck, rather than arriving individually. To co-ordinate it, I – as scrumhalf and skipper – used to shout a code word on identifying a potential ruck. As they headed towards it, the forwards would lift their arms to link with the nearest teammate and would end up running in this strange way. The code word was quite aptly 'airplanes', and it worked!

We got to a league final against Dublin's mighty St Mary's club, which featured numerous Lions and international players. We hadn't a chance. However, we started at great pace, and after moving the ball quickly a few times, a loose ball ensued. As our forwards converged on it, I duly shouted, 'Airplanes, airplanes!' at the top of my voice.

Suddenly, one of their players, a prop forward called 'Tojo' Byrne, fell on the ball shouting, 'Mayday, mayday!'

We had to stop for a laugh break after that. I still count it as a grand honour that this is one of the favourite stories of the great Lions captain, Willie John McBride.

Sometimes the funniest things occur when there is a misunderstanding. The Transvaal team of 1986 had just made it to their first Currie Cup final in a decade, and we were to meet Western Province at Newlands. They were hot favourites, and ultimately went on to win their fifth Currie Cup in a row. But we gave them a good go, in the first half at least.

Training the week before the game was tense and much of it consisted of scrummaging, because Province were exceptionally strong up front. Our coach was Prof Pa Pelser, very much of the old school of South African coaches. He was an academic and quite an elderly man, and a philosopher to boot. He rarely lost his temper, but the pressure began to show during a murderous scrum session.

I was there as scrumhalf, feeding the scrum, and the second team were giving our pack a good workout. After a scrum, Pa demanded a reaction from our Springbok hooker, Chris Rogers from Zimbabwe. 'Feedback, Chris, I want feedback!' he exhorted.

Chris, with that innocent look of his, turned to giant lock Lappies Labuschagne and shouted, 'Lappies, you heard the coach: feet back, get your feet back!'

It was deliberate, of course. Pa was totally confused, and we fell about laughing. After a minute, silence reigned again, only to be broken by Lappies, who had a slight stutter, saying in all seriousness, 'B-b-but C-C-Chris, m-my f-f-f-feet are as f-f-far back as they can f-f-f****** g-g-go!'

We collapsed again, and this time even Pa joined in.

So, remember to smell the roses as you play this great game, because long after you can no longer run, their wonderful perfume will linger on as memories.

JOHN ROBBIE played nine Tests for Ireland at scrumhalf, and one for the British and Irish Lions on their 1980 tour of South Africa. He enjoyed South Africa so much that he immigrated in 1981, and went on to represent Transvaal and win selection to the Springbok squad. John is one of Talk Radio 702's leading presenters, respected and hugely popular for his straight-talking interviewing style. He is also a regular rugby pundit for SuperSport.

ANDY CAPOSTAGNO

Did You Say France, or Frans?

The semifinals of the 1999 Rugby World Cup are forever etched in my memory. For some reason it was decided to play the matches back to back over a weekend at Twickenham. This meant that many touring parties of supporters had tickets for both games. From the press box I could look across the famous ground and see numerous patches of yellow, green and black, the colours of the Tri-Nations.

As fate would have it, South Africa played Australia in the first semi on Saturday 30 October, while the All Blacks, with the fearful Jonah Lomu to the fore, were expected to deal harshly with the French on the Sunday. However, that meant that one set of supporters was going to have to sit through that the Sunday game in the knowledge that their team was already out.

In my wife's family it is a ritual to meet in the West car park at Twickenham on match day to eat cold meat and hot soup, and to drink bitter beer and red wine. Experience has taught us that an early dive into Bloody Marys and gin and tonics is unwise, as the soporific effect of spirits inevitably leads to sleeping in the stands. This particular Saturday, I was greeted by the jovial commentator, Chick Henderson, who was also surrounded by relatives. Chick was of the opinion that the Springboks were narrow favourites, but that drop-goals wouldn't beat the Wallabies in the way they had seen off the English in Paris. But while we were chatting I saw a beaming Springbok fan swaying into the ground bearing a banner announcing, 'Only one beer. Jannie de Beer!'

That reminded me of the press conference that had followed the Springbok win at the Stade de France. Jannie had played a couple of seasons for London Irish, and so the English press knew him, and in particular they knew about his unshakeable religious faith. So one wag asked Jannie what part the Creator had played in a match dominated by the carrot-topped flyhalf's five drop-goals. His answer is one that I now pass on to any players who feel the need to proclaim their faith in post-match interviews.

'Well,' he said, 'God gave me the talent, but the forwards gave me the ball.'

Jannie's purple patch with the boot continued into the semifinal, and because of the drama of extra time few now recall that he had to slot a penalty from wide out and 40m back in the final five minutes to clinch the draw in normal time. And just as I remember the clenched fists of the Springbok supporters in the press box at that moment, I also remember the tremors of shock that ran through them when Stephen Larkham's outrageous drop-goal from halfway won the match for Australia. In the end, the team that lived by the boot died by the boot.

There were some glum faces on the train home, and many Springbok fans holding tickets for the second semifinal could not face the trip back to Twickenham the following day. They repaired to bars across the capital and sought ticketless French and New Zealanders, of whom there were plenty. The problem was that the tour groups couldn't simply jump on the next plane home: they had pre-paid for everything, and even those who hadn't signed up for the final weren't due to fly until Monday night.

And so, in the cold light of an autumn Sunday in London, Springbok supporters forgot their bitter memories of Saturday and trooped back to the same seats for the second semifinal. If the Boks were out, at least they could cheer for France.

As for the press corps, one among us, the writer for *Rapport*, could not bear the trip. A French supporter right to his Huguenot roots, he couldn't stand to watch his team humiliated by an unbeatable All

Blacks side. So he stayed in his room and missed the greatest World Cup match ever played.

Remember that in 1999 the All Blacks' finals bogey was in its infancy. They had won the cup at home in 1987, lost in the semis to the Wallabies in 1991 and in the final to the Boks (and Nelson Mandela) in 1995. They were expected to win in 1999, and shortly after half-time the semi was all but over, with New Zealand 24-10 ahead.

Then the fightback began, from who knows where. Maybe it was Fabien Galthié's tackle on the giant Lomu. The French scrumhalf eschewed the tried and trusted techniques of the oval-balled game; after all, they had proved utterly ineffective against the force of nature from New Zealand. Instead he leapt into the air and wrapped his body around Lomu like some demented feather boa, reasoning that constriction might work where power had failed.

Galthié's act of doomed gallantry struck a chord with me, but who knows where the rest of his team found the inspiration to turn the game on its head. Maybe they got it from flyhalf Christophe Lamaison, who kicked two drops and two penalties to bring France to within two points. And maybe, just maybe, they got it by looking into the crowd and seeing the hordes of green-shirted Springbok fans cheering them to the rafters. From 24-10 down, France scored 33 unanswered points. Jeff Wilson got a try in the dying minutes as scant consolation for New Zealand.

In quarter of a century of writing and broadcasting about sport, I have never seen a press box do what it did that day at Twickenham: when the final whistle blew, everyone got to their feet and applauded. In that heady moment, deadlines were forgotten and national loyalties set aside in order to celebrate the unique spirit of rugby union.

Other team sports can't do this. There is no such thing as a shock in a World Cup soccer match. On any given day the best side can lose because it's a simple game and goals are relatively easily created. Golf and cricket take too long to give the adrenaline surge of half an hour of sublime rugby. And no one ever said they were transferring to rugby league in order to play a better game.

There were, of course, a handful of New Zealanders in the press box not carried away by the moment. While the rest of us stood, half a dozen sat on their hands, too insensitive to the beauty of the game to step outside their narrow lives. And in the stadium around us the sea of black-clad supporters had melted away as though someone had squirted detergent onto an oil slick. But the green islands and the yellow islands stayed on to celebrate the moment.

I took time to look around and watch the glee, then made my way downstairs and out of Twickenham to the tent next door, which had been erected for post-match press conferences. John Hart and Taine Randell were first in, as coach and captain, respectively, of the losing side.

There is an unwritten code at press conferences: even when your opponent is down – in fact, especially when your opponent is down – don't kick him. And so we all skated around the periphery; let's face it, most of us were there for French quotes. But there is one thing you are not allowed to do in New Zealand, and that is to lose a game of rugby. So while the print journalists kept their heads down, a former All Blacks player at the back of the room got straight to the point.

'John,' he said, 'do you not think you made a few tactical errors before the game?'

There was a pause. The coach rolled his eyes and was about to answer when the dagger came in.

'I mean, John, you had a 14 playing 15, a 15 playing 13, a six at eight. Jesus Christ, man . . .'

It was a great moment for the connoisseur. Coaches are always happy to belittle media people who ask difficult questions; they hide behind the flimsy facade of 'you wouldn't be asking that if you knew anything about the game'. But that doesn't wash with former players, particularly highly respected former players who have been arguing all year that Jeff Wilson is a wing, Christian Cullen is a fullback and Taine Randell is an open-side flanker. No amount of bluster could get Hart out of this one, and I smiled inwardly at arrogance brought low.

When the French arrived in the tent, we all stood and applauded again. Coach Jean-Claude Skrela and captain Raphael Ibanez took the stage, and the first question was odd. Not how do you feel, or what was going through your mind at 24-10 down, but, 'Raphael, after the national anthems you took your team into their half and sang again. Why?'

A pause for the question to be translated into French and then the forthright answer: 'Sometimes soldiers sing before they go into battle.'

At this point I need to digress. When I was at school we were taught 'La Marseillaise', and it stuck. Now, whenever I hear the French national anthem sung a lump comes to my throat, despite the fact that I am half-Sicilian, not half-French. 'Fratelli d'Italia' doesn't do it for me, and neither does 'God Save the Queen'. 'Nkosi Sikelel' iAfrika' does a bit, but that's for what it represents, not because it's a great tune with stirring words like 'La Marseillaise'.

In the film Casablanca, there's a moment where a boorish group of Nazis start singing drinking songs in Rick's bar. The band goes quiet and then the female guitarist starts singing 'La Marseillaise'. Bit by bit the band joins in, then the patrons, and the Nazis are drowned out. By now I'm immune to the love story of Humphrey Bogart and Ingrid Bergman, but 'La Marseillaise' gets me every time.

In 1999, 'La Marseillaise' was 208 years old. Written in 1791, it was adopted by the French Revolution four years later, and it's a song that takes no prisoners. There's a line that, translated into English, reads: 'Let's march, let's march! That impure blood may water our furrows.' So when Ibanez said, 'Sometimes soldiers sing before they go into battle', everyone in his team knew what was required.

When the press conference ended, I packed my bag and walked back into the stadium. The South Stand incorporates a hotel today, but for years it was the last unenclosed part of Twickenham. You could stand on the concourse and see the field through the holes in the seating. As I walked along the concourse, I heard voices raised in familiar song.

Understand at this point that chilly night was falling and that the match had ended over an hour earlier. Unless you have a parking space in the West car park, no one hangs around at Twickenham after an international. They go to the Cabbage Patch pub or the Orange Tree or walk the three-odd kilometres to the train station and repair to the capital to celebrate or drown sorrows. So I was intrigued to know who was still here so long after everyone else had left.

I walked around the side of the stand and saw the most amazing sight. About a hundred green-shirted Springbok supporters were sat high up in the stand listening attentively to two fellows wearing the blue jerseys of France. There was a pause and then out it came: 'Allons enfants de la Patrie, Le jour de gloire est arrivé . . .'

I stood and watched a bunch of heartsore South Africans belt out the national anthem of France as though their very lives depended on it. The song ended, there was a pause for the raising of bottles and hip flasks and then off they went again. I imagine that they had been there since the final whistle, learning the words slowly at first, then running through a succession of musical duds. Sometime around when Ibanez was telling us why France sang their national anthem twice on the field, the penny dropped and 'La Marseillaise' entered their hearts and minds.

When I think about what makes rugby union a great game, I think about that moment at Twickenham, when I saw men and women from the other side of the world join in the joyful celebration of a

French win with two people who happened to have enough English to make a connection. Community singing happens in soccer, but it is frequently antagonistic. Mix alcohol with soccer fans and you get an explosion. Rugby is different.

I remember reading David Hands in *The Times* a couple of days before flying home. His review of the tournament made a telling point. It said that there had not been a single arrest in the six weeks given over to the fourth Rugby World Cup, and concluded by saying, 'Alcohol does not create hooliganism. Hooligans do.'

Three days after France beat the All Blacks, I drove to Wales to watch the Springboks drive the nail deeper into the New Zealand psyche with victory in the third-place playoff match. While queuing on the motorway to get over the Severn Bridge, my memory went back eight years, to when I made the same journey to see Scotland lose to the All Blacks in the third-place playoff game of the 1991 tournament. The kombi in front of me had suddenly disgorged six kilted Scotsmen, all holding bagpipes. They struck up 'Flower of Scotland', and for a magical minute time stood still. Angry commuters forgot their journey, wound down their windows and listened. Some were even bold enough to get out of their cars and take pictures. When the song ended, the six pipers jumped back into the kombi and continued on their way, having lightened the mood for us lucky few who were in the right place at the right time.

Music is a powerful drug. Ask Raphael Ibanez.

ANDY CAPOSTAGNO has worked in every section of the South African media since arriving from the United Kingdom in 1992, fleeing the evils of Thatcherism. He is best known for his rugby and cricket TV commentary for SuperSport, and for being a regular guest for ten years on the award-winning magazine programme *Super Saturday*. He has written three books: *Jonty in Pictures*, *Memorable Moments in One-Day Cricket* and *Fancourt: The Road to the Presidents Cup*. A fourth, collecting his humorous short stories set in the mythical *dorp* of Ystervarkrivier, is due out soon. Andy is the rugby correspondent for the *Mail & Guardian*, and farms in the Natal Midlands with his wife, daughter and three Dobermanns.

TONY LEON

The Argentine Affair

When I was growing up in Durban in the 1960s and 1970s, rugby, alongside cricket, was the crowning passion of my home province. In white, English-speaking Natal it was also the core symptom of lingering displeasure with Afrikaans-dominated national politics, from which the self-styled 'last outpost of the British Empire' was profoundly alienated.

Actually, the notion of the 'last outpost' gained much currency after the consistent overlooking of star Natal eighthman Tommy Bedford for the captaincy of the mighty Springboks. But my first brush with rugby was far more personal – and painful – than it was political. My early schoolboy attempts were deeply unsuccessful due to flat feet, which ensured that maximum passion for the game off-field was unmatched by any success on it.

I attended Kearsney College, one of the province's fine schools, where success at rugby determined the pecking order in a fiercely contested schoolboy hierarchy. My passion cooled when Friday nights at the boarding school were spent memorising the names of the first XV playing the next day, with any mistakes being swiftly punished by the business end of the prefect's cane! Unfortunately, I was often an unhappy recipient of this ancient and, I thought, somewhat cruel ritual.

But if Bedford was overlooked too often for the top Springbok job, then the man whose prowess on the field was matched by impeccable political connectivity off it was the Springbok captain and adroit scrumhalf, Dawie de Villiers. I first saw the blond dynamo in action when he captained Transvaal against my home team of Natal at a packed King's Park way back in 1972. Dawie had all the right stuff – and I was one of his legion of schoolboy followers. I never imagined back then that, some 20 years later, Dawie and I, on opposite political sides but sharing the same belief in our country's democratic redemption, would work closely together on negotiating South Africa's political future at the World Trade Centre in Kempton Park.

Dawie's rugby leadership was well recognised and much praised, but his sane and often sage chairing of our difficult and dramatic constitutional negotiations on behalf of the National Party government (alongside Joe Slovo of the ANC) was under-reported and too little heralded. He had equal measures of cool detachment and steely determination, and a clear ability to put himself in the shoes of his adversaries. I suspect that his attributes in rugby proved useful for the equally tough choices he confronted in politics.

Back in my school days I had a deep detestation of politicians interfering in sport. I – correctly – blamed the intransigence and racism of John Vorster's government for isolating South Africa from international competition. Many years later, when I became leader of the opposition in South Africa's Parliament, I had a lot to say about the successor government, the ANC, and its transformative imperatives in sport, which I often thought were a thin veneer for taking control.

About ten years ago, I found myself in the president's suite at Newlands, seated next to another schoolboy hero of mine, Mannetjies Roux, one of the celebrated Springbok legends of yesteryear. He was still sprightly, and told me he lived in Victoria West. South African rugby, at the time, was going through one of its periodic crises. Mannetjies, during the match we were watching against the All Blacks, then asked me, 'Tony, why do you think the ANC wants to control rugby?' All I could think of to say in reply was, 'Well, Mannetjies, it is one of the few things that they don't yet control!'

But, as ever, the sainted Madiba gave us a powerful example of the better and more noble admixture of sport and politics. I perhaps had the greatest and most unearned political and personal gifts of all time: my political leadership of the Democratic Party commenced and coincided with Nelson Mandela's presidency. I therefore had the opportunity to observe him at close quarters and receive both his friendship and counsel.

The significance, however, of Mandela was not sainthood, but shrewd political calculation matched by a genius for emotional intelligence and empathy. He once said, 'Sport has the power to change the world. It has the power to inspire. It has the power to unite people in a way that little else can. Sport can awaken hope where previously there was only despair.'

As we, and the world, famously learned, he went on to practise what he preached with the Springbok bravehearts of 1995 when he lifted the William Webb Ellis trophy after a tension-packed Rugby World Cup final. Alongside 62 000 other lucky ticket-holders, I bore witness on that autumnal August day in Ellis Park to the magic, heart-stopping moment in extra time when Joel Stransky's drop-goal off a splendid pass from Joost van der Westhuizen led to our famous victory. It was like a scene from a Hollywood movie, which of course it ultimately became when *Invictus* hit cinema screens worldwide in 2010.

It was actually Joost van der Westhuizen and *Invictus* that led to my more recent work, and the importance of rugby in it, as South African ambassador to Argentina. In early 2010, shortly after my arrival here as the newly minted South African envoy, courtesy of Jacob Zuma's inclusivity, my colleagues at the embassy thought it a splendid idea to arrange the screening of *Invictus* as an *avant-premier* (Spanish for 'opening night') to promote South Africa's image in the sports-loving city of Buenos Aires. After consulting my school-boy friend Gavin Varejes, today president of the South African Rugby

Legends Association, and with the generous sponsorship of Standard Bank Argentina, we secured Joost's attendance as the guest speaker at the opening. Whatever controversies dogged him at home, he and the movie were a huge hit with the *porteños* (as residents of this metropolis of 12 million people are called).

I thought it a good idea to arrange a dinner for Joost and living Pumas legend (and former Argentine ambassador to South Africa) Hugo Porta. Hugo is the most rare of human beings: arguably the greatest flyhalf of his generation (who can forget his demolition of the Springboks back in 1982 when he scored every winning point himself?), yet he remains an incredibly modest and gentle man. Hugo sized up the towering Joost in our dining room and observed, 'In my time scrumhalves were about half your size, but then they were only about half as good!'

Of all the bilateral ties which bind Argentina to South Africa, rugby is one of the most important, and often one of the less recognised (but hopefully not by the end of my ambassadorship). Actually, the importance of rugby in Argentina remains a matter of much unresolved contemplation by me, and doubtless by others. I often ask myself, and my Argentine friends, why it is that of all the countries in the whole of North, Central and South America, only Argentina plays really top-rate, internationally competitive rugby?

The obvious answer is the English influence, which has been vast and profound, in spite of the dispute over the Islas Malvinas, or Falkland Islands. Several of Buenos Aires's finest schools – St George's College, San Andreas and Cardinal Newman – were founded on the same ethos, and with similar reverence for rugby, as my own alma mater, Kearsney College. Indeed, Argentina's highly effective and rugby-obsessed ambassador to South Africa, the dynamic Carlos Sersale, recently told me that some 100 school and club rugby teams visit each other's countries in both directions every year.

Yet the English influence has been far greater in Canada or even in the United States, and neither of these much larger and resource-rich countries play rugby at the level Argentina does. Maybe it's the weather, but then again Argentina is hardly alone in the Americas in enjoying a surfeit of sunshine. Whatever the reason, or agreeable combination thereof, the fact remains that Argentina is the stand-out rugby nation of the Americas.

Of course, the sports isolation forced on South Africa by apartheid in the 1960s and 1970s, had a – forgive the pun – further, positive knock-on effect down here in the southern cone of South America. South Africa's shrewd rugby supremo, Dr Danie Craven, realised, I gather, that the development and modernisation of rugby in Argentina was a way out of the increasingly fraught and frozen ties with our normal rugby partners in Australasia and the United Kingdom. So there was much more than just fellowship and sports camaraderie behind South Africa's deep involvement with the game here. Indeed, the great achievements of Izak van Heerden (a former master at Durban High School and later Natal coach) with the Argentine national team, the Pumas, are fondly remembered in this country.

The huge success of *Invictus* in Argentina and surrounding countries has had many positive and personal spin-offs for my public diplomacy and South Africa's diplomatic projection. When I went in March 2010 to present my credentials as ambassador to Paraguay in Asunción, President Fernando Lugo pushed aside the diplomatic formalities and engaged me in a lengthy discussion about both the movie and Mandela's leadership role. He then said, 'I not only saw the film but went and read the book *El Factor Humano* too.' (This was the Spanish title of John Carlin's *Playing the Enemy*.) And, as he told me, 'The book is even better than the film.'

Which brings me to John Carlin, author of the book that was the inspiration and back-story for the movie. I knew John extremely well during the turbulent 1990s, when he was a frontline reporter on political developments in South Africa for London's *The Inde-*

pendent newspaper. I did not know of John's deep understanding and passion for sport, but was at the time deeply impressed with his first-rate, impeccably sourced political reportage. Imagine my surprise, then, to be informed in mid-2009 by the organisers of Argentina's biggest agricultural conference that John and I were to share top billing at their 5 000-strong gathering in September in the city of Rosario! And so it was through our discussion of *Invictus* moments and background that John and I were reunited, many years after the dust had settled on South Africa's democratic journey.

John's advantage as a speaker at the conference was not simply as the author of a widely admired book on Mandela and the 1995 Rugby World Cup. I discovered that, in contrast to my appalling Spanish (which I bravely stutter out at every public engagement), he was fluent in the language, since he grew up in Buenos Aires, where his father served as first secretary of the British embassy.

My agreeable reunion with John also yielded two additional insights. The first was his recollection that while he (and I and millions of others) thought *Invictus* a fine movie adaptation of the book, its name was Hollywood fiction. Yes, Mandela had a high regard for and made regular use of the excellent Victorian poem of that title, but contrary to the movie's depiction, he never wrote out the poem and gave it to Francois Pienaar for inspiration! Still, as Joost assured the large audience in Buenos Aires, 'Ninety percent of the movie really happened in real life!'

The second was John telling me that he had, in collaboration with ace South African director Cliff Bestall, produced a 45-minute documentary on the 1995 Springboks and Mandela's tilting of the arc of rugby toward building our nation anew, entitled *The 16th Man*. On receipt of a copy, I screened it for my staff at the embassy: there was not a dry eye among us by the end. In its way, it is even more powerful and real (and the rugby arguably much better!) than *Invictus*. Every South African, rugby enthusiast or not, should see that film.

With a rugby movie at the front end of our diplomatic projection in Argentina at the beginning of the year, and the brilliant 2010 FIFA World Cup occupying centre stage of our activities until July 2010, there seemed no way to up the ante even further over here. But rugby, and the sponsorship of Johan Roets of Standard Bank Argentina and others, ensured a grand finale for the year end. In discussion with Johan, we mused about how we could slake the Argentine thirst for more *Invictus* moments. And so we hit on the idea of hosting a South African festival in November in celebration of Argentina's bicentenary.

We flew the entire South African Rugby Legends team, led by Joost (this time in a playing, non-speaking role) and another veteran of 1995, Marius Hurter, over to Buenos Aires for a match against an Argentine Legends side. To discuss the political 'miracle' behind South Africa's transition, we brought in former President FW de Klerk and ANC senior negotiator Mac Maharaj to address a seminar after the exhibition match. And what a match it turned out to be: 15 former Springboks playing 15 ex-Pumas at the historic CASI Club, the headquarters of Argentine rugby, in the leafy northern suburb of San Isidro.

Unfortunately, the result fell just short of a perfect ending, and we lost by a single point – 20-19 – to the fired-up ex-Pumas. De Klerk then did the honours by handing over the Legends Cup to the just-made-it victors.

Rugby formed the backdrop to my childhood; South Africa's isolation from the sport helped change our country; and some of its greatest players have crossed my political path. Now I have the greatest fortune of being South African ambassador to a serious rugby-playing country, about to join South Africa, New Zealand and Australia in the Four Nations in 2012.

Not a bad place to be for someone who never made it out of the seventh and eighth XVs back in high school.

Ambassador Tony Leon and former South African President FW de Klerk
with the Legends Cup in Argentina, flanked by Guillermo Rivaben
of Personal (left) and Johan Roets of Standard Bank Argentina (right).

TONY LEON is the South African ambassador to Argentina, Uruguay and Paraguay. Prior to his diplomatic posting, he served for 20 years as a Member of Parliament in South Africa (1989–2009), and for 13 years as leader of the Democratic Party and Democratic Alliance. Despite having a home in Cape Town, he still supports the Sharks and uses rugby diplomacy to advance South Africa's interests in South America.

(This text reflects the personal opinion of Tony Leon and is not a reflection of the views of the Department of International Relations and Cooperation of South Africa.)

FAN NATION

The Surfer Who Loves Sharks

One crazy night not so long ago, this surfer felt like a fish out of water. It all started when my good friend, Ard Matthews from Just Jinjer, almost everyone's favourite South African band, came to stay for a few days to surf, party and cause a general ruckus in Durban. Being from the Bluff, Ard isn't known for his tact. This was going to cause us problems down the line, but let's start at the beginning . . .

Our first stop was to be a game of poker at John Smit's house, just north of Durban. I was very excited about this, as I am an obsessive Sharks and South African rugby supporter. John is one of my heroes and, I believe, this country's greatest-ever sportsman. But I never got the chance to tell him that.

After collecting Ard at the airport around lunch time, we went straight to my house in Umhlanga and proceeded to sample some Corona beer and Peligroso Tequila, a few cases of which had been kindly donated by my sponsors for our enjoyment. It was at least six hours before we needed to be at the poker game.

I met Ard in Los Angeles about five years ago, and we have been great friends ever since. He's just one of those guys . . . when you meet up, it's always full tilt. Soon the conversation got on to friends in common in the USA, like Reg the King of Hollywood, who always showed us the best time in one of the world's worst places. And Greg Long, the big-wave world champion, who had been hanging with us in Cape Town a few months earlier. Before we knew it, we were quite a few drinks down and it was time to go. We had a swim in my pool and got a serious warning from our girlfriends, whom we would be meeting later, not to embarrass ourselves.

Needless to say, by the time we rolled up to John's house Ard and I were pretty messy, but we were sure we could keep it together. But right away things didn't go well: as we arrived, we walked up some stairs that had just been concreted and were clearly marked 'DO NOT WALK'. Not a good start. John Smit is one imposing figure by reputation, and he's one huge guy in real life. He looked at us like we were crazy. All I could do was hope for the best.

He seemed to get over our little indiscretion pretty quickly, and once the cursory introductions and informal swapping of who, why and when were all handled with as much dignity as possible, I felt both welcome and empowered. I mean, here I was, a surf bum, invited to play poker with a bunch of my heroes . . . why wouldn't I feel on top of the world?

By a cruel stroke of fate, I found myself seated next to my least favourite Shark of all time – Englishman Andy Goode – and I just couldn't contain myself. Now we all know Mr Goode's story: signed in February 2010 for a season by coach John Plumtree to fill the gap after mercurial style-meister Frenchman Freddie Michalak had left our shores. And I don't think anyone would disagree if I said the two flyhalves couldn't have been more different in style or rugby finesse.

At first I tried to be civil, and because I am a rank amateur at poker and he seemed to know his way around a chip or two, Andy was friendly enough. But as we chatted, all I could hear in the back of my alcohol-riddled mind was the voice of the famous New Zealand rugby commentator, saying, 'Mate, I'm sorry, but I just don't know what to call that. What is that? It looks like a comb-over mullet! You have got to be kidding!'

I made some small talk, trying not to stare, and concentrated on playing poker. Some Sharks players take it pretty seriously and don't appreciate it if you hold up the table – especially if you're a loud, drunk surfer boy sitting next to Andy Goode. The other thing I discovered about poker is that it takes a long time to play. We had brought the Corona and a bottle of tequila with us, and were still drinking steadily. A few of the Sharks weren't scared of a drink either.

Amazingly, I managed to win a few hands and stay out of trouble. I even took out Keegan Daniel, another hero of mine, to make my way to the 'final table'. My new friend Andy hadn't punched me out either. But after holding my tongue for as long as possible, I finally succumbed to the drink and blurted out, 'Mate, I'm sorry, but I just don't know what to call that! What is that? It looks like a comb-over mullet! You have got to be kidding!'

Instead, he just laughed me off as a minor nuisance, all the while losing his money.

Andy finally bade us farewell, weakly stating some kind of family commitment. I tried to convince him to come out with us after the poker because we'd have a couple of girls with us who always liked to end up at the strip clubs. But no amount of coaxing could get around Andy's dedication to his family, or perhaps his disdain of me. It was probably for the best anyway, because my plan was to show him to my friends at Taco Zulu and have a good laugh at his expense even though he turned out to be a great guy and I supported him for the rest of the season.

I made it to the last three on the table, and got knocked out by Stefan Terblanche – who was getting very lucky on the river and, in-cidentally, seemed very competitive and unappreciative of some of my more snide, drunken chirps. By this time I was absolutely ham-mered and could barely hold things together, and all at once that was that. Ard had been knocked out a few hours earlier and was passed out on the couch. Once I managed to rouse him we were ushered – very politely, considering our state – out of the Smits' house and once again into rugby obscurity.

What happened after we left and met up with our by-now just as drunk girlfriends was ridiculous and not to be mentioned in public, but let's just say that we had a crazy night all wired up after having hung out with some of rugby's royalty.

And I'm still waiting for a poker night recall, but I guess I'll save holding my breath for some big waves instead.

GRANT 'TWIG' BAKER is a professional big-wave surfer, paid by Billabong to travel the world and surf the biggest waves possible. He played scrumhalf – bouncing between the A and B teams, depending on the state of the swell – until Grade 10, when a friend got a car and they became mobile on weekends, hunting waves and girls. Twig has gone on to win the highest-profile big wave competitions on the planet, but remains a committed Sharks supporter.

After the dust settled, we headed back to our suburban HQ.

I drove home with the South African flag flying proudly from my driver's window. This flag was then stolen from my hands. To be fair, waving a flag can often be mistaken for handing someone a flag.

All creeds and colours (literally) danced in the streets – an early World Cup parade. Naughty By Nature's *'Feel Me Flow'* replaced Eddie Vedder on the radio. Grunge may have been dead, but South Africa was reborn.

On arrival at our rendezvous point, my vampire friend spotted his earlier victim.

'Hey, that's the guy I bit!' he said, as if pointing out a spy.

'You bit my cousin?' asked another friend.

All was forgiven over a brandy and a tetanus shot.

The Rugby World Cup brought us together, tore us apart, then brought us together again. Sometimes, life and rugby are the same thing.

BRENDAN JACK is a writer, director, comedian and performer. At university, he discovered that he was too short to play in the Springbok front row and too slow to move to centre. After seven years in advertising, he co-created *Crazy Monkey*, which appeared on MTV around the globe. He then helped make movies like *Straight Outta Benoni* and *Footskating 101*. As a Lions supporter, Brendan equates watching rugby to riding an emotional roller coaster, but with beer. Visit brendanjack.com.

EVAN MILTON

The Horns of a Dilemma

He's easily 40kg heavier than I am, already out of school and is the leader of a little gang of similarly burly followers. He has me lifted off the ground by my throat. Added to this culturally rich slice of Pretoria's suburban white past (and to my immediate predicament), the afore-mentioned followers are forming a loose circle around my high-school sweetheart after forcibly prising apart our sweaty pre-teen hands. Not the evening one might have hoped for when she and I stretched the truth to our respective parents about a 'class party' and snuck a lift with one of her friend's older boyfriends to the Farm Inn. The muscled arm, the fingers around the larynx, the imminent peril . . .

Are these the foremost of my worries? No. The real problem is that I've been asked a question: 'WP of Bulle?' A direct translation is sim-ple: Western Province or Blue Bulls? What it means, though, is much more complex. And much more dangerous.

My relationship with rugby started early in life, as with most other things that defined cultural groups in South Africa's mad, bad segregated past. For my Pretoria East school friends and me, these groupings were simple, prevalent and governed by laws of birth. One either spoke English or one played rugby as a primary sport (with athletics and hitting English-speakers as tertiary pas-times) – preposterous stereotypes, of course, especially given what Pretoria represented to the rest of the world.

The seemingly black and white dichotomy in our world ignored the real divisions between black people and white people in pre-liberation times. But Pretoria was an architecturally perfect apartheid city, engineered so that one could live, work, be educated and socialise pretty much without meeting a person of another class or language group (let alone another race) as an equal. Hell, they'd brainwashed some of the kids at my English school so effectively that they'd joke they'd rather be friends with a black person than an Afrikaner. Although they didn't use the words 'black person'. Or 'Afrikaner'.

With the benefit of hindsight, it was an appallingly impressive masterstroke of social engineering. The black vs white, Christian vs Communist and South Africa vs the World propaganda was internalised so thoroughly that whatever group you were, you thought any other group was out to get you, and the only appropriate defence was a pre-emptive strike. And at the Farm Inn that evening, I was about to experience the full force of the other muscled arm into my all too clearly English-speaking face.

To reflect, for a moment, as one does in life-and-death situations when time slows: Western Province may now also be called the Stormers but, as far as Blue Bulls fans are concerned, they'll always be WP, and there will always be rivalry between the two teams. Back then, the antagonism ran deeper, and implied more. Province were a strong side, and a match could go either way. Most damningly, Province had English players. In Pretoria past, even though established English schools like Pretoria Boys High played rugger, the game was the birthright of Afrikaners, and treading on that turf was deemed a transgression – and certainly grounds for a drubbing.

In the combat theatre of the Farm Inn, my antagonist has just snarled the question again. 'Ek het gesê, WP of Bulle?' He's had the foresight to shift his grip so my voicebox can move sufficiently to permit words. Now able to speak (well, wheeze), I'm tempted to share the interesting observation of how I find myself on the horns of a dilemma. And how it is even more interesting that the Blue Bulls have an azure silhouette of a pair of horns as their symbol. I might even elaborate by observing that 'symbol', as used here, would be 'wapen' in Afrikaans – 'wapen' also meaning 'weapon' . . . and maybe that's why he, as a proud Blue Bulls man, is feeling a culturo-linguistic urge to punch me in the face.

Because that's the way this encounter is heading. If I say 'WP', it gives him immediate licence to hit me (and, by extension, to visit some unpleasantness on my girlfriend). If, on the other hand, I say 'Bulle' even in my most authentically accented Afrikaans, I'll be deemed a liar, a wise-ass and, worse, both a traitor to my assumed coastal team and an infiltrator claiming local allegiance. For while I can probably pass for an Afrikaner native on the telephone (I have enough cousins-twice-removed called Jannie and Boetie to have a fair command of die taal), the fact that I'm dressed in black, sporting an earring and wearing some or other overseas band T-shirt pegs me, unavoidably and undeniably, as a rooinek.

Things happen in slow motion when you're on the verge of being assaulted – and a possible escape suddenly becomes clear. It's a gamble, to be sure, but one that gives me a chance of escape without making matters worse. I dig deep, hack to clear my throat (and get the vice-grip to loosen a bit more) and affix an Oscar-winning grin of sincere befuddlement, with just the right amount of shit-eating deference, to my face. The plan is to utter the words, wriggle free in the moment of confusion I'm praying will follow, grab the girlfriend's hand and rush to the safety of somewhere I recall hearing a brace of English-speakers playing pool.

I review, and realise it really is a big gamble. But it also presents the classical answer to the bull's horns – and that is to refuse to enter the arena. 'I dunno, mate,' I say, mustering my best generically British accent and smiling even harder, partly to try and win him over, and partly because I realise my true lack of sporting knowledge may undo me, as I can't think of any of the right teams.

Time slows again as I scream through my mental database and –

hallelujah and insha'Allah – ferret out a team name that'll work. 'I dunno,' I say again, and somehow make the smile even broader, even more shit-eating (and fist-avoiding) and continue, laying on that accent even thicker. 'Me, I'm a Liverpool man.'

It worked! Despite the fact that the nascent civil war raging within the country's borders had spilled over into countless acts of barbarism, ranging from township necklace killings to security police family murders, South Africans are a fundamentally polite breed. For all that we're a socially traumatised nation, ours is not the poncey politeness of meaningless ceremony; rather it's a helpfulness that shows itself when a flat tyre needs fixing, a stranger asks for the last cigarette or, I suppose, when negotiating peaceful political change despite the world expecting a bloodbath.

Hitting some English-speaking guy in your bar and defending the revered Bulle against any and all reproach would be fair game and more or less entirely understandable. But rearranging the face of a visitor? Well, that would be being rude to a guest, and South Africans don't do that. Deep down, Mr Vice-Grip must have known that it was a bluff: just a handful of sand in the face of the bull, a song to placate a snorting bovine and a deft ruse to refuse the horns entirely. Still, we got away, and then faced the real dilemma – how to get back home, since her friend had left and we were supposed to be at the 5A class party.

Every South African has a Rugby World Cup tale from 1995, although some would argue that the way current sports administrators constantly overlook the nation-building power of sport suggests that the officials have forgotten their own after-dinner stories from that glorious time. Which is another way of saying that, eventually, I learned to respect and enjoy the oval-balled game, if not to love it or become anything close to an avid fan.

For a start, when I follow matches, it tends to be on the radio, while doing something else, much to the horror of my true sports-fan friends (although I've got a few to admit grudgingly that running the Radio 2000 commentary concurrently with a televised match is actually pretty good, on the rare occasions when there isn't a time-lag). Secondly, for me to say 'follow' is to cheapen the passion of the true enthusiast, because to be a sports fan is to follow a partic-ular team or nation, to live with their ups and downs, to soar as they triumph and despair when they fail. It is to follow the develop-ment of all that leads up to team selection and to understand the nuances of rule changes, the history of previous clashes, and the impact of terrain and temperature. In short, it's a lot of work when you're more interested in other things, like writing about jazz bands and reviewing rock festivals, or reading books that aren't about Tests and tries and kicking for touch.

It's especially the music-loving that presents a problem. With a live concert, you pretty much know what you're paying for. True, a band might be off-form on the night or a concert rig might be par-ticularly superb. But when you make the call to buy a ticket, you're basically guaranteed to get the good time you're shelling out for. With sport, though, all that money, time and queuing for bad beer in easy-to-spill plastic cups offers no guarantee. Live sport suffers the even more meagre risk-to-reward ratio of an audience that's entirely invested in an outcome they can't control, unless chanting rhyming couplets or wearing matching scarves counts as actually making a difference.

To the outsider looking in at sports-junkie logic, it seems that, even with a halfway decent team to support, in roughly 50% of the cases you're still likely to end up enduring a weekend loss and fac-ing a downcast week. Also, in the pie-chart world, precisely half the people watching a game are destined to delight in the very outcome that sees the other half reduced to misery. No, it makes far more sense to visit a stadium at night, hip-flask cunningly concealed, and watch a concert where everyone will be more likely than not to leave smiling and singing the same songs.

However, I did learn to enjoy the game, largely from two friends who are both published authors: University of Cape Town historian Nigel Penn and award-winning columnist, scriptwriter and author Darrel Bristow-Bovey. It was through their love of letters and mastery of language that I came to care about how the Springboks fare, and to worry about whether a game is good or not. When a good rugby clash is viewed as the unique arena that combines individual skill, brawn and flair with an almost unparalleled expression of teamwork, and when that view is seen through an existential lens that regards the clash as standing outside the humdrum and the uncertainty of the day-to-day world . . . well, then you can enjoy rugby as something a lot more than just people with massive forearms grabbing each other by the throat.

In the film *Amadeus*, the imagined voice of the embittered but enthralled Salieri enthuses about a composition by his rival, Mozart. Just as this widely popular film provided many people with an introductory avenue into classical music, so too the impassioned expressions of Messrs Penn and Bristow-Bovey provided me with a thread I could follow into rugby. Here was an erudite angle on a game I'd previously experienced as being only for boors. It allowed sport to sit less uneasily with a life's project of trying to explain, using the written word, the emotions produced by music. It also helped with a realisation about the tribes within the sport – the fans who feel so strongly about a team that they're willing to use that as an identity-bolstering excuse to inflict violence on someone else. It's like that in music too, although it comes to blows less often. Debates rage about what kind of jazz is better, and camps of mutual backslapping are formed around one genre, with dagger-eyes and dismissal heaped on the fans in another tribe of listeners.

Perhaps the most identifiable of those tribes provides the back-drop to my most memorable 1995 World Cup experience. It's hard to capture now the significance of the wave of national euphoria that swept all before it as the Bokke clawed and kicked their way to the top. Even just trying to find a big-screen television to watch the final had (the non-sport-viewing) me stumped. I gambled on the local alternative music bar, a gloomy den called the Purple Turtle, tucked off Cape Town's Greenmarket Square and a long-time haven for the city's Goths, punks and heavy-metal heads. There they were, in their black leather and mohawks, their shredded denim and their tattoos, all glued to a screen that normally showed videos by bands as likely to use a chainsaw or an angle-grinder as they were to wield a guitar or a keyboard.

Usually, by day, the only sport the Purple Turtle showed was English Premier League football (an extension of the self-same *rooinek* tribal identification that had somehow saved my English-speaking hide in Pretoria years before), but now the TV was tuned to the boys in green and gold. For once, the black faces in the club were not only those of the cleaners and kitchen staff. Passersby drifted in off the street, and all were welcomed into a place that normally implied, through the sheer unifying force of its self-badged clique, that you were not welcome unless you were one of them. But that was no-where near as astounding as what happened when it was time to sing South Africa's national anthem.

Here, in this enclave of contemporary European music and fash-ion, surrounded by a tribe that revelled in their sallow complexions and day-clothes patently unsuited to any corner of Africa, there was a revelation. To a man and woman, with pierced body parts glint-ing in the sunlight that filtered into what was normally a nightclub, and with their boots clicked together and their biker jackets fol-ded, they spontaneously stood and began to sing.

As a radio correspondent, I'd been shuffled off air for insisting on talking about Cape Flats hip-hop on an 'alternative' show, and had been told by newspaper editors that rock and jazz audiences didn't want anything to do with vernacular and indigenous music. Yet suddenly here was a unity that joined the country's white tribes with their black brothers and sisters, in the name of the same game that permitted one little self-identified tribe to regard beating up scrawny Goth kids as fair sport. That anthem was a song worth singing and a sporting moment beyond even the most scholarly of descriptions.

EVAN MILTON is a music and lifestyle journalist, radio DJ and South African Music Awards judge whose real job is to be a digital strategist doing business intelligence for internet and mobile marketing. Born and raised in apartheid-era Pretoria, he soon learned that talking to sports fans is just like interviewing rock stars. If you think on your feet and imply a general sense of knowing what's going on, ask the right questions and listen intently, the other guy will probably think it's a great conversation.

BRUCE FORDYCE

The Greatest Bok Supporter

As if alive, my cellphone clatters into my beer glass and leaps from the table. I have a message, and it's an angry one.

'@#$% that Stuart Dickinson!' the message screams. 'He deserves to have the word "Dick" in his surname!'

I'm in front of the television watching the Springboks play in a close Test match, and referee Dickinson has just given another of his dodgy decisions, and the most passionate rugby supporter in South Africa is venting her wrath. It wasn't a great decision, and I too am frustrated, but Lorraine 'Lor' Gibson is incandescent with rage.

It matters little that Dickinson was the Television Match Official (TMO) who ruled that Mark Cueto's foot had strayed over the touchline, thus disallowing his try against the Springboks in the 2007 Rugby World Cup final, or that it was the same referee who, again as TMO, called Jaque Fourie's crucial try against the British and Irish Lions at Loftus Versfeld as good. Lor operates in the present tense, and at this particular moment this referee is useless: he's made a bad decision against Lor's beloved Bokke and he deserves a torrent of abuse.

Lor is a great friend of mine, and is definitely one of the boys when it comes to rugby. She developed her passion for rugby after first watching her father play the game and then later while supporting her son Kerry, who was a very useful hooker for his school.

Lor is normally the picture of decorum, but when it comes to rugby, she can become a wild animal, and a vicious one at that. Her passion comes from a profound understanding of the game and its laws, despite the fact that she never played the sport herself. I played

CATHERINE MOORE

Welcome to the Club

Coming from a family of three girls and a father with zero interest in sport, and having chosen a string of boyfriends who were interested in the 'civilised' games of tennis and soccer, my introduction to rugby came fairly late in life. The timing was perfect though – the year was 1995.

I had moved into a house with my good friend Briony Borchers, and as luck would have it, she had a rather talented, Springbok rugby-playing cousin. It is therefore to Gavin Johnson that I owe my initiation as a committed rugby fan.

If the Springboks were playing in Cape Town, we would get match tickets through Gavin, or else through my other unlikely avenue into the sporting world – my connection with Brandhouse, who sponsored many of my fashion shows and had a box at Newlands. Once Mike Joubert, Brandhouse's marketing guru at the time, caught wind of my new passion, I became an honorary and unusual member of their little fan club in the quaint converted train carriages at Newlands.

We were plied with copious amounts of Smirnoff Spin, and discovered the wicked joys of mixing whisky and lime, while jostling for prime positions at the bar and in the stands. Weekend afternoons suddenly changed from sedate and sophisticated shopping excursions to raucous beer-swilling, leaping, swearing and shouting sessions, intoxicated with excitement and sometimes crushed with disappointment and despair. And always surrounded by young, healthy, virile men and the smell of the ever-present braai.

My rugby crush was Hennie le Roux. Regardless of how he was

performing on the field, I would greet any camera close-up of him most enthusiastically, much to the amusement of my male and female peers. We had our own nicknames for various players. Francois Pienaar was 'Mofkop' (for wearing his trousers too high, but having the most lovely manners); Kobus Wiese was 'Ol' Blue Eyes' (for obvious reasons); and André Joubert was 'Pronkperd' (for his amazing energy and all-round ability on the field).

My highlight of 1995 was being invited to a couple of events that afforded us the privilege of meeting South Africa's entire Rugby World Cup team and getting to know some of them, albeit briefly. I got to have a half-hour chat with Hennie . . . oh, heaven!

It was such an awesome time to be in South Africa and to experience the pride of showing the world how fantastic our sportsmen were, and also how it was possible to unite a nation against seemingly impossible odds . . . and all of this was made possible by a simple and fairly primitive game involving 15 grown men chasing after an oval-shaped ball.

My passion for rugby continued with the introduction of Bob Skinstad – to supplement the eye-candy quota – after Hennie's unfortunate retirement at the end of 1996. Once again, I came in for a lot of flak, but I was committed to the team, to the players and to a sport which was old and honourable, though brutish, physical and monumentally tough.

Sadly, my weekly support started to wane after the birth of my two daughters. It is fairly difficult to give a rugby game the consideration it deserves with two little people demanding your time and attention.

However, when I miss a match or two, I am now kept up to date by the personal trainers – all passionate rugby fans – at the gym that I attend. The mood at gym on a Monday is determined by the weekend's rugby results, national or international. Trainers and their clients eagerly discuss match details, and it can get quite tense, as

When Transvaal scored moments later, the ecstatic man stabbed his knife clean through a seat. We glanced at how far the blade protruded through the plastic chair, and then moved to a safer part of the stands – on the other side of the field.

What began as a promising and triumphant rugby moment once involved getting onto stage with Springbok stalwart Jean de Villiers. Our intention was to sing '*Ou Ryperd*' to a fairly large audience. It soon dawned on me that the only lyrics I knew were those in the title:

> *Ou ryperd, ons ry die pad tesame*
> [cue the improvised lyrics]
> *My pa se plaas is propvol haas*
> *en ek woon in Tsitsikamma.*

There was no appreciative cheer for my ad-lib. Rightly so. At least Jean knew his way around the Dozi classic and brought us home like a true champion.

Then there was that moment before kickoff when a fan took to the turf with his rugby ball, determined to run the entire length of the field. A security guard hunkered down for an ambush on the half way line, eager to stop the fan from achieving his field-length dream. The security guard wore sunglasses and crouched in a robot stance. We immediately nicknamed him The Du Toit-minator.

The scene was reminiscent of that Austin Powers movie where a steamroller takes an eternity to drive up to and over a screaming henchman. Instead of running over The Du Toit-minator, the fan used a sidestep he'd been saving for 40m.

The field cop was left sprawled flat on his stomach, arms outstretched, sunglasses and walkie-talkie on the grass. The crowd cheered as if the pitch invader had won the Currie Cup. We doubled our applause after he dived over for his try and successfully drop-kicked the conversion.

That was the same game where two hefty older men managed to sneak a Pick n Pay trolley into the stadium. Trolleyed in a trolley. One rode inside while the other pushed, unable to find their seats. It's not the destination, it's the journey – even in a trolley. I wondered if their kids were watching on TV. It didn't end well.

What did end well was the 1995 World Cup. We watched together with hordes of fans in a rugby village. Our large group had booked a table; things were a lot more civilised back then. The tense game got even more dramatic when Kiwi supporters at the bar performed a shirtless half-time *haka*. It was clear why they weren't selected for the All Blacks. Athleticism and sobriety weren't high on their priority list.

After Joel Stransky's 'Foot of God' incident, the village erupted into cheers, tears and jubilant air-punching. We climbed onto our table for an impromptu dance, probably to Leon Schuster's *'Hie' kommie Bokke'*, or *'We Are the Champions'*, or both songs at the same time. The table legs buckled under our beered-up weight and we crashed sideways onto a large table of strangers. It was reminiscent of the way in which pirates swung onto enemy ships, to seize and conquer. Air-punching was replaced with real punching. Both tables poured their pent-up emotions into one another's faces. We discovered that the overthrown table was manned by British fans, so we took delight in beating another nation that day. Retribution for the Anglo–Boer War.

Fathers and sons fought back-to-back, kicking and punching at the oncoming assault, very much in the style of that arcade game, Double Dragon. I saw someone get punched out of a wheelchair (OK, not in that fight, but weeks later in Roodepoort). I did see one of my friends draw blood by biting someone's forearm, long before it became popular in teen vampire novels.

Larkham at flyhalf, marshalling a lethal array of backline strike runners, they had such faith in their skills and in their bizarre and uncanny ability to come back from the death and win games they shouldn't. They just kept bouncing back. Dammit.

The Springboks haven't shown that kind of intense self-belief since 2009. It's the rugby gods, I tell you. Blessed with abundant talent in so many positions, even the South African Super Rugby teams never seemed to gel, not until those Heyneke Meyer-inspired Bulls got it together in 2007. Nor could the South Africans overcome the travel bogey on their over-long tours Down Under. No amount of whingeing could overturn that inequity. So we were forced to watch games at 9am or noon and listen to the sanctimonious drawl of the nether region's TV talkers. Laughing at them was all we could do to survive.

TOBY SHAPSHAK may be editor of *Stuff* magazine, but his first love is rugby. *GQ* bureau chief for ten years, Toby also worked as a senior newspaper writer, covering everything from news, politics and investigative reporting to the Truth and Reconciliation Commission and shadowing Nelson Mandela when he was president. Toby was also the *Mail & Guardian* sports editor (twice). Thanks to his column on thedailymaverick.co.za, he will never be invited to dinner at Peter de Villiers' place.

BRENDAN JACK

Back in Time for
the Game

Life, like a rugby game, can change in a moment.

Consider the moment Pieter Hendriks swooped across the try line to score against Australia in the opening game of the 1995 Rugby World Cup. South Africa suddenly believed that they could win the whole damn tournament.

Or the moment Japie Mulder silenced speculation about stopping giant All Blacks winger Jonah Lomu by clattering him into the advertising boards. They should edit that tackle into a video loop and display it on a wall in the Guggenheim Museum. That's correct. It's art.

There have been other notable, yet less explosive, moments. Like the time a mate and I watched Eastern Province vs Transvaal in the rain at Ellis Park. A few thousand spectators attempted to make the stadium look full. Alongside us an unhinged loner cut strips of biltong with his eight-inch hunting blade. If it was for biltong, then it wasn't considered a dangerous weapon. Security was more relaxed pre-9/11.

Studying for a liberal arts degree during the days of Pearl Jam meant that I had long hair. '*Vat bietjie soutvleis vir jou sussie* (Take some biltong for your sister),' said the wild-eyed man to my friend. He passed *soutvleis* to the *souties*.

We weren't sure if it was his sense of humour, or if he really thought I was a big-boned farm girl dressed in red flannel and a Lollapalooza T-shirt. I decided to hedge my bets by flicking some fringe across my eyes and thanking him in a high-pitched farm girl voice. '*Dankie, Oom.*'

(long ago when a try was worth three points, lifting wasn't allowed in the line-outs, and the ball was made of leather), but I bow to Lor's superior knowledge when it comes to rugby. Lor surprises male fans with her rugby knowledge, and at the risk of sounding sexist I certainly don't know many women who can spot a knock-on or a forward pass or who understand the subtleties of scrums and rucking and mauling.

And if Lor points out that the All Blacks are all camping offside, don't argue. They are.

But it's not only her understanding of the laws that makes Lor such a great rugby fan; it's also her understanding of the game itself. She can discuss the best Springbok centre pairing or which half-back combination works best. Yes, there might be a slight Sharks bias to her arguments, but we all have our provincial loyalties – and for a die-hard Sharks supporter to admit to a slight crush on Victor Matfield . . . that's honesty!

Many of us believe Lor would make a great coach, but if she were a coach her close friends would have to give up the pleasure of watching a big game at her house. A rugby afternoon at Lor Gibson's house is a treat, and invitations are highly prized. There is always Lor's fabulous cooking to enjoy, and of course there is plenty to drink. But the game itself is the highlight. From the announcement of the team selection ('He's not a fullback. We're in big trouble in defence,' and 'I'm glad they're giving that youngster a run. He's going to be a permanent fixture in the team by the end of the season') to the naming of the referee ('Oh, not that @#$%. He hates the Springboks!'), Lor's opinion is eagerly sought.

The match sees our hostess run the full gamut of human emotions. Lor's mood swings from despair to joy, from bitterness and anger to triumphant exultation. 'My boys are doing so well,' she'll boast when the Bokke are up. But if they're down, we're all depressed, and Lor's patient husband Brian has even been known to sneak out of the room and go to bed early. When we win, no Springbok supporter is as thrilled as Lor; when we lose, no supporter as upset.

But the true sign of Lor's commitment to our national team becomes evident when you're out of town and are unable to share an afternoon with her in front of the television. Lor is the undisputed captain of our small band of supporters and she keeps us close, as if bound together in a scrum, by sending profound SMSes to those who are away.

Lor once managed to track me down in Japan, where I was a guest at an international marathon. Rugby was the furthest thing from my mind when my phone growled angrily and I learned, via an irate message, that Corné Krige's Springboks had just suffered their worst-ever defeat at Twickenham.

Lor's messages are always an accurate summary of the state of play but are littered with colourful language. On more than one occasion, while watching a game alone in a hotel room somewhere, I have felt a little less lonely and have chuckled to myself as an SMS from Lor set off my phone.

I know the other members of our supporters' group feel exactly the same. Rugby would just be rugby without Lor, but with her it is an extra-special experience.

BRUCE FORDYCE ran his debut Comrades Marathon in 1977 and came 43rd. Four years later, he achieved the first of eight successive Comrades wins, with a ninth coming in 1990. Bruce is currently a sponsored athlete, motivational speaker, writer and columnist, coach, archaeologist and businessman. He also played scrumhalf until matric. Danie Craven would have been proud of his dive pass, and although he wasn't quite in the class of Gareth Edwards or Fourie du Preez, he was just as keen.

JAMES CAIRNS

A Weekend of
Higher Education

Students are the bane of any civilised community – rugby fans included. It's a miracle that those who go on to be leaders in business, government, academia and a host of other fields were once students. True, to call rugby fans civilised is a leap in the first place, but when the set including all rugby fans who are not students is placed adjacent to the set of student rugby fans, the depravity of the latter serves only to highlight the well-mannered gentility of the former. Surprisingly, you never hear of rugby disasters involving fans in the national press, because traditionally all disasters occur on the field. The other reason is that the national press didn't cover Eastern Cape student rugby in the mid-nineties.

The two major student rugby concentrations in the region at that time were UPE (the University of Port Elizabeth – now Nelson Mandela Metropolitan University) and Rhodes University. UPE won mostly, because they had money and no Humanities faculty to speak of. It is a well-known fact that your graduates of English, Drama, Fine Arts, Psychology and Classics are unable to fling the oval ball around as well as your graduates from faculties such as Metallurgy, Auto Mechanics, Police Science and whatever else UPE had hiding under their academic bonnet.

There was one area, though, where those of us who were more artistically inclined could really shine on match day, and that was in the hotly contested arena of fandom. We at Rhodes University at that time undertook to take fandom to places it had never been before. We realised that if there were any extra miles to go for rugby in Grahamstown, they were miles that could only be made up by the fans, because our players were not really up to the scratch we'd have preferred.

Now, the previous year, intervarsity had been a home game for Rhodes. Hordes of UPE students had travelled up the N2 to watch their first team dole out the customary hammering to the long-suffering Rhodents. We would stay up late in our res rooms and say the names of fearsome UPE first-team players out loud to each other to show that we weren't afraid. Vleis Visagie. Adri Geldenhuys. Pote Human. Satan. Anything would do – as long as it sounded big enough and rugby enough – but deep down we would know that we were beaten. Against names like that? Anyone would know they would be forsaken by the forces of victory.

All was not lost, because that previous year had given us a new war cry, one that echoed Peter Mokaba's hate-speech bonanza, 'one settler, one bullet'. At one point during the dark moments in the second half of the first-team game, when we trailed by an insurmountable tally, someone in the Rhodes pavilion shouted, 'One UPE!', and without fail the Rhodes pavilion thundered back, 'ONE BULLET!' Every time UPE scored, the chant would be picked up and roll across the field to strike fear into the vice-chancellor and his public relations person in their little tent as they tried to figure out ways to reassure the parents of their students that they weren't turning out a bunch of leftie bastards.

So, that year, we lost. Horribly. War cries, you see, aren't as good at winning matches as tries are.

The next year, the year in question in this particular anecdote, the intervarsity game was in Port Elizabeth. Spurred on by our inspired chanting the year before, some friends and I decided to take things to the next level. As we entered PE in a red Opel Kadett, the next level turned out to consist of Old Brown Sherry, Tassies and interesting haircuts. (A special note on the haircuts: many of the male supporters who made the journey from Grahamstown to Port Elizabeth that day shaved 'RU', the acronym of Rhodes University, into their hair. In our quest for ultimate fandom, we decided to shave off all my hair *except for* an RU in curly red hair at the back of my head.)

We rolled into PE and parked the Kadett in the middle of Govan Mbeki Avenue. We then plundered a local bottle store, as our supplies had already run low during the 80-minute drive. Street kids dancing to our banging tunes next to the Kadett shouted what sounded like 'Roux, Roux', but they were just repeating what was written in hair on the back of my head. Our supplies of Old Brown and Tassies replenished, we headed towards UPE.

The campus that the Port Elizabeth city planners bequeathed to the university is enormous. It is made to seem even more enormous by the way they ignored all that space and put everything into a concrete tower. (Then they had the gall to offer architecture as a subject.) Although some parts of the campus were cleared for sports fields and indoor basketball courts, most of it was covered by dense Port Jackson forest. Like little drunk Red Riding Hoods, we nosed our way through the forest towards that concrete tower in the hope that something rugby-like would reveal itself to us.

The only big bad wolf we encountered pointed us in the direction of some sort of activity, which turned out to be the women's first-team hockey game. This must have been just before midday, but we were already so spectacularly well refreshed that we felt creative enough to compose a song. Given the auspices of the day, this song should have been about rugby and Rhodes, but ended up being mostly about an alcoholic Port Elizabethan relative of mine, Uncle Rick. I am not sure how we got from the car parked at the side of the field into the goal mouth during a short corner, but I guess that we thought that this women's first-team hockey match needed a bit of pep, a bit of zest, a bit of a kick up the supporters' collective arses, because they were all very boring. There was nothing but the thwack of hockey sticks and a genteel round of clapping when things went well. If there was anything more uptight than that hockey crowd, it was the referee, who took umbrage at our impromptu song and dance number during the short corner, which is a very important moment in a hockey game. It wasn't that we wanted to detract from the gravity of the set piece; we only felt that it needed the sort of look and feel that only we could offer while we sang our song – loudly, with arms linked. Things didn't turn out exactly as we had intended and we were unceremoniously ushered off the pitch by security – security who, at that early point in the day's festivities, foolishly didn't take us into custody when they had us in their clutches.

We then bumbled off to locate our lodgings for the night: an old school connection who was at UPE had offered his res room. The idea of three of us and him sleeping in it didn't strike us as anything except damn well great at the time, so we dumped our bags and headed for the stadium on campus.

When we entered the stadium we had to admit that it was pretty grand of UPE to have an actual stadium of their own. Of course, we had also already started to accept that we would probably lose a game of rugby football within it once again. You could see that this was a place that cared about sport much more than Rhodes ever could.

The crowds had gathered in the stands long before the game started for the customary trade in insults, and it wasn't long before 'one UPE, one bullet' boomed out. They simply had no answer for it. I have a theory as to their lack of effective comeback. It is that Afrikaans rugby anthems (from which UPE drew their retorts) have always veered towards two basic styles: strange primary school cheerleader-led things that have their roots in interhouse swimming galas, and then actual songs that so few people know that they are rendered completely ineffective. Neither have what it takes to stand up to struggle-derived hate chants. Round one went to Rhodes.

Even though many Rhodes supporters had made the journey to

that would haunt the Springbok game plan for the next decade and beyond. Instead of flair in a flyhalf, successive coaches opted for a kicker who could reliably slot the penalties. Think back to the stilted backline play of Braam van Straaten, Louis Koen and Derick Hougaard. As good as they were (and two of them played in to a Rugby World Cup), they were kickers, not passers.

But at Loftus in 2009, the second Test of the revenge Lions series was a joyous occasion, although – like the first Test – it too almost went the other way. Late and unnecessary substitutions are never a good thing when momentum is on your side, especially not when John Smit is the heart, and sometimes the brain, of the team. In the first Test, Smit (already substituted) had to return to the field after a front-row injury, and in typical fashion his cool head won the game as much as determined defence did. It was one of those 'in spite of' moments. Like Jake White winning the 2007 Rugby World Cup in spite of the administrators, the Springboks in 2009 won in spite of their coach.

But in the second, decisive Test, it came down to Fourie du Preez being tackled in mid-air and a penalty, 53m out, being awarded to the Springboks as the hooter went. Morné Steyn, who had hardly missed all year in a run that included a Super 14 trophy, stepped up to take the kick. I was sitting not far from the halfway line, high in the stands above the press box. The stadium went silent. I don't think I have ever heard Loftus so ghostly quiet. And Steyn, in only his second Test, yet with ice in his veins, sent it sailing through the uprights. Loftus was a sea of Springbok joy.

For many years now, I have believed there is a small subset of gods – the rugby gods – who hate South Africa. They are the gods who make our life so painful, who dangle victory in front of us and then snatch it away. How else can you describe Smit's hundredth Test match, the first-ever Test in Soweto at the utterly spectacular Soccer City? Only the rugby gods could be that cruel.

Nicknamed the 'Calabash', it had hosted the FIFA World Cup opening and closing matches only a few months prior. When the Springboks visited Soweto, South Africa led until the last 30 seconds of the match, when an exhausted Smit fell off a tackle in the final move of the game, which resulted in the winning try. New Zealand clinched the match and the 2010 Tri-Nations. It was too painful to watch, and a bloodied Smit was the very picture of defeat. A week later, at Loftus, at least Victor Matfield was triumphant in his hundredth Test (against Australia), but the damage had been done.

The rugby gods seem to reserve special vindictiveness for South African fans, given the often bizarre choices as Springbok coach. Peter de Villiers may be the nadir, but don't forget that Harry Viljoen and mad Rudolf Straueli presided over eras characterised by, er, less than sober thinking.

One choice Aussie commentator wisecrack dating from those years concerned an electric young flank called George Smith, who had burst onto the scene: 'He's not the biggest guy on the field, and he's not the fastest. But he's got great anticipation.'

'Great anticipation!' I would savour the phrase, varying the context. Of a journalist friend who broke a big story: 'He's not the best reporter in the field, and he's not the smartest. But he's got great anticipation . . .'

And 'He loves to run' was transformed into 'He loves to schlep/ shop/over-research . . .'

They kept us sane some years, did those one-eyed Aussies. Such boundless optimism, unstoppable self-belief – in the face of all evidence to the contrary. That was what powered the indomitable Australian cricket team for a decade: sheer, bloody-minded self-belief. They exuded confidence; they sweated big-match temperament. Such insane self-belief made them invincible, almost All Black-like. Likewise the George Gregan-captained Wallabies. With Stephen the coast for the game, our numbers were significantly fewer than the opposition. We occupied only one section of the main stand, which ran along one side of the field, and then not even up to the top of the stand. The rest of the main stand and the stadium was full of UPE supporters – thousands of them, maybe tens of thousands. It was the Alamo, Rorke's Drift, Thermopylae – you name it. We were the lone Jack Russell and they were the pack of Rottweilers baying for our blood. Did we blanch at these insurmountable odds? Did we cast off the mantle of courage on this day of days? Did we even blink? Not at all. We were drunk, you see.

Our intake of Tassies and Old Brown had infused us with a certain dumb pluck. Myself and two of my comrades, overcome by zeal for victory, thought that if we ran around the field on the athletics track singing the Uncle Rick song we would seal the deal for our boys, kinda like Joshua did for his guys at Jericho. We didn't have an Ark of the Covenant with us at the time, but sometimes you just have to go with what you've got.

Well, we had insults and we had our pants, which could be pulled down to reveal our buttocks. This we executed in front of the UPE stand on the opposite side of the field. Insults and the sight of our buttocks worked really well in front of the massed ranks of UPE supporters because they got hopping mad and began to chase us. We got our pants up and set off at pace directly for our seats on the other side of the field, laughing like hyenas – until we noticed that the first-team game had just started.

The direct route would have taken us straight across the field, where the main game, the reason for all that we had undertaken that day, was now unfolding. Somewhere in the mess of alcohol, adrenaline and Dutch courage that our brains had become, there was something stronger than all of that – the respect for those white lines within the bounds of which a glorious struggle between two teams of 15 men was taking place. That was a Rubicon we were not prepared to cross even in ragged retreat from our committed pursuers, so we turned right to make good our escape along the track around the field, which, in a ghastly joke, turned out to be a steeplechase track.

The three of us ran that steeplechase course with an athleticism that will certainly never be seen again from me. I felt relieved and proud as I cleared the water jump, but, presented with the first of the barriers after the water jump, I felt that it looked a little too substantial to attempt and swerved in-field over the pole-vault run-up area. From there it was an easy trot into the shelter of the friendly grandstand. As I slowed and prepared to turn and vent derision upon UPE once more, I heard a squawk of pain behind me. I turned and saw that one of my comrades had, in his rush to reach safety, put a foot into the hole that the pole vaulters must stick the end of their pole in before they jump to get the necessary leverage. He'd gone down, and his pursuers were upon him. The remaining two of us reached the Rhodes stands and turned to see that the UPE horde was as confused with their prisoner as he was at being captured. They pulled him to his feet and jeered at him as he trotted sheepishly towards us. We helped him up and went to take our place in the stands as the game continued.

The details of the actual game are murky, and we were absorbed into the beast that is a rugby crowd, but the thing is . . . we won. That little Rhodes first team managed to engineer a victory against UPE. It was an unheard-of feat in those days. This was David and Goliath stuff. Biblical. Slaughter the fatted calf, stop all the clocks, bid the soldiers shoot, drink and be merry, because we *blerrie* won for once in our lives.

Our next move was clear and simple. Upon the blast of the final whistle, we barrelled down the stands to the field, ostensibly to congratulate our unexpectedly victorious team, but actually to steal the score from the scoreboard, which was on the opposite side of the field. Through sweaty players, celebrating Rhodes students and downcast, disbelieving UPE fans we shouldered and barged and, rather more easily than we had expected, reached the scoreboard. It turned out to be completely unguarded and assailable. We climbed up inside it and quickly removed the letters and numbers from their frame, threw them to the ground, climbed down and gathered them up. Our Kadett had been brought round to the back of the scoreboard; we loaded it up and gunned it out of there with our loot into the early twilight.

As the hangovers started to kick in, the rest of the evening went downhill. A depressing party in a shed on the campus and an incredibly uncomfortable 'sleep' on the floor of a UPE res room topped off our stay in the Windy City.

The hangovers were even more substantial the next day as we made the journey back to Grahamstown, but the knowledge of the hallowed trophy in the boot made it all worthwhile. Every now and then, we'd lean back to stroke the dusty metal plates to make sure they were still there. I can't even say for sure which Rhodes res bar they ended up in – Matthews or Botha – but we basked in the infamy.

It was almost as good as the time some guys went through to the Kei in a bakkie with a couple of chainsaws and sawed down the 'Welcome to the Ciskei' road sign on the night that particular Bantustan ceased to exist as a state. I have always argued since that as our booty was associated with a victory against the old enemy at UPE – not the failure of a relatively new enemy, Oupa Gqozo in the Ciskei – ours was all the more meaningful.

Rugby union has already lasted longer than the Ciskei did, and while children will ask their fathers what the Ciskei was, that question will not be asked about rugby, because rugby – unlike Bantustans – will be with us for some time to come.

JAMES CAIRNS is a writer and performer from Johannesburg. He has written a number of critically acclaimed works: *Rat*, *The Sitting Man*, *Brother Number* and *The Groundsman* among them. *Brother Number* (co-written with Rob van Vuuren) was nominated for Best Comedic Play at the 2007 SA Comedy Awards. James's short story, *Ossewa Mulaudzi*, was one of the four winners of the Vlaams-Nederlands Huis de Buren's Writing Beyond the Fringe competition in 2009. James played mediocre rugby at various levels from 1986 until 1997 and is an avid fan of the game. He still struggles to keep it together on weekends when the Springboks lose.

MARK BOUCHER

The Proteas' Rugby Fan Club

I was in Standard 6 at Selborne College in East London when Mark Andrews was in post-matric. He was huge and very intimidating. As his skivvie, I'd clean his boots and do the odd chore for him – all part and parcel of initiation at a traditional, all-boys school. Still very wet behind the ears, I once walked into the post-matrics' room and Mark just picked me up (I must have weighed about 40kg back then) and hung me on one of the coat hooks on the back of the door.

That was my introduction to Mark Andrews. I later got to know him a bit better, and he was a great guy to be around. I played scrumhalf until Standard 9, when I broke my arm, and from then on I focused on cricket and squash. That was the end of my rugby career, but most definitely not of my interest in rugby.

At Selborne, I played first-team cricket with Andre Vos, who went on to captain the Springboks in 16 Test matches. As cricket and rugby are two of South Africa's main sports, it was natural that cricketers stayed interested in the Springboks, wherever we were. During the 1995 Rugby World Cup, I was on a South African U19 tour to England. We watched the final on a big screen at an athletics stadium, taunting the Kiwis and doing a lap of honour around the athletics track. There must have been close to 5 000 people there and quite an after-party. It was like watching the match at a home away from home, because it's not often that a World Cup is held in your own country.

A year or two later, I was at the National Cricket Academy and we had drawn numbers out of a hat in preparation for watching the big South Africa vs Australia Tri-Nations game. Every time the Bok player with your number on his back touched the ball, you'd have to sink a Springbok (half a tot of peppermint liqueur, half a tot of Amarula or Cape Velvet). The guys who drew 11 and 14 were pretty happy, but I landed up with No. 9. Needless to say, at half-time I was taking strain and had to ask the guys if we could do a re-draw as I couldn't handle No. 9 any more. So we drew again, and I got No. 2, which was probably just as bad. It ended up being a long day.

The Proteas always take a couple of rugby balls on tour. We often kick a ball around during our warm-ups, just to get the blood going, or we'll play a bit of touch rugby. Funnily enough, if we lose a match, you'll often find the boys playing touch rugby, mixed up with a bit of tackle, to work out their frustrations. When we lost the first Test of the 2001–02 series against Australia in Adelaide, we played touch for about two hours afterwards. By the time we were finished, we'd finally got all that anger out of our systems.

The camaraderie between rugby and cricket players is very good, especially at national level. We've got a lot in common, and often end up talking about our different sports over a couple of beers, or about the things that happen on tour. The Proteas and the Springboks do plenty of socialising when we're at the same functions. A lot of the Titans cricketers are good friends with the Bulls players, likewise with the Cobras players and the Western Province rugby guys. We're regularly invited to their after-match drinks, or we'll be at the same golf days or see each other out at nightclubs. At one of the Ernie Els Foundation golf days, Ernie came over and sat with us – the rugby players and the cricketers – and after a few beers, he ended up teeing a ball off one of the tables into the side wall of the marquee!

I've become good friends with Schalk Burger. Playing for the Warriors and being an East London boy, I obviously supported the Sharks. But one night Schalk and I were having a drink, and he sort of hinted that he wanted me to start supporting Western Province now that

I'd been living in Cape Town for eight or nine years. I said, 'If you become captain of Western Province, then I'll support you.'

A week later, he phoned to tell me that he'd just been made captain! It's always difficult when you're really good mates with a guy who plays rugby, and you support a different team – even more so when he's the guy who's running the show. I couldn't go back on my word, so I'm a Western Province supporter now. But the Sharks are still my second side.

The Proteas always make a big effort to watch Springbok matches when we're overseas. If you have to, you can usually pull the game off the internet, and project it via a laptop onto a big screen or a wall. We did that for a Tri-Nations game against the All Blacks in a little hotel bar in Grenada when we were touring the West Indies in 2010. That's probably the strangest place that I've watched the Springboks. That, and a dingy pub somewhere in Colombo, Sri Lanka.

On the day of the 2007 Rugby World Cup final, we actually played a One-Day International against Pakistan in Lahore. I think some of the SuperSport boys who were working on the tour stole some coverage somehow, and the whole team gathered to watch in the team room. Pakistan is the last place where you'd think we'd be watching rugby, but there we were jumping up and down when the Springboks beat England.

When it's Super Rugby or Currie Cup time, there's a lot of rivalry in the team. We always have bets on, and there's plenty of niggle when the Sharks play the Bulls, or the Bulls meet Western Province. There are probably eight or nine guys in the side who are quite big into the rugby. A bunch of us even made it to the match against the All Blacks at Soccer City in Soweto for John Smit's hundredth Test. Being there was awesome. We said to each other how much we'd love to play cricket there; it's just a pity they didn't make the pitch slightly bigger. We spoke to a couple of the Boks afterwards and asked how they felt running out in front of 95 000 people; we get the same kind of questions about what it's like playing in front of almost 100 000 fanatical India supporters at Eden Gardens in Kolkata.

One of the things that rugby players and cricketers see eye to eye on is the pressure of always being in the spotlight. When we're watching rugby in a bar and a player makes a mistake, it's tempting to get excited and start shouting at the TV like every other South African rugby fan. But it's easier for us to acknowledge that we actually don't know what we're talking about – not *really* – and we should just sit back and watch the rugby. When it could be you out there the next day making an error, you definitely get a sense of perspective. No South African sportsman ever goes out there to lose.

What I really admire about the rugby guys is how they get themselves up for a game, week in and week out, considering what their bodies go through. In cricket, you play for five days in a row and you certainly get fatigued, but then you see how these guys take the hits and put in the big tackles . . . you can actually hear the crunching noise of the collisions on TV. You think to yourself: if that were me, I'd be in hospital already!

But one of the biggest things for me is that the Springboks have picked up two World Cups. I have been part of three Cricket World Cup campaigns where we haven't managed to bring it home, and a lot of people say, 'Ja, well, go to the World Cup and just win it.' But it is not that easy, I can guarantee you that. And the way that the Boks won those tournaments has been really impressive – especially the 2007 tournament, which they approached so professionally. Jake White and John Smit led from the front; they had a group of senior players who really dominated; and the team were able to play their own brand of rugby, which is why they ended up on top.

The Springboks can be proud of their record and of how they have conducted themselves. And that is something that our Proteas cricket team can look to, and take heart from, as we pursue our own goals on the world stage.

——— *As told to Angus Powers*

MARK BOUCHER is the finest wicketkeeper South Africa has produced, with over 500 Test dismissals and more than 400 ODI dismissals in his 14-year international career. He is a three-time winner of the South African cricketer of the year award, was Wisden Cricketer of the year in 2009, and hit the winning runs in the famous '438' ODI against Australia at the Wanderers in 2006. Mark is a former SA junior squash champion and one of the biggest rugby fans in the Proteas cricket team.

CHRIS ROPER

From the Sidelines

I think it was Bob Dylan who sang it best: 'How many games must a rugby fan watch/Before they call him a fan.' The answer, my friends, is a little more complicated than the ones you usually find blowing in the southeaster at Newlands. But what's simple is the truism that all kinds of people in South Africa are affected by rugby, and, in my case, in some strange and tangential ways. And the evolution of a fan, or, more accurately, what converted me into a fan, is a fascinating process.

It's become a cliché of sporting passion to say that rugby is like a religion. But as with most clichés, it has a kernel of truth beyond the obvious. Rugby is like a religion, but not because its devotees congregate in large, worshipful groups one day a weekend and spend the time in either abject prayer (Lions fans, for example), ecstatic praise (Bulls fans, unfortunately) or trying to *bliksem* people who don't follow the same team as them (you know who you are). No, rugby is most like a religion because the different types of fans are analogous to different sorts of believers.

There are three sorts of fans. The first are the devout fundamentalists, attending every match they can, and watching the rest on television. They're the ones who actually PVR the matches they physically attend so that they can watch them again when they get home. They know the holy scripture inside out; in the same way that your more committed Catholic knows all the minor saints, they'll be able to name every Bok captain from Herbert Castens to Victor Matfield (our most recent captain at time of writing, thanks to a John Smit injury). And in the spirit of rugby fans everywhere, some of them will be able to tell you what was wrong with every one of those captains, too.

The second type are those who only attend the major, meaningful matches, like a final, or one that's being played at Soccer City for the first time. They're like those folk who only go to church a few times a year, on Christmas Day perhaps, or for a wedding. They consider themselves fans, and they carefully watch their favourite teams' results, but they wouldn't go to war for them.

The third kind of fan is one who doesn't even realise how much of a fan he or she is. They're part of a society that's imbued with a certain culture and belief system, and they experience everything that comes from that system – like taking Christian holidays off, for example, or sharing the euphoria of the 1995 Rugby World Cup – but they wouldn't really think of themselves as fans. I used to be the third type of fan, and I've now become the second kind. How that happened is kind of weird, and says a lot about the power of rugby to convert.

The first time I realised how important rugby is in our country was 1983, during my two years of national service in the army. I spent most of that year putting my life on the line for my country by playing table tennis to raise funds for a Defence Force rugby team to tour Argentina. Not the most effective use of army resources, if you think about it. I seem to remember that Naas Botha was somehow part of that touring team, but my memory is hazy. We could have made that bit up to cajole people more easily into donating money.

The deal was that we'd set up at a shopping centre that housed a Pick n Pay (they must have been a co-sponsor) and then start playing endurance table tennis and see how many hours we could rack up. You don't get more surreal than a bunch of shaven-headed soldiers in brown fatigues playing table tennis in a suburban mall, I promise you. But the most striking memory I have is of how much money people were willing to donate to a rugby cause. It was almost as if they were donating to a war effort. As a Western Province supporter brought up to hate Northern Transvaal, it was the first indication I had that rugby people were a community, and not just an assortment of warring tribes.

Fast forward twelve years to 1995, and the tribalism was a bit more pronounced. A nation fresh into democracy was asked to support a team called the Springboks, in defiance of the majority of the population's wish to change all the old symbols into new ones. In hindsight, a bunch of rugby heroes called the Proteas weren't going to work that well. Mind you, a springbok isn't exactly a ferocious killer either, but we've managed to overlook that minor issue. The fact that (according to AC Parker's 1970 history of the Springboks) the symbol was originally embroidered onto the national team jerseys in mouse-coloured silk (yes, mouse) hardly adds to a general air of herbivorous menace.

The 1995 Rugby World Cup took place during contentious times, something most rugby fans have probably forgotten. After all, with such a highlight (note to Aussie and Kiwi readers: we won), only the most churlish would remember the negatives. One fairly humorous incident, which was an indication of how far South Africa still had to go as a democracy – and how much we needed a unifying moment like Nelson Mandela donning a Springbok jersey – occurred when a South African rugby commentator referred to the Ivory Coast as 'the only African team to make the finals'. However, the Springbok has been with us since time immemorial (OK, 1906 in the case of rugby, which is the same thing) and with such symbols you tend to forget that they have a history other than the one that the marketers are pushing.

While most Springbok supporters will remember 24 June 1995 as one of the greatest days of their rugby-watching lives, my memories are a little more troubled. This is mainly because I found myself watching in a room full of tipsy Springbok supporters, and one All Blacks supporter, who happened to be my partner. Fairly uncomfortable, I assure you. Especially if said All Blacks supporter, like Trevor Manuel in 1996, is vocal about why she's supporting the All Blacks.

And yet this too is what makes a rugby fan. I realised that there are several complicated things going on when you choose to support a rugby team. Are you supporting 15 men on a field, or are you showing allegiance to a certain geographical affiliation? Are you showing solidarity with your fellow fans, or to a greater ideal that represents a certain kind of culture? It's something that most fans probably never have to think about. They just are fans, and they needn't bother to explain how they got there. As with belief in any religion, taking that 'leap to faith', as the great Danish rugby commentator Søren Kierkegaard called it, is a vital part of supporting a team. After all, as the accepted wisdom has it, if you don't believe in them, they can't win against the odds.

At 9-9 going into extra time in the World Cup final, you don't want unbelievers in the room – trust me. Especially in a room where the Windhoek Lager has been flowing. Luckily, the Springboks edged it. I don't think it would have been very pretty if the All Blacks had won. Forget the nation – I'd have been the one needing the rebuilding. What I learned, however, was that you can't support a team for political reasons. It just doesn't taste right, and it's joyless. Rather start watching badminton. It's like being at a revivalist church where everyone is dancing and singing rollicking gospel, and you're just humming along.

The final stage of my ascent to fandom occurred in that most unlikely of rugby places, America, where I had to spend time in a San Francisco hotel room with an ex-Western Province prop sitting in his underwear and talking dirty. Not as exciting as it sounds, you'll be glad to know. He'd probably prefer to remain anonymous, so let's call him Buffel.

We were in San Francisco to work on a few websites that streamed video on demand. (Well, we were actually in San Carlos, just outside San Francisco, a small town a bit like the cosmopolitan metropolis of Parow, outside Cape Town. But San Francisco sounds more glamorous.) One of these websites showed Super 14 and international rugby matches live. When you're far from home, in a country where scoreboards at sports venues are extra large in order to fit all the numbers in, and people go to ice hockey matches to spend half their time in the gift shop, you need a fix of Super Rugby (formerly known as 'high-scoring Super Rugby') and of gritty Test rugby, where the outcome is decided by one or two mistakes.

The only problem, of course, was that the matches took place in the wee hours of the morning, so watching South Africa face England required a commitment to hollow eyes and exhaustion. And also a commitment to huddle around a small laptop with a massive, beery ex-prop who was partial to farting disdainfully and swearing violently at the minuscule referee and the inadequate scrummaging.

To push the religion analogy a little further (hell, we've gone so far now there's no turning back), it was like being sent off to a retreat in the desert with a hermit, a holy man who has devoted his entire existence to contemplating the meaning of life and the arcane minutiae of holy rituals. You don't want to try and do what that holy man can do, because you need years of training to achieve that level of knowledge and spirituality. Or, as Buffel put it to me when I first met him in the airport before we left South Africa, 'We're going to be drinking a lot of beer in the next three months, so I just want to warn you – don't try and keep up with me. I'll drink three beers for your every one. I've practised.'

As with many holy men, he lied. It was more like five beers to every one I could drink, with the added problem that I had to stop after three or four, whereas he could keep going all night. But when you come out of that desert, you've either ascended to a higher plane, or decided to run away to the city and change your name. In this case, I was converted.

There's something a little bit special about being treated to your own personal running commentary by someone who has actually been at the bottom of a scrum and has actually spilt his blood for a team at a professional level. It's always a sobering and humbling experience when you realise that you're not as clever as you thought, and that being a fan of something doesn't necessarily mean you know anything about it.

And it's not just the technical aspects of what was going on, although that was enlightening enough. For example, I had no idea that I'd never actually *seen* a scrum. Sure, I'd watched a bunch of big lads pushing up against each other while some hyperactive midget chucked a ball under their feet and insulted their mothers, but when you have someone like Buffel telling you what's going on, a whole new world opens up.

There's another aspect of being a fan, and that's being aware that – just like the hermit in the desert – you have to devote your life to understanding a sport inside out. Buffel understood exactly the emotional state of the players on the field, and could say things about the opposition like, 'This is a good time to push him mentally. His wife's busy divorcing him because she caught him with a teenager.'

A dark, freezing cold morning in a grey hotel room, huddled in front of a small laptop, watching tiny players scurrying around on a flickering screen, with tinny crowd noise bleating from minute speakers . . . not exactly the optimal way to watch rugby. And yet it's probably the moment I realised that the real definition of a fan is someone who loves a sport rather than a team.

Which isn't to say a fan is not discerning. In Buffel's case, he'd watch any top-class rugby, but never any games from the American league (which didn't endear us to our American rugby colleagues). It's not really rugby, is it?, he'd sniff. But in the same way that religious people are pro-humankind, a true fan won't make a plan to watch only if it's his team playing – he'll be a fan of rugby in general. It took me a while to figure that one out, but once you get it, you get it.

CHRIS ROPER, although primarily a soccer fan, also likes to support teams who actually win, which is the best reason to be a South African rugby supporter. He is the editor of *Mail & Guardian Online* and a Stormers fan and misses the days when top teams were allowed to wear *streeptruie*. The most poignant rugby shrine he has seen is the Mannetjies Roux Museum in Victoria West, which salutes the days when rugby represented a lot more than just a meal ticket.